Lowco
and C

Lowcountry Agricultural and Convivial Societies

Where Planters Came Together in Antebellum Georgetown, South Carolina

Christopher C. Boyle

McFarland & Company, Inc., Publishers
Jefferson, North Carolina

LIBRARY OF CONGRESS CATALOGUING-IN-PUBLICATION DATA

Names: Boyle, Christopher C., author.
Title: Lowcountry agricultural and convivial societies :
where planters came together in antebellum Georgetown,
South Carolina / Christopher C. Boyle.
Other titles: Where planters came together in antebellum
Georgetown, South Carolina
Description: Jefferson, North Carolina : McFarland & Company, Inc., Publishers, 2022 |
Includes bibliographical references and index.
Identifiers: LCCN 2022011613 | ISBN 9781476686264 (paperback : acid free paper) ∞
ISBN 9781476644219 (ebook)
Subjects: LCSH: Plantation life—South Carolina—Georgetown
County—History—19th century. | Plantation owners—
South Carolina—Georgetown County—Social life and customs. |
Clubs—South Carolina—Georgetown County—History. | Agriculture—
South Carolina—Societies, etc.—History. | Winyah Indigo Society—
History. | Plantation owners—South Carolina—Georgetown
County—Biography. | South Carolina—Politics and government—1775-
1865. | Georgetown (S.C.)—History—19th century. | BISAC: HISTORY /
United States / 19th Century | SOCIAL SCIENCE /
Agriculture & Food (see also POLITICAL SCIENCE /
Public Policy / Agriculture & Food Policy)
Classification: LCC F277.G35 B69 2022 | DDC 975.7/89—dc23/eng/20220310
LC record available at https://lccn.loc.gov/2022011613

BRITISH LIBRARY CATALOGUING DATA ARE AVAILABLE

ISBN (print) 978-1-4766-8626-4
ISBN (ebook) 978-1-4766-4421-9

On the cover: Winyah Indigo Society Hall.
Photograph by Rich Taylor

Printed in the United States of America

*McFarland & Company, Inc., Publishers
Box 611, Jefferson, North Carolina 28640
www.mcfarlandpub.com*

For my beloved D'Andrea Lynn

Table of Contents

Acknowledgments

Many people deserve credit for assisting in the production of this book, as I have leaned upon many people throughout the creation and editorial phases of this work. Mrs. Kelsy Kay Dailey served as my chief editor. She served as a grammarian and provided indispensable styling support to the entire manuscript. Without her assistance, I simply could not have completed this project. For her assistance, my primary scholarly indebtedness for this work is to her.

Dr. Jason Silverman, professor of history at Winthrop University, and Dr. Lynn Willoughby, professor of history at Winthrop University, helped to guide my thesis research in the mid–1990s. Dr. Silverman volunteered his time to read the final manuscript, as well. I extend a very special thank you to Dr. Silverman for continuing to mentor my progress as a historian.

Several of my former professors assisted me in developing into the historian whom I am today. Without their guidance in research, and understanding of the bigger picture, I would not have been able to produce this work. Dr. Silverman and Dr. Willoughby deserve credit for helping me shape the early stages of this work into my master's thesis. Dr. Charles Joyner, professor of history at Coastal Carolina University; Dr. George C. Rogers, professor of history at the University of South Carolina; and Professor James L. Michie, associate director of the Waccamaw Center for Cultural and Historical Studies at Coastal Carolina University and associate principal investigator and program director of the South Carolina Institute of Archaeology and Anthropology, University of South Carolina, have all passed on to their heavenly rewards, but their lessons and memories remain close to my heart. They all guided me with research and questioned my findings in their own individual ways over the years.

My close personal friends J. Benjamin Burroughs, director of the Horry County Archives Center at Coastal Carolina University, and Robert T. Oliver, senior instructor of American history at Coastal Carolina University, provided me with outlets for very serious historical discussions and helped to keep me focused on this project by challenging my knowledge of local history and pushing me to dig deeper into primary sources. Both gentlemen read the entire manuscript of this book prior to publication and offered several suggestions which prompted further research. For their assistance, all readers of this book are indebted.

Trusted friends Rich Taylor and Paige Sawyer photographed for this venture. They also worked with archival photographs and helped me to select the best shots to include in this work. I am very thankful for their expertise and willingness to share their time, talents and enthusiasm to help complete this project. My lovely wife and best friend D'Andrea Lynn Boyle sketched pieces of art for this volume. Her time and efforts are very appreciated beyond measure or expression.

My former boss and mentor, James A. Fitch, director of the Rice Museum in Georgetown, South Carolina, allowed Rich Taylor to photograph the entire museum and permitted me to use the pictures at my discretion. Amanda Breen, collections manager, Gibbes Museum of Art, Charleston; Julie Warren, collections manager, Georgetown County Library; Jennifer McCormick, chief of collections and archivist, Charleston Museum; McKenzie Lemhouse, library specialist, South Caroliniana Library; Michelle McCarthy-Behler, reference librarian, Frick Art Reference Library; James A. Fitch, Georgetown Rice Museum; J. Benjamin Burroughs, Horry County Archives at Coastal Carolina University; and Jonathan Eaker, reference librarian, Prints & Photographs Division, Library of Congress, all provided valuable archival pictures, artwork or historical artifacts for publication.

In researching the history for this work, I leaned on the help of many people at numerous libraries. Employees and volunteers at the following depositories helped by retrieving documents and published works: South Carolina Historical Society, South Carolina History and Archives, Southern Historical Collection at Chapel Hill, Louis Round Wilson Library at Duke University, South Caroliniana and Thomas Cooper Libraries at the University of South Carolina, Kimbel Library at Coastal Carolina University, South Carolina State History and Archives, Chapin Memorial Library and the Horry and Georgetown County Libraries.

I would also like to extend a warm debt of gratitude to thank the officers and members of the Winyah Indigo Society who trusted me with their archives and supported this endeavor.

To my extended family, like my innumerable students both at the high schools and Coastal Carolina University who have endured my historical lectures and rants, I thank you all for your patience and dedication.

I would also like to thank my little patchwork family for their support and toleration in listening to my stories of the past over the years of my research and for helping divert my attention from my studies when I needed breaks. My beloved bride D'Andrea Lynn has taught me the true definition of devotion and love. Her dedication and support for me and my work have been immeasurable, and it is through our love that I receive the strength to push forward with my scholarly pursuits. My oldest daughter Veda Dailey is an amazing beacon of what is good in the world today. Her dedication to follow her own path to success in Japan is as admirable and as pure as any path that any man or woman has ever walked. I treasure the time that we spend together. My daughter Hannah Grace also provides me with great pride and has often helped me with public presentations. As she prepares to finish high school, we all sit back and watch her discover her passion and blossom in adulthood. I have nothing but admiration and love for her and cherish the time we share. She is a blessing to everyone who knows her and a symbol of hope for humanity which grows brighter as she matures. My thanks and appreciation are also extended to my son Brandon Joseph. A true inspiration of strength in my life, Brandon has always proven himself to be a true leader who listens twice as much as he speaks. He is a true gentleman in the nineteenth-century terminology: he is one who mingles with all but remains tarnished by none. He is a law student at Charleston Law, a graduate of Coastal Carolina University with a major in political science and double minors in history and prelaw, and his rise to prominence and leadership in this family I joyfully await. It is with great pleasure that I sit back and watch him blaze his own path to scholarly success. I also wish to extend my appreciation to his lovely bride Megan Leigh Boyle. Megan has supported Brandon's love of history, politics and law by traveling to historic places, attending lectures, taking classes with him and engaging in family talk for years. She is the source of much of his scholarly pursuits as D'Andrea is to mine, and I now understand my father's position when he told me, "she's the one."

My mother Annette Boyle has always supported my efforts. She has nurtured my mind, body and soul throughout life with her unwavering support and love for me. She and my father encouraged my love and understanding of history at a very young age with dinnertime historical talks and by taking me to historical places and in adulthood engaging in polite historical conversations, attending my public lectures, taking my classes at Coastal Carolina University, and buying me first-print editions of my favorite books as birthday and Christmas gifts, something that was cost restrictive for me. Instead of presenting me with senseless gifts upon these celebrated occasions, they provided me with special opportunities to touch, smell and feel the past. To my deceased son Benjamin Charles, I thank you for your gift of life, although it was a short life (a little over a year), during which you taught me to value every day that God gives us.

Lastly, I extend my appreciation to my deceased beloved father Gerard Boyle. It is finally published, Dad. That dream that you told me about in one of your final days about me finally publishing my thesis, that one publication which I have struggled with for over two decades to complete—well, here it is. I thank you, my father, for instilling within me the old Irish work ethic and never-give-up attitude.

Family and friends: I thank you all for your gifts of love.

Preface

Technically, I started writing this book in 1994 as a graduate student at Winthrop University, Rock Hill, South Carolina. I submitted my thesis to the College of Arts and Sciences in partial fulfillment of the requirements for my Master of Arts degree in the Department of History. I titled my thesis "Social Organizations and Leisurely Activities of the Georgetown Rice Planters 1840–1861." The main readers for my work were Dr. Jason Silverman and Dr. Lynn Willoughby. Each gave constructive criticism and asked if I was going to further develop it into a doctoral dissertation. I carefully considered expanding the thesis in two ways. First of all, I considered comparing Georgetown planters' clubs to those throughout the state of South Carolina (a project which I would have completed at the University of South Carolina) or to compare the Georgetown, South Carolina, clubs to those of the cotton planters of the Natchez District, Mississippi (I would have completed this task at the University of Mississippi). However, after working on the topic for two years, I tired of studying the social organizations and found other historical interests about which to research and write.

After working on some other publications, nearly a dozen articles in various magazines, another dozen blurbs on local history in the *Sun News*, a compilation of *Georgetown County Slave Narratives* that I edited and published in conjunction with James A. Fitch through the Georgetown Rice Museum, writing for James L. Michie at Coastal Carolina University on one of his archeology manuscripts, editing the *Independent Republic Quarterly* (the magazine of the Horry County Historical Society) for five years and publishing *Mansfield Plantation: A Legacy on the Black River* through the History Press in 2014, I felt ready to get back to my earlier study and search for deeper meanings to the social clubs. My additional research on the clubs caused me to look further into local calls for secession. By the time that I completed research on the causes of secession locally, I realized that my manuscript was really two books. In 2017, the first part of the study was published as *The Road to Secession in Antebellum*

Georgetown and Horry Districts by Arcadia Press, but my history on the clubs, the basis of my master's thesis, remained largely unpublished.

As I was reading over my earlier manuscript and digging back into the primary sources, I realized that the agricultural and convivial organizations of the Prince George Winyah and All Saints Parish planters were much more than simply a place for planters to gather to talk about farming, enjoy fine wine and dine. The societies and clubs explored in this book served as South Carolina Lowcountry "think tanks" which guided civilization and eventually led the region and influenced the state into secession. The gentlemen did not always agree upon the best road to travel to meet their concerns; thus the organizations served as debate and oratory clubs for the leaders of their civilization to work out their differences and come to a consensus on their visions for the future. In that sense, the organizations served as debate clubs used to fine-tune political thought and acceptable behaviors and make educational, livestock and agrarian improvements which would be used to steer civilization: the populace of their voting districts, the Lowcountry and eventually the state of South Carolina.

Essentially, the social organizations were places where gentlemen could enjoy a day with their contemporaries, drink choice wine and spirits, smoke cigars, dine on exquisite meals, talk politics, agriculture and social concerns without alarming the constituents of their community until they fine-tuned their ideas and without offending their ladies with their strong talks or any individuals whose input was not warranted. Planters and their allies met year-round for decades to provide continuous forums for the leading men of the day to assemble and discuss their concerns. Without having a technologically advanced media to share information, community leaders came together to examine, digest, debate, and disseminate the implications of the latest news and forum responses. After polishing their thoughts, and upon special occasions, the organizations sponsored large gatherings where the people of Georgetown, Horry and sometimes Williamsburg District met to listen to the great orators of the day explain the challenges to their civilization which rallied the masses to defend their traditions and agriculturally based way of life.

To place the organizations within the context of their importance I provided an overall history of rice in Georgetown and on the South Carolina coast as the introduction to this work. Next, I included two chapters on social, economic and political challenges to the rice planter class of the era. In constructing these two chapters I relied heavily upon local newspapers for the regional response to national challenges. It was very clear to me that the newspapers were a mouthpiece of the planter class which were being used to expostulate their conservative morals, values and visions for the future. I provided numerous examples of how the media assisted in shaping and molding the mindset of the people of Georgetown and the surrounding region and was instrumental in bringing forth the war. Rather than address this subject chronologically, I have chosen to address the media's influence upon issues which concerned the planters topically. For example, I tried to express the social, moral, economic and cultural concerns in the first of these two chapters and the political and some economic issues within the pages of the next chapter.

To better explain the challenges to the planter class, the next chapter in this work is an essay which explains the lifestyle of the planter class. The remaining seven chapters deal exclusively with the social organizations of the era. I have chosen to analyze the history and importance of each organization in chronological fashion rather than to provide the reader with a single timeline. My thought process for this method is such that exploring the clubs and societies individually allows for greater details and nuances to be included, and hopefully the reader will better understand the purpose of the association and gain greater appreciation for each organization's form and function. In that sense, the history of each club and society addressed in this work is designed to stand upon its own merits.

To further explain this study, I have placed biographical information on leading men within the text where the gentleman made his most important contributions rather than simply the first time that he is mentioned or to provide a biographical section within this work. Three individuals discussed in this book reached very high-ranking positions in South Carolina politics, so I biographized them in the chapter on political challenges to the region and state. Having reached the office of the president of the state senate and South Carolina governor, Robert F.W. Allston's contributions to state politics, I felt, were larger than his contributions to any of the organizations, and likewise Joshua John Ward and Plowden Charles Jennett Weston, who each reached the post of lieutenant governor of South Carolina during the late antebellum era. I feel that this approach allows the reader to better understand the importance of the individual members and helps express the impacts that leading gentleman had upon politics or an organization in assisting it to reach specific goals.

Introduction:
The Rise and Fall
of the Georgetown Rice Culture

The history of South Carolina's rice culture is one of the most colorful stories in American history. It reminds us of simpler times when agriculture controlled the economy and rice was in its golden age. How rice initially got to America, however, is a question historians have argued over for generations. One theory is that the duke of Albemarle, one of King Charles II's eight Carolina proprietors, originally set up the colony to produce rice. Other historians claim that Dr. Henry Woodward started the rice culture in the 1680s with a single bag of Madagascar rice. Still others claim West African slaves brought rice to America and grew it to subsidize their meager diets.[1] Whether it was Albemarle, Woodward or hungry slaves who began the rice culture, we will probably never know. We do know that beginning in 1691, the general assembly of South Carolina permitted colonists to pay their taxes in rice, and in 1700, Charles Town exported 330 tons of the staple to England and the West Indies.[2]

During its experimental stage, planters grew rice in river swamps around Charles Town. Preparing the land was difficult. Cypress, tupelo and gum trees had to be removed and the land ditched and diked. Planters increased their slaveholdings to perform these chores since a sufficiently large labor force was not already on hand. The rice crop was responsible for a drastic increase in the slave trade. The slave population increased to a point where the slave population eventually outpaced the population of free people and the colony, in fear or rebellion, placed a moratorium upon importing slaves until the population of free persons increased.

Throughout the first century of South Carolina's settlement, rice was an important crop, but it was not the colony's most important export. Tar, pitch, turpentine, timber and the Indian-assisted deerskin trade controlled the early colonial economy. Not until the 1720s and 1730s did the rice industry experience its first boom. At that time, production of the crop advanced to creek bottoms and inland swamps throughout coastal South Carolina. Then, during the 1730s, rice planters began to grow rice on every river in the Lowcountry and experiment with tidal flooding, using the ebb and flow tides to flood and drain fields.[3]

The expansion of the crop led directly to an increase in the number of slaves. By the 1730s, two-thirds of the colony's population were African slaves. Most bondsmen came from the west coast of Africa where rice growing had been a dominant part of African culture since 1500 BCE.[4]

In 1740, Charles Town merchants exported 80,000 barrels of rice, while the districts north and south of Charles Town—Georgetown and Beaufort—exported a combined total of 4,795 barrels. Due to rice crop failures between 1740 and 1746, and interference in shipping due to the British Empire's war with France (known as the War of Jenkin's Ear—a part of the much greater European war known as the War of Austrian Succession), prices dropped, and insurance rates increased. Exports remained small throughout the 1740s, and the 1710 shipping figure was not surpassed until 1755. After a few years of peace, France and England went back to war in the Seven Years' War/French and Indian War (1754–1763). Finally, in 1766, after 25 years of inconsistency, the rice trade stabilized, and prices remained high for ten years.

During this lull in the rice market, South Carolinians (led by Eliza Lucas) developed a profitable indigo market which quickly surpassed the profitability of rice since it was sold and used within the British Empire exclusively. The South Carolina Lowcountry, with its abundance of rich, high, loose soil between the rivers, provided a perfect environment for indigo production. To the north and west of Georgetown, townships had already begun to develop: Williamsburg on the Black River, Queensboro on the Pee Dee River and Kingston (now Conway) on the Waccamaw River. Williamsburg, with its superior soil, became the production site of the finest-quality indigo grown in the English colonies.

In 1747, South Carolina had its first indigo export, and the following year the crop established credit in the London banking houses. In 1748, shortly after the restoration of peace between the colonial powers, the King of England offered a bounty of six pence per pound for quality indigo to exclude French indigo from the British Empire. The bounty stimulated a boom in production. Indigo production expanded until 1760 when production leveled off.

South Carolina planters eventually manufactured three types of indigo: a copper-colored variety used for dying wool, purple for linen and blue for silk. In most cases, planters grew rice and indigo on the same plantations: rice on the tidal flood plains and indigo on the upland. It was almost natural for planters to grow both crops because slaves cultivated indigo in the summer and cut, cleaned and milled rice in the autumn.

Although indigo planting was highly profitable in South Carolina and helped to keep wealth within the English colonial system, indigo grown in the tropics was far superior in quality. Spanish Guatemala grew the finest indigo in the world, followed by the French West Indies. In those areas, four or five crops could be harvested each year, while South Carolinians, due to differences in climate, could produce only two, and in addition to having a shorter growing season, South Carolina's indigo cakes tended to be hard on the surface and not fully cured in the middle. Despite these shortcomings, the crop produced the area's first aristocracy.

Profits from indigo supported the growth of an intellectual center in Georgetown: the Winyah Indigo Society. The society grew out of a convivial club which met monthly at the Old Oak Tavern on Bay Street (now Front Street). As early as 1740, planters met to eat and drink, to discuss the latest news from Europe and to compare notes on agriculture and livestock. In 1755, this informal group became a society and two years later was incorporated as the Winyah Indigo Society.

As the English and French battled for supremacy over the North American continent and the high seas, as well as influence in Europe, South Carolinians worked on improving the rice culture. In 1758, McKewn Johnstone used the ocean's ebb and flow tides to flood and drain his rice fields with river water. Planters had been damming rain and creek water into reserves to systematically flood their rice fields since 1748 without great success. Johnstone's method held out hope to the rice industry.[5]

On the eve of the American Revolution, Northern Europe, mainly Holland and the German states, imported as much as 65 percent of the rice exported from South Carolina and Georgia. Southern Europe, primarily Spain and Portugal, imported only 17 percent of the crop, and the West Indies, with a large slave population to feed, accounted for the remaining 18 percent.[6] Generally, English consumers refrained from eating rice and remained dependent upon wheat products. France and Spain (England's main competitors for world empire), for the most part, relied primarily upon cheaper rice from Turkey and Brazil.[7] On the contrary to England, transplanted Englishmen in South Carolina and everyone and everything else in the colony consumed rice or used rice by-products. The parts not consumed by people were used as bedding for slaves and fodder for animals. Horses, pigs and cattle ate the straw and bran, fowls the refuse.[8]

In 1770, King George III reduced the bounty on quality indigo to four pence per pound and abolished it when the American Revolution erupted in 1776; both the indigo and slave trades collapsed. With closure of commerce with England, indigo lost its only market, and rice became the area's top cash crop again.[9]

During the 1780s, after suffering through the American Revolution, the rice industry underwent a revolution of its own. In 1783, Gideon Dupont perfected the tidal flooding method of growing rice, which allowed planters to utilize fertile flood plains for cultivation. With the tidal flow method of irrigation, fields were flooded by freshwater rivers which pushed water upstream during high tide and dropped it during low tide. Soon, planters expanded rice production to the tidal lands on each of the Lowcountry's rivers.

In 1787, Jonathan Lucas built the first water-powered rice pounding mill, and in 1792, the first tide-operated mill. Jacob Motte Alston, a Waccamaw River rice planter, recalled the function of these mills. He wrote:

> The mill was erected near the river, and the fields in the rear were flooded at high water. Then the floodgates were closed, and when the tide fell in the river, the water held back in the fields was some four or five feet higher than the river.
> This then was the motive power which set the machinery of the mill's water wheel in motion; huge stones to rotate and the heavy pestles to pound. The grain, when under the rapidly rotating stones, would not lie side-wise but on end, and so escaped being broken. The former [the stones] were [so] set as only to grind off the outer hull of the grain, called chaff; and the latter [the pestles], the inner coverings, which was the coarse flour used for feeding stock. The flinty grains of rice were then carried by elevators through screens of various dimensions and, last, polished on rapidly revolving drums, covered with prepared sheep-skins.[10]

Prior to Lucas's inventions, slaves used the ancient African mortar and pestle method of removing the outer hull from the grain. A few animal-powered rice pounding mills, mostly oxen, had been used before Lucas's inventions.[11]

However, it cannot be disputed that his inventions helped to foster the crop's position in South Carolina's economy. In fact, most Lowcountry historians agree that Lucas's mills had an impact on the rice industry comparable to the impact Eli Whitney's cotton gin had on the cotton trade.

With these new technologies, rice planting became so profitable that many merchants, physicians and attorneys left their professions, purchased land and slaves and plated rice. Soon, Georgetown, South Carolina, became the center of American rice production, cultivating almost half of the nation's annual rice crop on 46,000 acres. The number of slaves increased proportionately. By 1810 nearly 90 percent of the district's population were slaves.[12]

The new profitability of rice planting also brought a sudden rise in land prices. Improved rice land sold for roughly $200 to $300 per acre;

virgin swampland sold for roughly $100 per acre, as compared with pine land, an area non-conducive to rice planting, which sold for only 25 cents per acre. Soon, it became nearly impossible to buy into rice planting. By the antebellum era, most planters were born into rice planting families as an aristocracy of planters controlled the rice lands.

Year	1820	1830	1840	1850	1860
Male	7,851	8,381	7,589	8,748	9,143
Female	7,695	9,417	8,413	9,505	8,966
Total	15,546	17,798	15,993	18,253	18,109

Georgetown Slaves according to the Census Reports.

The primeval forest (courtesy Rice Museum, Georgetown, SC, photograph by Rich Taylor).

Though profitable, there was a great risk involved in planting rice. One in three crops were swept away by freshets (sudden flooding of streams) and autumn gales. Other enemies of the planters were the bob-olinks (also known as rice birds), blackbirds, crows, grubs, rice worms, ducks, maggots, rice weevils, rats, crayfish, snakes and alligators. The process of transforming virgin swamps into tidal-flooded rice fields was difficult work. Fields had to be low enough to be flooded at high tide yet high enough to be drained when the tide went out.

Slaves measured the land and felled and burned trees. Next, they cut a four- or five-foot ditch through the clearing to form an enclosing bank with mud, leaving a 15- or 20-foot-wide space surrounded by a canal. In the third phase of construction, slaves installed floodgates (or trunk docks), drained and completely cleared the fields of stumps and underbrush. Finally, the fields were ready for the first season. The second season, slaves dug quarter divides, smaller ditches two feet wide, three feet deep and a quarter-acre apart (50 to 75 feet apart) running the length and width of the field. Cross banks served as dividers for the different fields and were kept above the highest point of the field so the land could be covered without overtopping the enclosing banks. Slaves also repaired banks so that the outside remained a few feet higher than the spring tide and constructed smaller banks to divide fields. Finally, slaves dug ditches four or five feet deep around the entire field and put in small drains, about two feet wide and the same depth, in place so the fields could be drained. The resulting product was a field of beds from 50 to 75 feet wide. When completed, a large plantation with 500 acres of rice land had about 60 miles of ditches and canals.

Clearing the land (courtesy Rice Museum, Georgetown, SC, photograph by Rich Taylor).

Planting the fields (courtesy Rice Museum, Georgetown, SC, photograph by Rich Taylor).

Slaves harrowed and plowed the fields for cultivation in March, using either mules or oxen. Oxen, with their divided hooves, negotiated the lower fields easier; mules required rawhide or wooden "boots" tied to their feet. The fields were laid off in trenches about 12 to 15 inches apart to receive seed. Slaves clayed seeds by soaking them in wet mud and allowing them to dry before planting to prevent the seeds from floating when the sprout flow, the first flooding of the fields, was applied.

The sprout water remained on the fields until the grain sprouted, usually between three and six days. Next, by opening the floodgates, slaves drained the fields so the seeds could emerge. When seedlings were visible above ground, trunk minders opened the floodgates again and flooded the fields for another three to six days. This point, or stretch flow, encouraged the rice to grow. When trunk minders drained fields, field hands lightly hoed the acreage. Twelve days later, slaves strong-hoed fields and allowed the sun to dry out the plots for two or three days, enough time to kill weeds and grass exposed by hoeing. Then, slaves opened the floodgates once again and applied the long flow or deep flow, sometimes called long water, completely submerging the rice.

By this time, it was midseason. This flooding killed insects such as rice worms and grubs and floated trash left over from previous hoeing, which slaves raked out of the fields. After three or four days, slaves opened floodgates and dropped the water level to six inches then slowly drained the remaining water. When the ground dried, slaves hoed the fields again. About three weeks later, slaves hoed the fields for the last time. Then they

Harvest (courtesy Rice Museum, Georgetown, SC, photograph by Rich Taylor).

applied the lay-by flow, the last flooding, and fields remained submerged for seven or eight weeks. When they drained the fields again, usually in early September, the crop was ready for harvest.

Slaves used sickles, known as rice hooks, to cut down the grain one day before it fully ripened and allowed it to dry for a day. Then laborers tied the rice in sheaves, loaded the harvest onto small boats called flats and moved it by river to threshing yards. Next, slaves stacked the harvest in barns to dry. When thoroughly dry, rice was either sold in this rough form or processed by plantation slaves using a flail stick. Slaves placed bundles of rice in rows on the ground with heads joining each other. Then, laborers walked between rows,

Rice threshing with flail sticks (Georgetown County Library, Georgetown, SC).

The water-powered rice mill (courtesy Rice Museum, Georgetown, SC, photograph by Rich Taylor).

swinging flail sticks above their heads and then down on the heads of rice. This beating, or threshing process, removed the grain from the straw.[13] This primitive African method of threshing gave way to animal-powered mills, followed by water-powered and wind-powered mills.

Finally, in 1830, Calvin Emmons produced a steam-powered threshing mill which threshed 700 bushels of rice per day and cost about $8,000. This invention utilized a multiplicity of machinery, including beaters, rakes, screens and fans. Despite their cost, many planters owned steam-powered threshing mills by 1860. However, all seed rice was still threshed by the flail stick because the mill cracked the grain and often injured the germinating end. After threshing, slaves either winnowed the rice in fanner baskets, separating straw tailings from the grain, or brought it to a winnowing house.

A winnowing house was about 16 feet square, built high on posts of 12 to 15 feet, and stood about 20 feet high. Slaves took threshed rice up into the structure and dropped it through a grating or hole in the floor. The breeze blew away light and unfilled grains and short pieces of straw. Next, the grain was either sold as brown rice, pounded in a mortar and pestle set, or brought to a pounding mill for polishing.[14]

Separating the straw tailings or chaff from the grain with a fanner basket (courtesy Rice Museum, Georgetown, SC, photograph by Rich Taylor).

During the 1840s, steam power was applied to rice pounding mills at a cost of about $20,000. Robert F.W. Allston, a rice planter on the Pee Dee River, explained his steam-powered pounding mill's function. He wrote,

> By steam power the rough rice is taken out of the vessel which freights it up to the attic of the building—thence through the sand screen to a pair of (five feet wide) heavy stones, which grind off the husk—hence into large iron-shod pestles, weighing 120 to 350 pounds, for the space of two hours, more or less. The rice now pounded, is once more elevated into the attic, whence it descends through a rolling screen, to separate whole grains from the broken, and flour from both; and also through wind fans, to a vertical brushing screen, moving rapidly, which polishes the flinty grain and delivers it fully prepared, into the barrel or tierce, which is to convey it to market.[15]

Plantation work was not confined to the March through September planting season. Slaves worked year-round. Preparing the crop for market took a considerable amount of time. Also, ditches had to be cleared, stubble burned, floodgates mended and replaced, banks rebuilt, and new fields cleared. Fields were rarely left fallow or manured. In 1840, on hundreds of plantations, South Carolina produced 66,897,244 pounds of the nation's 88,953,468-pound rice crop.

The winnowing house (courtesy Rice Museum, Georgetown, SC, photograph by Rich Taylor).

The antebellum era proved to be the most profitable decade for South Carolina rice planters, who, thanks to mechanical advancements in preparing rice for market, produced 159,930,613 pounds of rice (5,753,000 bushels) in 1850 alone.[16] Many planters sold more than 1,000,000 pounds of rice each at $2.75 to $5.00 per hundred pounds for clean rice and $0.75 to $1.00 per bushel for rough rice. By 1860, the planting class, the wealthiest 3 percent of the Southern population, owned more than 50 percent of the land in the Lowcountry, and Georgetown, South Carolina, led the Lowcountry in production.

Mortar and pestle method for polishing rice (Georgetown County Library, Georgetown, SC).

The inner workings of a rice mill (courtesy Rice Museum, Georgetown, SC, photograph by Rich Taylor).

Georgetown District	36,360,000 Pounds
Charleston District	11,938,750 Pounds
Beaufort District	5,629,402 Pounds
Colleton District	5,483,533 Pounds
South Carolina Total	59,411,685 Pounds
United States Total	80,841,422 Pounds

South Carolina Rice Production, 1840.

Although the Civil War disrupted the production of rice and crippled the economy, some planters continued to produce the staple. However, now only able to cultivate about one-third of their rice land (due to a shortage of skilled laborers willing to stay at their former slave jobs), planters steadily lost influence over the economy as railroad companies, public utilities, banks, lumber companies, turpentine producers, phosphate

Mending a flood gate (courtesy Rice Museum, Georgetown, SC, photograph by Rich Taylor).

Corporate rice mill on the Sampit River, Georgetown, SC (courtesy Rice Museum, Georgetown, SC, photograph by Rich Taylor).

mining and corporate-owned rice mills became the new foundations of the economy and often employed the best workers. The new employers could pay employees weekly or biweekly due to their production and frequent sales of products and services and at higher rates of pay than planters could possibly afford due to the depressed condition of the rice market because of the disruption of war and because planters could only pay employees upon selling their crop.[17]

Because of the shortage of laborers, exorbitant interest rates and lack of capital (due to crop failures), rice yields were very small. Nonetheless, planters still profited because the shortage of production led to an increase in price to between seven and eight cents per pound, double prewar prices. Despite higher prices, South Carolina's supremacy in the rice market quickly waned.

In 1881, when railroads connected New Orleans to Houston, land speculators and Midwestern farmers moved into Louisiana and used methods of wheat agriculture to improve the existing rice culture. Farmers employed harvesting machinery, improved Japanese seed, steam engines, gang plows, seeders, disks and twine binders to achieve dominance over South Carolina. An agricultural revolution came to rice production, but because of the South Carolina Lowcountry's soft, boggy soil, South Carolinians could not mechanize. After completion of the Southern Pacific Railroad, Texas and Arkansas joined Louisiana in developing the "Prairie Rice Culture."[18]

By 1909 the three prairie rice-growing states produced nearly 99 percent of the nation's rice crop (22,877,000 bushels of the 23,586,000 produced in the United States). At the time, Louisiana cultivated more than 400,000 acres of rice land. Texas planted 286,847 acres, while South Carolina worked only 35,041 acres.[19]

In addition to labor problems and competition from mechanization, a series of environmental catastrophes sped along the decline of South Carolina's rice culture.

Between 1893 and 1913, hurricanes and ten violent storms destroyed annual crops, and severe freshets topped flood banks and washed away the barriers to saltwater circumvention and took their toll on the land. By 1920, South Carolinians planted fewer than 500 acres of rice, and the crop ceased to be an export. The age of magnificence had passed, and the empire built on rice had fallen.[20]

State	1839	1849	1859	1869	1879	1889	1899	1909	1919	1929
Arkansas	-	2	1	3	-	-	-	1,264	7,600	7,956
California	-	-	-	-	-	-	-	-	9,300	5,719
Florida	17	39	8	14	47	36	81	20	33	-
Georgia	445	1,401	1,889	801	913	524	402	139	58	-
Louisiana	130	159	228	570	834	2,721	6,213	12,617	19,005	18,832
Mississippi	28	98	29	13	62	24	27	-	-	-
North Carolina	101	197	273	74	202	210	284	22	-	-
South Carolina	2,180	5,753	4,284	1,162	1,873	1,091	1,704	528	131	-
Texas	-	3	1	2	2	4	259	8,996	6,784	7,027
All Others	7	93	20	10	29	16	33	-	-	-
U. S. Total	2,908	7,745	6,733	2,649	3,962	4,626	9,003	23,586	42,911	39,514

Rice production in the United States, 1839–1929, in thousand bushels.

ONE

Georgetown's Response to Social, Moral and Economic Challenges

Agriculture is our wisest pursuit, because it will
in the end contribute most to real wealth, good
morals, and happiness.—Thomas Jefferson

Antebellum South Carolina was a state under siege, and Georgetown rice planters rallied the populace against a triple threat from the North which endangered the South's traditional lifestyle. The growing tide of liberalism associated with the Second Great Awakening (an outpouring of social reforms that took place in the North and West), the growing industrial sector in the North which challenged the South's traditional agricultural lifestyle, and the federal government of the United States' willingness to modify in order to accommodate the demands of the proponents of change (brought on by a continuous stream of immigration to the Northern states) prompted South Carolina to react.

Agricultural societies and social clubs served as places for planters and their allies to meet, compare notes on matters of importance and develop their arguments in countering the rising tide of national and international, moral, social and economic changes. Within the sacred walls of their organizations, and on the pages of their newspapers, members discussed local, state, and national politics, advancements to their educational system, agricultural and livestock improvements in order to better compete with the industrial North. Within the protected confines of their convivial organizations, planters felt safe discussing politics and sharing disfavor for the changes sweeping the North and West. Jointly, in conjunction with their newspapers, planters used their organizations and convivial clubs to craft a political alliance with the yeomen farmers and forged Southern Nationalism.

Rice planters and their allies were on the defensive during the antebellum era. Religious and social reformers criticized their lifestyle and

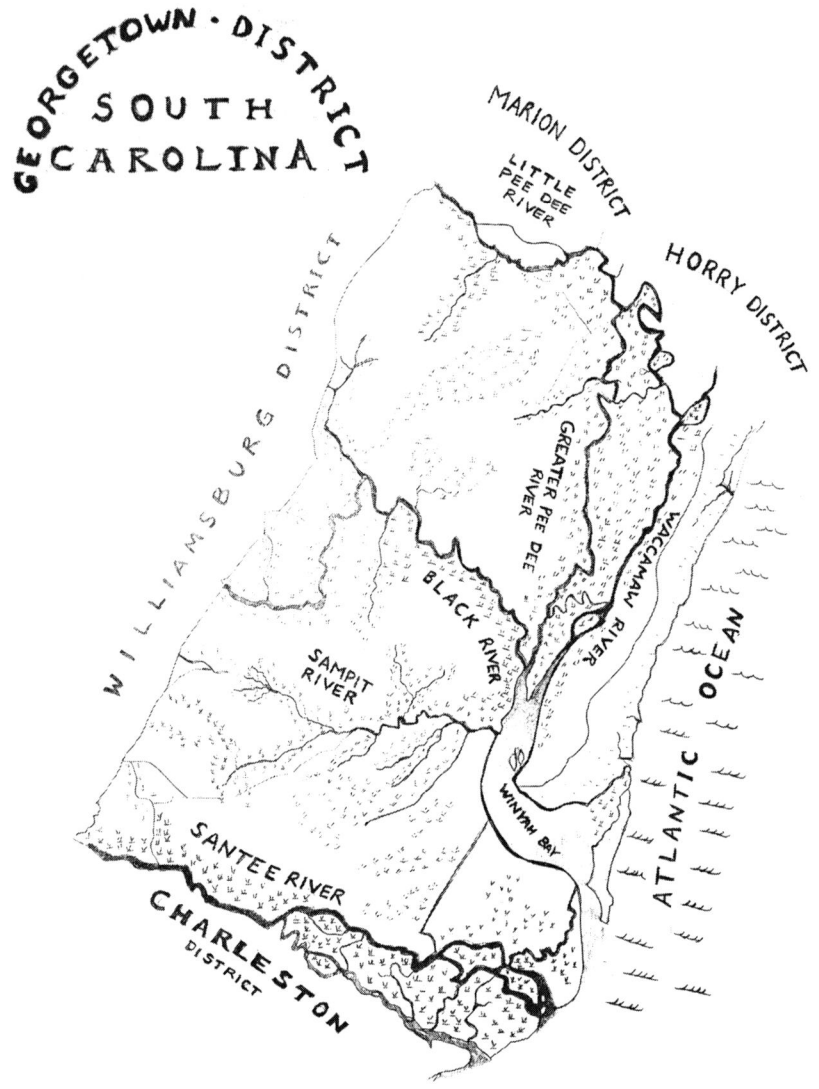

Georgetown District, 1825, by Robert Mills, reproduced by D'Andrea Lynn Boyle and photographed by Rich Taylor.

their patriarchal code of chivalry as a medieval holdover of European tyranny. Activists protested the planters' social, political and economic arrangement, first established on the North American continent in the Virginia colony and inherited from the earliest settlers of Carolina, as oligarchical and promoting male-dominated authoritarianism.

Like the Founding Fathers at the Continental Congress, rice planters held in esteem the enlightened argument put forth by English philosopher, John Locke, the rights to life, liberty and property. However, although they claimed to be resolute in their maintenance of traditional values, the reform movements of the Second Great Awakening did prompt the rice planters to bring forth change in many aspects of their cherished culture. Unlike the North, however, which wanted to use the central government to bring forth social and economic changes, the rice planters believed that change should come from their state and local governments.

Planters agreed with the social contract that men create governments to serve and protect themselves. They held close to the idea that if government fails to deliver basic rights to citizens (in this case derived from God and defined by the government's founders) or through shear population imbalance forces the will of the majority of the citizenry upon the minority of the population, they have the rights, in the words of Thomas Jefferson's Declaration of Independence, "to alter or to abolish it, and to institute new government, laying its foundation on such principles, and organizing its powers in such form, as to them shall seem most likely to affect their safety and happiness."

The great Southern agriculturalists clung to the American Revolution-era political ideas passed down to them by their fathers, concluding that local autonomy was better than a strong, central authority and keeping the ideas espoused in Jefferson's Declaration of Independence. They held fast to the ideas of the framers of the United States Constitution and the Bill of Rights that the American governing documents intentionally set forth limitations upon the central authority in order to preserve the powers of the states and the people. They cherished the Tenth Amendment which clearly states that the powers not delegated to the United States by the Constitution, nor prohibited by the states, were reserved to the states or, respectively, to the people.

In short, the United States was in the midst of great social and economic changes, and the conservative planter class, which produced the Founding Fathers and framers of the United States Constitution, such as George Washington, Thomas Jefferson and James Madison, were accused of being barbaric and tyrannical for remaining devoted to the Founding Fathers' ideals.

To planters, their lifestyle was not barbaric or tyrannical at all but rather gentile and based upon the founding principles of the United States. However, although they clung to "American ideals," their code of chivalry was certainly rooted in medieval values of gentility.

While Americans North and South debated the actions of their leaders, and the difference between barbarism and gentility, Georgetown's *Pee Dee Times* asked its readers, "What Constitutes a Gentleman?" After considering if gentility revolved around wealth, dress and manners, the author of the article concluded that wealth and fine clothing had nothing to do with gentility. The author concluded, "Gentility is not wealth; it is not in dress, nor genius, nor any other attribute of man, unless it goes hand in hand with a cheerful disposition, an amiable temper and a philanthropic will. There are real bonafide Gentlemen in all classes of society, and he is the greatest gentleman who mingles with all and remains untarnished." Later on in the same article, the author wrote, "Real gentility is moral freedom; it respects no particular person, as a class beyond their merits; it does not exclude one man because he is poor; but embracing all who are worthy, it regards them as kindred souls who should ever dwell harmonious together. This constitutes a gentleman."[1]

The Second Great Awakening reforms took root in Puritan-inspired New England's rocky soil and the growing cities of the Northeast. As the reforms expanded and diversified over time, and more people were swept up by the spirit of change, the traditional mentality of what was gentile continuously morphed. As immigrants fled the reemergence of the European monarchies after the fall of Napoleon Bonaparte and sought refuge for their French Revolutionary liberal ideas in the Western Hemisphere, the Northern seaport cities swelled with unskilled laborers with the new ideas for social justice.

The Second Great Awakening was born in Northern churches, but it was clearly more than a religious movement; it included a plethora of radical social reforms. The abolitionist movement, women's rights movement, prison and asylum reforms, national education reforms, anti-dueling legislation, the temperance movement, utopian societies and new religious sects were all seen as threats to the planter class who dominated the American South and desperately wanted to retain their traditional ways of life. These social modifications conflicted with the traditional values and family structure of the planter class. However, although they stated they wished to hold onto their traditional livelihood, it cannot be denied that the various movements did affect the Georgetown rice planters and did cause them to alter their own civilization even though they insisted that they were steadfast to defend their traditions.

By the antebellum era, the rice planters of South Carolina's Lowcountry had spent over 150 years developing their civilization. The world that they carefully constructed centered upon the Episcopal Church, and the people lived by the propositions suggested in the *Winyah Observer* articles titled "Profanity—don't do it," "Depend upon yourself and God will lead you," and articles on the apostles, their wives and children.[2]

The Second Great Awakening saw the expansion of the Methodist and Baptist and to a lesser extent the Presbyterian sects among the farming and merchant classes through camp meeting revivals and evangelical circuit riders. The expansions of these Christian sects were not necessarily seen as threats by the Episcopalian planters, but the development of the Mormon religion (the Church of Jesus Christ of Latter-day Saints) was disdained. The Mormons boasted of ties to a lost tribe of Israel and claimed to possess another testament of the Bible. *The Winyah Observer* informed its readers that the origins of *The Book of Mormon* or "Golden Bible" and "its claim to a divine origin is wholly unfounded."[3] Later, The *Pee Dee Times* published an article titled "An illustration of Mormonism—the Truth is Stranger than Fiction."[4]

Planters also eschewed the expansion of religious utopian communities such as the millennial optimistic Seventh Day Adventist and Advent Christians whose leaders prophesied the end of time and claimed to have mathematically figured out the return of Jesus Christ. They also questioned the beliefs of the Shakers (United Society of Believers in Christ's Second Coming), a group who eventually had 19 communities by 1820 and 60 by 1860 scattered throughout the West and a few in the North (with a combined population of over 6,000) who alleged that all men and women were created equal and, as a result, banned sex (even for reproduction) because they claimed sex was a tool that men used to dominate women. They recruited members and "demarried" converts as part of their mission of celibacy, self-discipline and their belief in devotion to God's will. On the contrary, another utopian group, the Oneida community of upstate New York (a community that began as the Putney Association in Vermont in 1840 and moved to New York in 1848) raised concerns among the planters due to their beliefs in complex marriage, sexual partner swapping, and eventually, after the publication of Charles Darwin's book titled *On the Origins of Species*, began eugenic selection. These less-developed Christian sects and communities offered new ideas that seemed outlandish and contrary to conservative Episcopal beliefs. Another group, Brook Farm in West Roxbury, Massachusetts, was a transcendentalist communistic model experimental community which grew to about 100 members over its six-year existence from 1841 to 1847. The group had collective ownership of all land and properties. It began as an agricultural collective, but it attracted mostly urban dwellers who did not have farming skills; thus the community resorted to hard labor and was eventually not very attractive to potential converts due to the hard work required to live in the community.[5]

Adding to the religious deviations developing in the North and on the Western frontier, atheism rose. A group of antireligious people in Boston, Massachusetts, held the Anti-Sabbath Convention. William Lloyd Garrison and Lucretia Mott led the convention and "spoke to a packed house and their message was very well received." They proposed that honoring Sunday as a holy day and a day of rest violated their First Amendment right to freedom of, and freedom from, religion. The convention, supported by industrialization, proposed that steamboats and railroad traffic commence on Sunday and that factories and businesses conduct trade as normal. William Lloyd Garrison went so far as to declare that "ministers are wolves in sheep clothing" and accused them of being "Christian Tyrants."[6]

At the same time of these religious upheavals and broadening of religious diversity in Christian sects and utopian communities, women reformers challenged the planter class's patriarchal society. The female reformers called for a convention to "discuss the social, civil, and religious condition and rights of women" for the right to vote and to be treated equal to men. Elizabeth Cady Stanton published and read her *Declaration of Sentiments* to a crowd of 300 men and women at the Seneca Falls Convention. Nearly 100 in attendance signed her document, including William Lloyd Garrison, Lucretia Mott and a runaway slave turned orator and autobiographer, Frederick Douglas. Female agitators continued to hold conferences and demand their rights until the outbreak of war in 1861.

The world the rice planters created inspired boys to become gentile country gentlemen who mandated a society in which girls supported the men in their lives—not competed with them as equals. Their children started their formal education early and learned the art of manners, grace, and conversation. Ladies married young, bore several children and expected their husband to head the household.

The planters of South Carolina's rice coast certainly loved their mothers and daughters but believed that females occupied a different place in society than men in several ways. They held that women were to be honored for educating and raising children, providing a moralistic model for the family unit, running the homestead, and serving and supporting her husband's career. The planters' notion of paternalism required them to shield the women in their lives from politics and economic concerns to keep them untarnished from the anxieties of business. As a result, gentleman had their social clubs and societies where they could address business and politics, drink alcohol, use foul language and smoke cigars outside of the home and away from their wives and daughters without offending ears and noses.

Although they attempted to cloak their wives from business and politics, Southern ladies, whether they liked it or not, lived right in the middle of their planter-husband's agri-business. Though wealthy, they were still burdened with the traditional duties of wife of one and mother of many. Meanwhile, plantation mistresses helped supervise the slave labor force, nursed the sick, gave out rations, clothing and medicines, cut out garments, sewed, spun, and knitted.[7]

One Georgetown merchant from this time period explained the demeanor and lack of political involvement among the ladies of Georgetown. He wrote, "Politics were rather ignored in the drawing room, not because the ladies were supposed to be ignorant or out of sympathy with the questions of the day (on the contrary they rather cultivated a taste for public affairs), but as a matter of good form, because Southern Gallantry held that social occasions should be devoted mainly to the amusement of polite society."[8]

In an article in the *Winyah Observer* titled "A Good Wife," the author wrote, "The Place of Women is eminently at the fireside. It is at home that you must see her to know what she is. It is less material what she is abroad; but what she is in the family circle is all important."[9] Other articles in the same journal such as "Woman: Her Mission and Destiny," "Diffusion of Christianity," and a poem in the same newspaper titled "The Worth of a Woman" reinforced the female position in planter society.[10] On November 1, 1848, *Winyah Observer* published "Domestic Training" which advised women how to train their daughters to become good wives and "Women" which explained their role in uplifting their husband and helping to keep him focused upon his trade by taking care of him.[11]

The *Pee Dee Times*, the most prominent Georgetown newspaper of the 1850s, promoted the same mentality in a series of articles such as, "A wife's devotion; or the chivalry of love," "A receipt for getting a husband," "Devotion of a true woman," and "Marrying advice to ladies."[12] In an article titled "How to treat a wife," the newspaper explained how a man should act towards his wife. The article explained that men must be patient. The report expounded, "you may have great trials and perplexities in your business with the world; but do not therefore carry to your home a clouded or contracted brow."[13]

Another assault upon the patriarchal structure of the planters was the temperance movement—an undertaking to limit or ban the use of alcohol. The American Temperance Society started in 1826 with the intention of "saving the American family" and by the 1840s consisted of over 8,000 local groups with more than 1,500,000 members who had taken the pledge to abstain from consuming alcohol. Most rice planters enjoyed their brandy and cigars, wine, champagne and spirits. They consumed spirits at home and at their social clubs and society meetings, which were always occasions for celebration.

Eleazer Waterman, proprietor of the *Georgetown American* and later the *Winyah Observer,* explained that his paper would publish the views of all and not be conformed to support any agenda.[14] He published

"The Drinking, Vending and Making Ardent Spirits" and "The Temperance Oath" by Mary L Gardner and later the Washingtonian's temperance oath.[15] Georgetown rice planter, John Izard Middleton, explained the planters' view of temperance, which, like most other issues, was based upon their view of small, localized government. He said, "I am opposed to a prohibitory law against the sale of ardent spirits. I deplore the evils which arise from the excessive indulgence in the use of strong drink, but fear those evils are beyond the reach of legislation."[16]

To the planter class, the abolitionist crusade was the largest, most visible, concentrated and dangerous reform movement spawned by the Second Great Awakening. The abolitionist movement originally began during the colonial period under the tutelage of the Quakers but spread throughout the North. Abolitionists' publications ran from the mundane, which simply asked for the release of slaves, to the radical. Boston freeman of color, David Walker, was among the most radical. He called for a race war in his 1829 publication *Walker's Appeal* to free slaves. William Lloyd Garrison, the radical proprietor of the magazine *Liberator*, proposed that the virtuous New Englanders should secede from the United States if the federal government would not intervene and end slavery. Garrison's publications, as well as other abolitionist papers, were banned from the mail south of the Mason-Dixon Line. At the same time, the United States House of Representatives adopted a "gag rule" on the issue of slavery from 1836 to 1844. The Senate was still open to debate the "peculiar institution," but the house, which was dominated by the Northeastern states due to their population, banned discussing or debating the issue.

By the 1830s, the abolitionist movement became more centralized. William Lloyd Garrison and his abolitionist friends formed the American Antislavery Society, a national organization with branches throughout the North and West determined to end slavery in the United States. Some radical abolitionists refused to eat rice or sugar, wear cotton clothing or smoke tobacco because they were all produced by slave labor. By the 1840s other abolitionists openly defied the fugitive slave laws by assisting runaways along the Underground Railroad, a system of safe houses along trails leading north. Abolitionists claimed that they were serving a higher power and rule, while they cognitively plotted and willfully broke the law by instilling and promoting insurrection and by aiding runaways and their guides on their journey to Northern states and Canada. In April 1851, the prominent Georgetown newspaper of the day printed an article in reaction to the work of the Underground Railroad, where it claimed that the "People of South Carolina are ready for secession—only strict adherence to the fugitive slave law can prevent it."[17]

At the dawn of the 1850s, Southerners were completely enraged with the changes taking place in the North and with the way that Northerners were attempting to enforce their ideas of reform upon the rest of the country. The *Winyah Observer* published an article titled "The Slavery Question," which was a complete defense of the institution of slavery and the Southern way of life.[18] With the South continuously closing in on itself in defense of its civilization, and having called for the Nashville Convention with all 15 slaveholding states for the coming summer, Northern reformers incessantly called for change, the population in the Western territories expanded and pushed for statehood, and it appeared that the United States was careening towards insolvency if not violence.

In the midst of the 1850 crisis, the *Winyah Observer* published articles such as "Slavery and the Constitution" where the paper explained to its readers that slavery was legal in the Constitution and that the people of the South had the right to maintain the institution. The paper furthered the defense of slavery by stating that Northern agitation of slavery would not cease and expressed the need for citizens to prepare to defend their civilization.[19]

One of the major topics explored in the early 1850's editions of the *Pee Dee Times* was the issue of combatting the abolitionists and the promoters of change in the North and West. Articles such as "Can an Abolitionist be a Gentleman," numerous articles on their perspective of benevolent "charity" and "philanthropy," and reproachful articles on fanaticism, such as "New York Conventions," were common.

In the article, "New York Conventions," the paper indicted New York as the new leader in the various reform movements by saying, "The Empire State has distinguished itself for holding conventions of every stripe and color—Women's rights, Greeylite, anti–Christ, temperance, abolitionist and political." Another article played on the fears of the people by warning of "More Abolitionist Outrages" and decreed that the North is full of fanatics who will injure those Southerners who travel outside of the South. The article stated, "It is now a settled matter that Southern citizens going into the Free States are considered fit game for robbery and assassination."[20]

On May 11, 1853, less than a year after the publication of her book, *Uncle Tom's Cabin*, the newspaper published an article on "Harriet Beecher Stowe's Charity" where it accused her of having a lack of philanthropic concern for slaves. The article described a story of a slave owner in Virginia who recently contacted a benevolent society in Philadelphia, explaining that he would like to sell 30 slaves into freedom. He asked if the society could help him by raising funds necessary to free them since he had a mortgage on the chattel property. Stowe and other leading abolitionists were contacted by the benign society to help raise money for the cause.

Some people contributed to the fund; however, Stowe did not offer any financial support. Instead of helping to finance the effort, apparently she returned a "sweet sympathy card with the charity of advice and approval, but no money." The *Pee Dee Times* chastised Mrs. Stowe for her lack of financial support by stating, "Her mission is to make money out of Negro philanthropy and not for it."[21]

Another inflammatory article concerning abolitionists was "Condition of the Colored Population of the North," which informed citizens that they were not only lawful in keeping slaves under the Constitution but doing God's duty by keeping their slaves in good health. The article described the free persons of color in the North as living in abject poverty, "half-starved and left to die in the gutter." The tabloid explained the actions of the abolitionists as self-serving and non-philanthropic. The newspaper complained, "the illustrations of their own directions are the very reverse of their preaching" and once again accused abolitionists of not living up to their preaching and dismissed their actions as "an example of the difference between the profession and the practice of abolition."[22]

By late 1853, the Lowcountry's interpretation of slavery changed again. As the collective mentality shifted from the "humanitarian idealism" of Thomas Jefferson to the "economic realism" of John C. Calhoun by the mid–1820s, the rhetoric of the mid–1850s turned to a proslavery defense of slavery as a positive good. According to the Lowcountry's new stance on slavery, all persons, slaves, masters and non-slaveholding persons had a vested interest in seeing slavery defended and upheld, and slaves were Christianized to save their souls from damnation.[23]

During the antebellum era, slavery was certainly different than it was in the Lowcountry prior to the reforms of the Second Great Awakening. The abolitionists, although not able to bring freedom to the slaves, were able to convince planters to better provide for their human chattel through political and social pressure. Visible changes in the overall system of slavery in the Georgetown District can be seen in the transformation in housing standards for slaves. Most planters built wooden two-family duplex homes for their slaves on raised platforms to promote better health by keeping slaves from sleeping on the ground as they had in the earlier African designed huts. Many planters also reserved half of the workday on Saturday for slaves to clean their whitewashed homes and belongings to avoid sickness. Also, by this time period, slaves on many plantations had regular medical attention provided by either their master (many planters became doctors at this time period for the sole purpose of taking care of their family and slaves) or a traveling doctor, used store-bought porcelains for eating and house servants wore tailored livery, not homespun. Ultimately, planters brought Christianity to their slaves to save their souls. The

Methodists and the Episcopalians had missions to the slaves in Georgetown during the era.

One citizen of Georgetown explained that slavery was not a perfect situation and that "there were cruel masters, just as there are cruel fathers, and hardheaded overseers in the mills and factories North and East, but the comforts of well-treated Negroes far surpassed those of the best regulated factories."[24] One South Carolina politician later explained his state's view comparing immigrant hirelings and the treatment and welfare of African slaves. "The Senator from New York said yesterday that the whole world had abolished slavery. Aye, the name, but not the thing; all the powers on Earth cannot abolish that." Later he compared Southern slaves to Northern hirelings and said, "Yours are hired by the day, not cared for, and scantily compensated, which may be proved in the most painful manner, at any hour in any street in any of your large towns. Why, you meet more beggars in one day, in any single street of the city of New York, than you would meet in a lifetime in the whole South."[25]

In November 1854, in another attempt to rally the masses against the abolitionists, the paper ran a two-part series deflecting the South's responsibility in the slave trade. In the article titled "Who were the Slave Traders?" the newspaper pointed out that the New England shippers were responsible for the slave trade and reminded its readers that Southerners were farmers, not seafaring people, and had no way to obtain slaves without the help of Northern shippers and slave dealers.[26]

The *Pee Dee Times* continued to play on the fears of its readers and to further convince them to rise to the defense of Southern culture. One article offered a glimpse at what could happen if slaves were set free, in an article titled "Abolition of Negro slavery—its Results in the British Colonies." The journal reported that British abolitionists declared that with abolition, Jamaica would become a Garden of Eden. The newspaper blamed the abolitionists for turning Jamaica into a "waste, howling wilderness." The account explained how the exports from Jamaica were once vast but that within a generation of abolition in the country (England banned slavery in 1833), it had become "an economic desert."[27]

With a perceived continued assault upon slavery, the *Winyah Observer* went on the offensive against the reformers and industrialists and published a scornful article titled , "A Day at Lowell" to expose factory working conditions in the North and to reinforce their validation of slavery. The article thoroughly explained how 25,000 workers (9,000 of whom were mill girls between the ages of nine and 14) lived in the upstart textile mill town of Lowell, Massachusetts. It explained how the mill town had 24 churches which took a role at service and that church attendance was mandatory for employment. The accusations continued. Workers lived in cramped barracks designed exclusively for the employees by the employ-ers, who also provided stores to sell the employees everything they needed. At the end of the week, men could expect $4.00, and women earned a minuscule $1.75 for their six-day, 12- to 14-hour commitment to Lowell. The paper asked its readers how the factory system was anything but an industrial model for slavery, as employees gave all their money back to the factory through purchases and rent.[28]

During the second half of 1857, the *Pee Dee Times* published several more stories assaulting abolitionists. One article titled "Life in Northern Cities" described a hateful civilization built upon greed, while another one titled "White Slavery in Massachusetts" explained the life of indus-trial workers as receiving poor pay and living in almshouses. According to the article, nine out of every ten hands who are disqualified to work in the factories due to injury are sent off to the almshouses or have their labor sold in a public auction where their work is purchased for a year. The article further accused the industrialists of abusing their employees by saying that the immigrants were worked 14 hours per day and lived in squalor. The article ended with a poignant denunciation of the industri-alists and the reformers who were quick to judge the South but unwilling to protest the problems of industrialization. The charges leveled, "What do they care for human suffering? What is their philanthropy but a fash-ionable excitement which they substitute for drinking liquor and smoking tobacco, because it is cheaper and more the vogue?"[29]

The major reforms of the Second Great Awakening were in full swing during mid-century and picking up momentum in the Northeast and West. Wilderness utopian transcendentalist writers protested American ideals, social structure, and organization as they championed civil disobe-dience to the law. They not only protested the values of the planter class but retreated in protest from the demands of the new industrial world as well. Fredrika Bremer, a Swedish woman who stayed at Joel Roberts Poinsett's *White House Plantation* on the Pee Dee River when she visited the United States, boasted that she introduced him to transcendentalist literature. When she read Ralph Waldo Emerson to him, Poinsett explained how he felt that the transcendentalists were "unpractical" and criticized the entire literary movement. His antagonism promoted Bremer to say, "It is remark-able how very little, or not at all, the authors of the Northern States, even the best of them, are known in the South."[30]

Other reforms of the era stemmed from the personal experiences of the reformers. When Dorothea Dix visited a prison in Massachu-setts, she was inspired to lead a movement for prison asylum and orphan-age reforms. Eventually, Georgetown would see to the construction of an orphanage for its wayward youths, but they used local funding through the Winyah Indigo Society, not tax dollars raised by the central government or even state government to accomplish this task.

Still another movement, the push for anti-dueling legislation, drew distain from the planter class. In 1838, in response to a call to ban dueling, former South Carolina governor and Georgetown resident, John Lyde Wilson, published his chivalrous eight-chapter pamphlet titled, *The Code of Honor, Or, Rules for the Government of Principals and Seconds in Dueling* to bring an official set of rules for the practice of dueling in hopes that the act would be accepted universally as more chivalrous than barbaric. In Wilson's work, men of similar social status were

John Lyde Wilson, 1803, by Robert Field, watercolor on ivory (gift of Margaret Haswell in memory of Charlotte Alston, 1983.005, Gibbes Museum of Art).

encouraged to settle their differences in acts of combat. His work includes chapters on what to say in a challenge letter, how to properly respond to a letter offering a challenge, chapters on the duties of the challenger and the person challenged prior to the duel, the duties of the principals and seconds, a chapter on arms and the manners of loading and presenting them, and a chapter on the degrees of insults and how one's honor was compromised based upon the particular insult. Again, although the local planters were not willing to ban their practice, they did modify it based upon the influence and denunciations of the Second Great Awakening.

Still another Second Great Awakening reform proposed by Northern citizens was a nationalized education system designed to assimilate immigrants. The local planters did not see a nationalized education system as a reform. They created their own education system through the Winyah Indigo Society and eventually private schools, which educated sons and daughters of planters, merchants and yeoman farmers alike paid for by funds raised locally. The schools taught a classical education filled with courses in history, languages, the arts and sciences as pertaining to agronomics.

Collectively, these reforms infuriated the conservative rice planters and their allies who yearned for small, localized government and a return to the social norms of their father's revolution. The local planters wanted to be left alone on their plantations where they could mandate civilization in the conservative fashion of their predecessors.

Traditionally, the Lowcountry rice planters of antebellum South Carolina were captains of agriculture in a time when industry was in its infancy and agronomy and husbandry dominated the economic, political and social structure of the South. The economic challenge to the South Carolina planter-dominated civilization at the time was the introduction and expansion of industrial textile manufacturing. Agriculture dominated human civilization for an estimated 12,000 years, but the economy of Western civilization was quickly changing. England introduced the new economic model which quickly spread to the European continent and the Northern cities of the United States. Industrialization in manufacturing and transportation brought forth rapid urbanization and the subsequent development of Wall Street in New York City and the expansion of corporate banking.

Contrary to New Englanders and those in the Northern cities who subscribed wholeheartedly to industrialization, Southerners only utilized mechanization when it supported agriculture. Like cotton planters who accepted the cotton gin and cotton press to help them make agriculture more profitable, rice planters, such as Dr. Francis S. Parker, embraced a steam-powered rice threshing mill for removing chaff from rice. Other rice planters, such as James Heyward Trapier, Ralph I. Izard, William A. Alston, Joseph Blythe Allston, John Izard Middleton, John Hyrne Tucker, Joshua John Ward, and Daniel W. Jordan, constructed steam-powered pounding mills for preparing their rice yield for market. Rice planters, John Harleston Read, Jr., Sextus T. Gaillard, Maurice Harvey Lance and Stephen Ford, employed water-powered pounding mills on their plantations. As industry expanded throughout the United States, it began to challenge the supremacy of agriculture, and planters began to rely upon new industrial inventions to keep their trade profitable, until the two ultimately locked into a death struggle for omnipotence in the American Civil War.[31]

With the expansion of manufacturing, the Northern states pushed for continuously increasing tariffs (taxes on imported goods). The tariffs were a draw on Southern wealth and essentially a bounty for Northern industry. Tariff-driven sales swelled the coffers of manufacturers and also increased the already-great economic distance between the Northern capitalists and their wage-earning laborers.[32] The South protested that the North was buying the West's votes by providing them with internal improvements funded by the tariff. Frustrated, South Carolina took the lead and declared John Quincy Adams's Tariff of 1828 unconstitutional. The "Tariff of Abominations" imposed 45 percent taxes on certain items, and England again forced a readjustment to the world cotton market by decreasing the value of cotton from 32 cents per pound to 18.

The rice planters understood that the Northern industry needed protection from European producers, and in fact, South Carolinian John C. Calhoun had originally promoted the 1816 tariff in an attempt to defend and protect the growth of Northern industry, but they believed that the current tariffs were too high and hurt the Southern economy and were fearful that the South would outvote the manufacturing states and end all tariffs, leaving the manufacturing sector unprotected. The *Winyah Observer* calmly appealed for a compromise tariff. "As to the tariff, the whole country is in favor of a reasonable one, and almost any that is not prohibitory, can be reconciled to all parties in a week's debate on the subject with honest politicians."[33]

With the stress of competing, of reaching and maintaining progressive market status, along with the burdens of mandating social order and politics and unifying the yeomen farmers to the planter's cause, rice planters formed several agricultural clubs and societies to compare notes on agriculture and husbandry and address their varied concerns of national and international, social, moral and economic changes.

Although the rice planters criticized industrialization every chance that they could as being immoral and contrary to the traditional lifestyle of man, they revolutionized the international rice market by empowering new industrial tools such as steam-powered threshing and pounding mills. They continuously reinvested their profits into rice mills, more land and slaves, which resulted in large agriculturalists buying out smaller planters and becoming masters of multiple estates. With the smaller rice producers removed from the industry, larger planters were drawn closer socially and formed tighter political alliances.

From a twenty-first-century glance, the professional and social positions of planters would appear to be a stress-free existence. They had slaves to do the physically demanding work on their plantations and kitchen staffs, maids, butlers, gardeners and coachmen to tend to their daily needs. The planter class enjoyed extended stays at the beach throughout the growing season, spent the holiday season at their plantations and enjoyed the social season in Charleston or took extensive vacations abroad. However, every highly effective aristocrat had to be a good businessman with enough aptitude, vigor, and luck to stay ahead of the masses in a highly competitive and intensifying economic system which required meticulous detail to agronomics as evidenced in their journals that they made for operating their estates.[34]

The rice planters were successful businessmen who benefited financially from their occupation and place in society but stayed busy year-round by directing their plantations and civilization. Besides being agro-capitalists who adhered to Adam Smith's philosophy of laissez-faire free trade as described in his book, *Wealth of Nations*, planters served their community, state, and nation as politicians, agricultural scientists, physicians, and civic leaders. They promoted education, internal improvements, and the betterment of the general public. Collectively, the planter class held a great responsibility to maintain social order, to provide for their families, slaves and for their less-fortunate neighbors. And, in order to successfully defend their civilization in the face of economic and social change, they had to convince their less-fortunate neighbors that they were, indeed, brothers of the soil and that they shared the same interest in upholding Southern traditions.

Unlike the rice planters who lived along the tidal-flooded rivers, the yeomen farmers lived on family-operated farms which they carved out of the pinelands. The yeoman farmers were hardy agrarians who tremendously outnumbered the minuscule (about 3 percent of the total population) planter elite. The yeoman farmer was an average man who lived and worked his own land with the assistance of his family. His homestead was the most common economic, social, and cultural locale in the Old South. They had very limited resources, but they lived in a land of great white mobility, and, like anyone else in a free economic society, dreamed of advancement. Like farmers everywhere in the United States, they were independent and proud.[35] The life of the yeomanry revolved around family and community. They did not vacation and spent their social time helping neighboring farmers. Their social activities were corn husking, quilting bees, clearing fields, building barns, and going to court to witness their government in action. For leisure they rode horseback, participated in contests of speed and skills, and competed for marksmanship with firearms. They bet on horseraces, cockfights and dogfights and played card games.[36] Like their husbands, the women worked hard, too. They cooked, sewed, washed, cleaned and bore and raised large families of children, around five on average and sometimes as many as ten or 12.[37]

The antebellum period was a time of mass democracy throughout the United States. Universal male suffrage was an icon of the era as one by one states expanded democracy by dropping property ownership as a requirement for voting. Americans North, South and West took a greater interest in politics than ever before and thoroughly enjoyed participation in the political process. The Southern yeoman, in particular, reveled in politics, followed political affairs and voted in large numbers. They were usually literate and enjoyed conversation and rhetoric. They attended all-day political rallies where political parties provided barbeque and strong drink, and politicians and planters gave long fiery speeches on economic, moral, social and political issues which newspapers reported.[38]

Without social media, musicians, sports stars or movie actors to emulate, the yeomanry looked to the planter class for role models. They aspired to become just like them, and even though social mobility to that level was impossible, they supported the system that the planters created because they knew that they had social status over free blacks and slaves and therefore did not fill the lowest position in the social stratification of the South.

Although most yeomen farmers did not own slaves, the planters launched a huge public relations campaign to convince them that they had a vested interest in seeing slavery upheld. James DeBow published an article in his *DeBow's Review* magazine titled , "The Interest in Slavery of the Southern Non-Slaveholder," where he gave several reasons as to why the yeoman class should fight to defend the delicate social structure of the South. He started by reminding the non-slaveholders that they received higher wages in the South than they would make in the Northern factories, reinforced the mindset that the yeomen farmers were above blacks in the Southern caste system, and told them that since they were farmers, they did not have to compete with European industrial workers who lived in cities and worked with loud, dirty machines. They also reminded them that if they saved their money that they, or their children, could someday be able to buy their own slaves. Lastly, the planters reminded the yeomanry that they would all be overrun by freedmen if emancipation took place and that they would be forced to compete with the free blacks for jobs.[39] DeBow finished his essay with "I think it but easy to show that the interest of the poorest non-slaveholder among us, is to make common cause with, and die in the last trenches in defense of, the slave property of his more favored neighbor."[40]

The Georgetown districts were comprised of two political parishes. Georgetown included Prince George Winyah Parish (which was very heavily populated with yeomen farmers) and Lower All Saints Parish. All Saints Parish, Georgetown, had a very small population and was dominated by rice planters. It was a thin stretch of land bound by the Atlantic Ocean to the east and the Waccamaw River to the west. Upper All Saints Parish was part of the Horry District. A few of the Horry District men participated in the Georgetown social and economic structure as the rice industry did not cease at the politically drawn district line. They belonged to the Georgetown agricultural, social and convivial clubs and were better connected to the Georgetown families and societal structure than the Horry District social structure, which was predominantly yeoman in nature.

In the planter societies, farmers, merchants, bankers and others were welcome to join the planters in shaping and molding society. The societies had elected officials, and their rules were serious in nature. Unlike the societies, the convivial clubs were for planters and their immediate allies only. The clubs featured looser-organized gatherings which were closed to the public, where planters took turns holding offices and served both political and convivial purposes. As their occupation became more and more specialized and competitive against the rising tide of industry and the central government increased tariffs to make industry more profitable, planters organized to share strategies designed to increase the quality and quantity of their crops.

The first planter-dominated society formed in Georgetown was the Winyah Indigo Society. Planters formed the society in the 1750s to provide a forum in which to share agricultural successes and failures as well as to share news and gossip. By the antebellum period, the Winyah Indigo Society was a powerful organization. Not content in having the only free school between Charleston and Wilmington, the order opened a school in the All Saints Parish portion of neighboring Horry District and also sponsored and directed the establishment of the Georgetown Library Society. The society's focus was to provide the best education possible but also to teach discipline and morality to defend religious beliefs as well as to promote unity, patriotism and tradition in response to changes threatening their civilization. The Winyah Indigo Society also addressed women's rights by providing education to girls as a means of promoting nationalism and education in the home and to secure the place of women in society as educator and nurturer to the family. An organization for philanthropic work, as well as for serious discourse on politics and the needs of society, the society grew increasingly important to not only the planters themselves but to the general public and linked the wealthy planters to their neighbors. From the early days of South Carolina's history, Georgetown preferred to exercise local authority over education and government agencies.

The gentlemen of All Saints Parish formed the Hot and Hot Fish Club. The men would spend the day fishing or hunting and then would feast upon their catches of fish and wild game which their slaves prepared while they drank wine and spirits. It was originally designed as a convivial club for gentlemen to relax and enjoy hunting and fishing excursions and to experience comradery, but the form and function of the club changed as a new generation in politics dawned. Soon, by the 1840s, the club became a forum to discuss societal needs, a place to safely debate their fears and to advance agriculture as well as to provide seasonal settings for a male-only social order.

In 1839, planters in Prince George Winyah formed the Planters' Club on the Pee Dee, in an attempt to further agricultural pursuits. Unfortunately for the country gentlemen, the State Agricultural Society would not recognize the Georgetown organization. The Planters' Club, like the Hot and Hot Fish Club, soon focused upon convivial pursuits and building political alliances. Unlike the Hot and Hot Fish Club which met during the summer months while planters moved to the beach to escape the malaria of the swamps and rice fields, the Planters' Club on the Pee Dee was for fall and winter entertainment while the planters lived at their plantations.

A couple of years after creating the Planters' Club on the Pee Dee, planters and their allies formed the Winyah and All Saints Agricultural Society to promote agronomic research and improvement to stock. Although the Hot and Hot Fish Club of All Saints Parish and the Planters' Club on the Pee Dee always welcomed members from both All Saints and Prince George Winyah Parishes, the new fraternity unified the communities by naming it in honor of both voting districts. The society also developed to serve as a communal link between the wealthy rice planters and the yeomen farmers of the pine barrens. The Winyah and All Saints Agricultural Society met three times per year. The spring meeting was the Society's annual agricultural fair where members shared agrarian advancements and treatises. The organization sold livestock and fauna at the fair and judged livestock and staple crops for honors and awards, provided the community with a barbecue, entertainment and delivered an agricultural address. The address focused upon a topic related to agriculture or animal husbandry but also reinforced the ideas and virtues taught at the Winyah Indigo Society to unite farmers and planters alike in an economic war against the industrialists and bankers who dominated Northern society and were seen as responsible for the changes in social norms.

The young men who matured to be the great planters of the era experienced these challenges firsthand. They grew up seeing their very civilization, social structure and moral values challenged by the ever-growing and ever-changing Northern states and as a result developed a defensive posture to these deviations. The conservative mindset that surrounded their civilization was fostered by a stagnant population growth and the lack of immigration to the South. Spawned by the social modifications of the day taking place throughout the North, the planters of Georgetown looked inward and prepared for a life struggle to save their civilization.

Many of the great planters of the era attended university in the Northern states, where the Second Great Awakening was clearly visible, and in Europe where the French Revolution had sowed the seeds of change throughout the continent. They were exposed to the reforms underway; however, when the cavaliers of the Lowcountry returned home to their plantations, they quickly resumed their Southern mindset of master and slave and their feudal, chivalrous code of ethics championing knights and ladies fair.

Thus, the formation of South Carolina College in 1805 signaled that South Carolina would educate her own sons. Fittingly, education began the task of unifying the Lowcountry planters with the up-country farmers within the walls of South Carolina College.

As they matured, many of the rice planters entered politics in order to steer and protect their civilization. Colonel Richard Lathers, a leading merchant of Georgetown, explained the role of planters in shaping society. He said, "The rice planters on the Black, Pee Dee, Samput [sic], Waccamaw and Santee Rivers were gentlemen of culture, educated at northern colleges or in Europe, who rarely sought the high and remunerative offices, but accepted without reluctance local appointments as school, charity, and road commissioners, and were ready to represent their district in the State legislature. The choice of candidates for the Senate offices, for Congress and for Federal appointments depended on the initiative of friends and neighbors who gave public notice of their selection in the local journals. There were no nominating conventions or political caucuses."[41]

The disproportional population growth between North and South was hard to ignore and had a large impact upon the coming of war. In 1800 the two regions had similar-sized populations. However, the 1850 census revealed that the population of the United States was continuing to expand at a disproportional rate. The United States at mid-century contained 23,000,000 people, of which 7,250,000 lived in the South. Within ten years (1860), with the continued influx of German and Irish immigrants to the West and North, respectively, the population of the United States grew to 31,000,000, of which roughly 9,000,000 (4,000,000 of which were slaves) lived in the Southern states.[42]

In 1860, the North had over 140,000 factories which employed over 1,500,000 employees (mostly women and children). Immigrants from Ireland and the German states continued to pour into the Northeastern cities, which already teemed with unskilled labor. The huddled masses packed into tenement houses with poor sanitation and ventilation, without sewage systems, with rat and insect infestations, dimly lit streets and dealt with soaring crime rates and gang fights for turf in the overcrowded ghettos. Dirt roads, piled high in trash, were clogged with street vendors, unemployed mobs of men and animal-drawn carts, dead animals, meat cuttings and entrails from butcher shops and human and animal waste. Thomas Jefferson's prophetic warning to steer clear of industry in fear of becoming as corrupt and polluted as Europe came to fruition. The two regions had become two divergent civilizations.

The war which led to the fall of the planter class bears much greater significance than merely a contest to maintain slavery or even a challenge over the rights pronounced in the Declaration of Independence or the principles expounded in the United States Constitution and Bill of Rights but was rather a contest between old world and new. The American Civil War was a clash and struggle between the traditions of millennia and a technological industrial sector that was barely 100 years old at the time of conflict. It was the tried and true ways of living off the land versus the unsure and untested ways of modernity.

At the epicenter of the contest was a question of identity. Southerners—planter and farmer alike—sought answers to the lifelong question, where do I fit in in this new world order? With a competition brewing which pitted the continued social and economic conditions versus wholesale structural change, Southerners looked to the planter class (their politicians) to defend their traditional agricultural culture. In turn, the rice planters used their agricultural societies and convivial clubs to prepare the answers to the questions of their constituents as well as to quell their own fears of change.

Two

Georgetown's Politicians and Media Promote Southern Nationalism

At this time, the quill is out of vogue, and everybody has resigned himself to the glory that clusters around the sword and the plume.—Richard Dozier

The Treaty of Ghent ended the War of 1812 and ushered in the "Era of Good Feelings." Hallmarks of the era included economic cooperation between the regions of the United States and open markets abroad. Soon, ships loaded with American cotton and other goods sailed to Europe and returned with finished products. Filled with good will and patriotism for the United States as a whole, the South (led by Henry Clay of Kentucky and John C. Calhoun of South Carolina) agreed to the first tariff in American history designed to both protect American manufacturing from foreign competition and promote the development of infrastructure intended to stimulate Western settlements. Congress agreed that the rate of the tariff was a temporary cost and would be reduced in 1820, after the American manufacturing sector proved able to contend with foreign competition. However, the rate was not reduced in 1820, and the era of positive relations was shattered when Northern congressmen blocked the admission of Missouri into the Union because it supported slavery and would upset the balance of slave to free states in Congress, giving the slaveholding states a majority in the United States Senate.

Immediately, the regional challenge, which had been brewing before the War of 1812, reemerged. Henry Clay resolved the gridlock over Missouri with his famous Missouri Compromise of 1820, and the United States tried to regain trust between the sparring regions with the nationalistically motivated Monroe Doctrine, but the impasse reopened sectional wounds which were amplified by the new social challenges of the Second Great Awakening and the economic trade barriers. Rather than reduce the tariff rate as promised in 1816, Congress increased the trade levee in 1818 and 1820 under President James Monroe and yet again in 1824 under John Quincy Adams. In 1827, Adams designed another increase to tariff rates which would eventually pass under President Andrew Jackson in 1828; however, this time South Carolina was no longer complacent with protectionism. In 1828, Georgetown erupted in protest.

On January 8, 1828, the city of Georgetown held a political rally to discuss the newly proposed federal tariff. Intendant of Georgetown, Abram Myers, on behalf of the town council and citizens of the town, addressed the crowd while Solomon Cohen recorded his speech. Myers started his oration by reminding the gathering that South Carolina initially supported tariffs designed to help manufacturing to help the entire country "without complaint, trusting to that wisdom and patriotism which have heretofore so signally advanced the real interests, happiness, and glory of the country."[1] The essence of the complaint was that "the law cannot throw its protecting mantle around one, but must contain within its ample folds the whole national family. No privilege can be extended to any, from which the many are excluded; and all burdens for the support of government are to be borne alike by all."[2] Myers complained that since 1816 the federal government tariffs were essentially a bounty for the manufacturers at an expense of the producers of raw materials and that the federal Congress had assumed the "power to protect or prohibit at pleasure." In his argument, Myers protested that tariffs caused the value of cotton to decrease in the world market as European producers of finished products attempted to beat the tariff by paying less for cotton. (Cotton value diminished from 32 cents per pound to 18 cents per pound due to the tariff.) He grumbled of a transfer of wealth from the South to the North when he said, "The taking of money of A, to give to B, leaves the sum of the individual and consequently of national wealth the same." He continued, "bounties may give relief; but all interference of this kind adds nothing to the wealth of the nation; it will only impoverish one branch of industry to enrich another."[3]

He reminded the gallery that when King George III repealed the bounty on indigo, coastal growers did not complain and ask the congress to add protection but rather switched to rice cultivation. And, he stated, that shippers and agriculturalists did not receive aid during the time of the embargo, Non-Intercourse Act and war years of the War of 1812. To those means, he stated, "We formed no peace societies; had no conventions to drive the government into such measures as would have sullied the national honor. We bore the inconvenience and submitted to the evil without a murmur." He then claimed that the North was making ample enough profit off of the South's cotton. He said that he was "yet to be convinced of the fact that the manufacturers of coarse woolens have any claims to further protection duties" since clothing producers in the North were currently (1825 figure) already producing 30 to 70 percent profit upon their capital invested in making their wares.[4]

Myers concluded his oration by stating, "Let the agriculturalist proceed in his employment, and enrich the country by his labor; let the merchant pursue his present profitable occupation; and whenever the proper season shall arrive, to disenthrall ourselves from foreign supplies, there will be a greater capital to invest in manufactures, the country will be flourishing, and the nation prosperous. But by forced means, and improvident legislation, to bring forward prematurely a particular branch of industry at the expense of all the rest, produces a situation by which nothing is gained, but much is lost."

In the age of President Andrew Jackson, South Carolina was politically divided into three camps, as social and economic disputes between North and South became political jousting points of contention. One group, mostly slaveless yeomen farmers, were Union men who did not necessarily agree with the pendulum shifts of social and economic change but did not want to leave the safety of the United States. Two other groups were both secessionists. One group, the nullies (short for nullifiers—those who wished to nullify federal tariff laws during the nullification crisis), believed in immediate secession from the United States and promoted the idea of an independent nation of South Carolina if the other Southern states would not secede with South Carolina. The other group, known as cooperationists, believed that South Carolina should wait on the other Southern states to secede and form a Southern Confederacy.

In 1832, in reaction to another new tariff, Georgetown nullies formed the States' Rights and Free Trade Association.[5] The group held meetings throughout the year to discuss their options in the Union and whether the time had come to act upon secession. That year, Georgetown selected Thomas Pinckney Alston and four others to represent the district in the statewide States' Rights Convention in Charleston.[6] The assembly agreed that there was no hope for compromise in either branch of Congress since the legislature soon passed another tariff under Jackson.[7] South Carolina seemed destined to withdraw from the Union and for civil war to break out. On November 6, 1832, United States Secretary of the Treasury Louis McLane sent letters to the tax collectors of Georgetown, Charleston and Beaufort explaining that South Carolina was in a state of upheaval and that it needed to be ready for any emergency. The letters reminded the tax collectors of their duties and powers as described in the 1799 "An act to regulate the collection of duties on imports and tonnage."[8] Thankfully, Henry Clay proposed a compromise tariff which reduced tariffs and avoided bloodshed, but many in the region had become radicalized by secession talks over tariffs, Second Great Awakening reforms and political strife.

Many of Georgetown's leaders were ready to declare independence from the United States; however, Georgetown was not yet united for secession or even nullification of federal tax laws. Georgetown had two very politically driven newspapers during this time period. The *Winyaw Intelligencer,* which began publication in September 1817 and lasted until April 1835, was the newspaper of the States' Rights and Free Trade Association during the nullification crisis.[9] The nullies controlled All Saints Parish and attempted to expand their influence over the much larger and much more heavily populated Prince George Winyah Parish (which included the port city of Georgetown). Unionists from throughout the region called All Saints Parish the "rotten borough."[10]

When the *Winyah Intelligencer* wrote, "Any citizen appearing in arms against the State (meaning South Carolina) would be guilty of treason," some pro–Unionists threw bricks through the windows of the newspaper office and broke down the doors.[11] The Unionists had their own paper in Georgetown. The *Georgetown Union* began publication in 1830 by John Matthews and Company and later Taylor and Matthews. It ran until August 1839. The paper, which printed George Washington's famous quote—"United We Stand—Divided We Fall" across its masthead, was the paper of the moderate planters, immigrants, the town's middle class and Northern-born men.[12]

The *Georgetown American* (another pro–Union newspaper) succeeded the *Georgetown Union* on November 9, 1839, with William Chapman as the editor. In the first edition the newspaper explained that all topics except religion and abolitionism would be discussed. The *Georgetown American* printed a lot of world news and history but not much politics or local news. Its motto was "Nothing extenuate … nor aught set down in malice." Eleazer Waterman became the publisher by December 9, 1840, and, eventually, gained full ownership of the paper. Waterman was from Connecticut. He ran a variety of businesses in town and served in various positions in local government, including intendant (mayor) of the town. The paper ceased publication in March 1841, and Chapman died the following August. A week after closing the paper, on March 10, 1841, Waterman rolled out the *Winyah Observer* with his son Eleazer Waterman, Jr. J.W. Tarbox later joined the production.

The *Winyah Observer* was not politically charged at the time, but it did encourage citizens to get involved in organizations, societies and clubs. In an article titled "The Welfare of our Town," the editor reminded the readers that they must "serve the community."[13] Perhaps the greatest service that one could provide to their community was to serve in the local militia. The South Carolina legislature passed the Basic Patrol Law in December 1839 to protect the people from slave insurrections and domestic and foreign forces. Two years later, in 1841, Georgetown's two beat companies of the lower battalion, known as the upper and lower beats, consolidated.[14] All told, Georgetown had four units: the Georgetown Rifle Guards (incorporated on December 20, 1826), the Columbian Blues, the Washington Greys and the Wee Nee Dragoons.[15]

The *Winyah Observer* printed nearly 100 articles from 1840 through 1850 on the Wee Nee Dragoons and the various infantry militia units. Some articles were simply advertisements for members to meet at certain locations for review and drill, and others were reports of patriotic militaristic displays such as "Military Parade at Black Mingo" and "Celebration of the 22nd."[16]

The age of Whig presidents William Henry Harrison and John Tyler was relatively calm and without great sectional conflict, but the recollections of the power-hungry Federalist Party was still close in memory. One politically charged article from this time period pertained to the proceeds from the Democratic States' Rights Party in June 1841. The article complained that the old Alexander Hamilton "Federalists ideals of big government were surfacing again and must be fought."[17]

The 1840s was a time period of great expansion for the United States, and growth of the country caused many problems, one of which was how to divide the newly admitted states into the Union: free or slave. Texas was one of the most pressing questions of the first half of the 1840s. On the Fourth of July 1844, the Pee Dee community celebrated American independence in grand style at the Pee Dee muster field. After the audience was seated, John Harleston Read, Jr. (Pee Dee planter and cooperationist representative) commenced the annual exercises by reading the Declaration of Independence and giving a few pertinent "remarks and reflections upon the causes which led to the publication of that manifesto and declaration which has been so justly styled the character of Liberty." After the reading and patriotic speech, "the company partook of a very bountiful repast (pic nic)." Apparently, a rumor began to circulate that Pee Dee Senator Robert F.W. Allston was soon to arrive and would address the crowd. Allston did eventually arrive and address the gathering. He spoke of the need to annex Texas, and by the time he was through with his oration, the crowd had given up nine rounds of cheers. The newspaper reported that there "was not a single instance of intoxication, and not a quarrel, while we remained on the grounds."[18] If Texas was not going to be annexed, Lowcountry South Carolinians touted that they should secede from the Union and start their own country.[19] After much debate and political wrangling, the United States welcomed Texas into the Union as a slave state.

In April 1846, the United States entered war with Mexico over the annexation of Texas, and again the nation came to a crossroads. A few short months after the onset of war, Pennsylvania's Democrat Senator, David Wilmot, shattered the short period of nationalism when he proposed the Wilmot Proviso. In his proviso, Wilmot suggested that all land gained in the war be closed to slavery since the land was currently slave-free under Mexico's control. Wilmot claimed that allowing slavery to enter the region was not promoting democracy to the region but rather promoting the "slavocracy" of the South. Southerners assumed that Western expansion would naturally continue the extension of the Missouri Compromise dividing line between the North and the South to the West Coast. The measure easily passed the House of Representatives because representation in the house is based upon population but did not pass the Senate where each state had two votes. Although the measure did not pass, it caused a reopening of political and mental wounds between North and South and showed that the United States, although a nation at war with Mexico, was far from united.

In February 1847, the Wilmot Proviso was again introduced to the legislature. The measure once again passed the House of Representatives but was again defeated in the Senate. The *Winyah Observer* reminded its readers of the ramifications of the Wilmot Proviso in an article titled "Ruin of the Slaveholder and the Slave" if the South did not expand with the rest of the Union. In April, the paper printed a much more precise and scathing attack upon the Wilmot Proviso when it stated, "The Wilmot Proviso is an attack upon the constitutional rights of all the states, and the Democracy of this state." By this time, the newspaper replaced the slogan "Published every Wednesday at Three dollars per Annum" with "We will cling to the Temple of our Liberties, and if it must fall, we will perish amidst the ruins."[20] Georgetown was clearly radicalizing.

On February 2, 1848, the Mexican-American War officially ended with the Treaty of Guadalupe Hidalgo. In a last-ditch effort to pass the Wilmot Proviso, Northern politicians again attempted to pass the measure as part of the treaty. Again, the Wilmot Proviso failed; however, fear of federal government legislation such as the Wilmot Proviso caused the 8th South Carolina Cavalry and the various South Carolina infantry regiments to hold regular military exercises throughout the Lowcountry and Pee Dee Region that spring. Reminiscent of the Boston countryside in the spring of 1775, the area was alive with military preparations that spring. The Kingstree Light Dragoons and the 31st Infantry Regiment (Upper Battalion) drilled in Kingstree on May 5, and the Wee Nee Dragoons and the 31st Infantry Regiment (Lower Battalion) trained in Georgetown on May 9. The Horry Hussars drilled with the 32nd Infantry Regiment in

Conwayborough on May 13, and The Marion Light Dragoons trained with the 3rd Infantry Regiment at the Marion Courthouse on May 16. All militias lined up for review at 12:00 p.m., and drill followed.[21]

That spring, the Democratic Party started holding meetings in Georgetown, and by late May, the Whig Party followed suit.[22] In August, the *Winyah Observer* published an editorial titled "North and South: Van Buren, Cass and Taylor: Which can the South Support?" Colonel John Harleston Read, Jr., stated that he supported Zachary Taylor because Taylor "has 300 slaves which he intends to keep." He also reminded the citizens that if the South does not band together to all vote for Taylor, the election could go to the House of Representatives, which the North dominated due to their numeric superiority. Read concluded that Northerners with their, "fanaticism would elect Van Buren" to further their agenda of free soil.[23] Fortunately for Read and his supporters, Taylor did win the election.

Despite Taylor's victory in the election, the mistrust created by the Wilmot Proviso compelled the South Carolina legislature to unanimously resolve that the time for discussion with the federal government had passed and that it was time to seek a union with the other Southern states. The elder statesman, John C. Calhoun, made it very clear when he said, "Though the Union is dear to us, our honor and our liberty are dearer."[24]

While Mexican War hero, General Winfield Scott, pled for nationalism and called for annexation or conquest of Canada to distract the nation from sectional conflict and bring forth unity, the Georgetown District's politicians and the *Winyah Observer* called for Southern Nationalism. On April 9, 1849, leading statesmen of the Georgetown District met in the city of Georgetown to discuss John C. Calhoun's call for a meeting of Southern states in Jackson, Mississippi, and to plan a unified stern resistance to the federal government. The newspaper said, "the Government of the Confederacy cannot of right impose upon the people of any States or territory any particular scheme of internal policy, except to the extent of the authority expressly delegated to that government by the Constitution of the United States." The assembly expressed their love for the "Union entered into by our fathers we are ardently attached; for it was a Union of friendly communities for common purpose of mutual defense." But, the committee continued, "when we witness the war-ill-disguised which is waging against us under the screen of this Union, we cannot but regard it with alienation and distrust." The group reminded the people of Georgetown that each of the great sections of the country had their own "peculiar scheme" of civilization and vowed to never attempt to influence decisions made in the North, asserting that each section of the country must be "permitted to work out for itself the great problem of its political salvation undisturbed by the other."[25]

The committee then adopted six resolutions designed to bind the Southern states together in defiance to the federal government. They called for a confederacy of "co-States" for mutual, "maintenance of our rights." Perhaps the most pressing of the resolutions was number four. The resolution stated "That the adoption by the Federal Government of the measure in reference to the Territories called the Wilmot Proviso, would absolve us from our federal obligations, and compel us and our co-States to resort to such means of defense, as the great law of self-preservation may require." As a final measure, Chairman Robert F.W. Allston, much like his forefathers had done in preparation for the American Revolution, appointed a group of 13 (which included Joshua John Ward, Dr. Edward Thomas Heriot, Dr. John D. Magill and Benjamin Henry Wilson) to constitute a Committee of Correspondence and a Committee of Safety for Georgetown.[26]

On July 25, the *Winyah Observer* published an article titled "Who has betrayed the South?" The essay accused former president, John Quincy Adams, as being the man who was to be blamed for the heated regional rivalry since he had passed high tariffs. Most Southerners did not support him or his father (John Adams, a founding member of the Federalist Party) as presidents. The article also claimed that the Northern Whigs were to blame for making abolition a political pillar of their political party whereas before that time the abolitionists were regional extremists who did not have a political party who was willing to commit support for their goals.[27]

On October 1, 1849, representatives from the Southern states met in Jackson, Mississippi, to demand the end to slavery agitation in the Northern states, to curtail the Underground Railroad and to encourage Southerners to migrate west. At the end of the day, they agreed to reconvene in Nashville, Tennessee, in the summer of 1850 to form a Southern Confederacy if the agitation did not cease.[28] Also in 1849, Robert F.W. Allston represented South Carolina and served as a vice president at the great Railroad Convention in Memphis, Tennessee.[29]

By the time the delegates finally met in Nashville during the summer of 1850, Henry Clay's 1850 Compromise had much support in both the House of Representatives and the Senate. With the compromise destined to pass, the movement for secession lost much of its momentum, but the gentlemen made relationships at the meeting which would later help in Southern nation-building. Robert F.W. Allston penned a letter to his son, Benjamin, then a cadet at West Point Military Academy, from the Nashville Convention. He wrote that he had made several new political allies in Nashville where they met, "respecting the course of legislation in congress on the subject of the territories acquired from Mexico by the close of the late war."[30] He wrote a letter to his wife from the same location in which he stated, "Unless the Northern people now come to be reasonable people,

Revolution will be unavoidable. It were (sic) better to settle the matter now than to leave it to our children."[31]

Upon returning home from the Nashville Convention, South Carolina Lowcountry planters again beat the drum of secession and attempted to lead the state down the fiery path to disunion. As they had done in 1832 and 1844, many Lowcountry planters called on South Carolina to act alone. However, the two regions of the state continued to be at odds and remained split along old division lines. Lowcountry planters called for secession, and up-county farmers called for moderation and compromise. A divided South Carolina once again backed down from independence.

However, although South Carolina backed down from secession, the local media published an article explaining that the design of the originators of the Nashville Convention was patriotic as they were meeting for secession in the name of defending the rights of all citizens as they were explained in the United States Constitution. Other articles focused upon the lives of the signers of the Declaration of Independence—their births and occupations, the history of the Missouri Compromise, and how the North's attempt to block the admission of Missouri shattered the Era of Good Feelings. The paper also addressed the traditional division within the state by publishing an article about the American Revolutionary Battle of Kings Mountain where South Carolinians fought against each other under the names "Patriots" and "Loyalists."[32]

Right after the passage of the Compromise of 1850, the Georgetown and All Saints Southern Rights Association announced the formation of committees of safety for Georgetown, Black River, Sandy Island, and All Saints for defense.[33] The group resolved to move for separate state action and demanded that their senators and representatives in the legislature vote for independence. They also resolved "That although it would be an occasion of great pleasure and satisfaction to have our sister slave holding states act in common with us, we can see no reason in their backwardness, why the State of South Carolina should fail in carrying out her declared intentions." The convention proposed that the planters, or anyone who had disposable income, invest in the program already at hand, open direct lines of trade with Europe, and boycott Northern trade.[34]

Following the meeting, the *Winyah Observer* published a small article titled "Divisions of the South." The article addressed the division in South Carolina and blamed the divisiveness between the immediate secessionists, and cooperationists as the cause of most of their problems. The author stated, "Southern people, upon the subject of our own misconduct; arising from our jealousies and rivalships among one another. It is our own divisions which have enabled the Northern section of the Union to encroach upon the rights of our constitution."[35]

Year/ District	All Saints Parish (Includes Horry and Georgetown Districts East of the Waccamaw River)	Prince George Winyah Parish (Georgetown District)
1832	Joshua John Ward	Anthony White Dozier, Peter William Fraser and Solomon Cohen, Jr
1833	Joshua John Ward	Anthony White Dozier, Peter William Fraser and Solomon Cohen, Jr
1834	Joshua John ward	Allard Henry Belin, John William Coachman and Solomon Cohen, Jr.
1835	Joshua John ward	Allard Henry Belin, John William Coachman and Solomon Cohen, Jr.
1836	Joseph Alston	Allard Henry Belin, Thomas G. Carr and John William Coachman
1837	Joseph Alston	Allard Henry Belin, Thomas G. Carr and John William Coachman
1838	Joseph Alston	Allard Henry Belin, Thomas G. Carr and John Izard Middleton
1839	Joseph Alston	Allard Henry Belin, Thomas G. Carr and John Izard Middleton
1840	Thomas S. Randall	Allard Henry Belin, Thomas G. Carr and John Izard Middleton
1841	Thomas S. Randall	Allard Henry Belin, Thomas G. Carr and John Izard Middleton
1842	John Ashe Alston	Allard Henry Belin, Thomas G. Carr and John Izard Middleton
1843	John Ashe Alston	Allard Henry Belin, James Ritchie Sparkman and John Izard Middleton
1844	John Ashe Alston	Peter William Fraser, John Izard Middleton and John Harleston Read, Jr.
1845	John Ashe Alston	Peter William Fraser, John Izard Middleton and John Harleston Read, Jr.
1846	John Ashe Alston	Samuel Taylor Atkinson, John Izard Middleton and John Harleston Read, Jr.
1847	John Ashe Alston	Gabriel Manigault, John Izard Middleton and John Harleston Read, Jr.
1848	John Ashe Alston	John B. Easterling, John Izard Middleton (Became Speaker of the House) and John Harleston Read, Jr.
1849	John Ashe Alston	John B. Easterling, John Izard Middleton and John Harleston Read, Jr.

Year/ District	All Saints Parish (Includes Horry and Georgetown Districts East of the Waccamaw River)	Prince George Winyah Parish (Georgetown District)
1850	Daniel William Jordan	Gabriel Manigault, John Izard Middleton and John Harleston Read, Jr.
1851	Daniel William Jordan	Gabriel Manigault, John Izard Middleton and John Harleston Read, Jr.
1852	Allard Belin Flagg	Gabriel Manigault, John Izard Middleton and John Harleston Read, Jr.
1853	Allard Belin Flagg	Gabriel Manigault, John Izard Middleton and John Harleston Read, Jr.
1854	Thomas S. Randall	John Izard Middleton, John Harleston Read, Jr. and Benjamin Henry Wilson
1855	Thomas S. Randall	John Izard Middleton, John Harleston Read, Jr. and Benjamin Henry Wilson
1856	Plowden Charles Jennett Weston	John Izard Middleton (Resigned to fill Robert.F. W. Allston's seat in the Senate when he became governor) Richard Dozier, John Harleston Read, Jr. and Benjamin Henry Wilson
1857	Plowden Charles Jennett Weston	Richard Dozier, John Harleston Read, Jr. and Benjamin Henry Wilson
1858	Peter Vaught, Sr.	Richard Dozier, John Harleston Read, Jr. and John Hyrne Tucker, Jr.
1859	Peter Vaught, Sr.	Richard Dozier, John Harleston Read, Jr. and John Hyrne Tucker, Jr.
1860	Peter Vaught, Sr.	Richard Dozier, John Harleston Read, Jr. and Plowden Charles Jennett Weston
1861	Peter Vaught, Sr.	Richard Dozier, John Harleston Read, Jr. and Plowden Charles Jennett Weston (Weston was Elected Lieutenant Governor in 1862)

Georgetown, South Carolina States Representatives.

Year	All Saints Parish (Includes Horry and Georgetown District East of the Waccamaw River)	Prince George Winyah Parish (Georgetown District)
1832	Joseph Waites Allston	Robert F.W. Allston
1833	Thomas Pinckney Alston	Robert F.W. Allston
1834	Thomas Pinckney Alston	Robert F.W. Allston

Year	All Saints Parish (Includes Horry and Georgetown District East of the Waccamaw River)	Prince George Winyah Parish (Georgetown District)
1835	Thomas Pinckney Alston	Robert F.W. Allston
1836	Thomas Pinckney Alston	Robert F.W. Allston
1837	Thomas Pinckney Alston	Robert F.W. Allston
1838	Edward Thomas Heriot	Robert F.W. Allston
1839	Edward Thomas Heriot	Robert F.W. Allston
1840	Edward Thomas Heriot	Robert F.W. Allston
1841	Edward Thomas Heriot	Robert F.W. Allston
1842	Joshua John Ward	Robert F.W. Allston
1843	Joshua John Ward	Robert F.W. Allston
1844	Joshua John Ward	Robert F.W. Allston
1845	Joshua John Ward	Robert F.W. Allston
1846	Joshua John Ward	Robert F.W. Allston
1847	Joshua John Ward	Robert F.W. Allston
1848	Joshua John Ward	Robert F.W. Allston
1849	Joshua John Ward	Robert F.W. Allston
1850	Joshua John Ward (Elected Lieutenant Governor–Resigned Seat)	Robert F.W. Allston (Served as President of the Senate)
1851	Andrew Hasell	Robert F.W. Allston (Served as President of the Senate)
1852	Andrew Hasell	Robert F.W. Allston (Served as President of the Senate)
1853	Andrew Hasell	Robert F.W. Allston (Served as President of the Senate)

Year	All Saints Parish (Includes Horry and Georgetown District East of the Waccamaw River)	Prince George Winyah Parish (Georgetown District)
1854	Andrew Hasell	Robert F.W. Allston (Served as President of the Senate)
1855	Andrew Hasell	Robert F.W. Allston (Served as President of the Senate)
1856	Andrew Hasell	Robert F.W. Allston (Elected Governor-Resigned Seat) John Izard Middleton
1857	Andrew Hasell	John Izard Middleton
1858	Charles Alston	Benjamin H. Wilson
1859	Charles Alston	Benjamin H. Wilson
1860	Charles Alston	Benjamin H. Wilson
1861	James J. Wortham	Benjamin H. Wilson

Georgetown, South Carolina States Senators.

In 1850, Georgetown was well represented in the state government. That fall, All Saints Parish rice planter, Joshua John Ward, took the position of lieutenant governor (Waccamaw rice planter, Dr. Andrew Hasell, filled

Joshua John Ward (by D'Andrea Lynn Boyle, photograph by Rich Taylor).

his vacant seat), and Pee Dee rice planter Robert F.W. Allston retained his senate seat representing Prince George Winyah Parish but also served the state as the president of the senate.[36] Allston was the largest rice planter on the Pee Dee and Ward the largest rice planter on the Waccamaw. They had been working together for two decades to unite the region under the banner of separate state secession, and now the election assured that they would work together to push the entire state towards separatism.

The new Lieutenant Governor Joshua John Ward was

known as an ardent supporter of nullification and independent South Carolina secession. He started his political career as justice of the peace and justice of the quorum in Georgetown. He won two elections to the state legislature representing All Saints Parish, and beginning in 1842, the people of Georgetown and Horry Districts elected him to South Carolina's State Senate. He served in the state senate until December 7, 1850, when he resigned to accept the lieutenant governorship of South Carolina, a position he held for one term.[37] He was a trustee of All Saints Summer Academy and South Carolina College as well as a commissioner of free schools.[38]

Allston spent nearly his entire adult life in public service, culminating in his governorship of South Carolina in 1856. Allston graduated from the United States Military Academy at West Point in 1821, and in June 1821, was commissioned lieutenant in the 3rd Artillery, Topographical Service, a position he held for only a few months. In 1822, he was elected to his first public office, surveyor general of South Carolina, a position which he held for two terms (four years). In 1827, he assumed the management of his estate and officially became a rice planter. The following year Allston was elected to the South Carolina House of Representatives where he served from 1828 to 1832.[39] In 1832, a strong supporter of John C. Calhoun's Nullification Doctrine, Allston became the state senator from Prince George Winyah, an office he held for 24 years (serving as the president of the senate from 1850 to 1856).

Allston won many easy victories to the state senate, but the 1850 election was very interesting and controversial. Although Allston won his bid for reelection, the victory did not come without a challenge from the cooperationists camp. In fact, Allston's good friend, Dr. Edward Thomas Heriot, opposed his reelection. The *Winyah Observer* reported, "someone's name was placed on the ballot without their approval to challenge Allston." The newspaper went on to say, "Colonel is elected by a very handsome majority." The other candidate "whose name was placed on the nomination" stated that the whole matter "was without his consent, and that the use of his name for the purpose of being used against Col. Allston in his absence met with his most unqualified disapprobation."[40] One week later the same newspaper released the official results. Dr. Edward Thomas Heriot received 45 votes. Allston carried the day with 171 votes.[41]

While serving in the state senate, Allston attended the Nashville Convention in 1850 and contributed to a fundraiser to send slaveholders to Kansas in 1856.[42] He resigned his seat in the state senate to accept the governorship of South Carolina on December 10, 1856. Allston, who served one term as governor, was a huge proponent of state-funded education.[43] He was colonel of the South Carolina State Militia, commissioner of Free

Schools, trustee of All Saints' Academy, South Carolina College, General Theological Seminary in New York, chairman of the House Committee on "The College, Education and Religion," president of the South Carolina Art Association (Allston bought and placed the bronze replica of George Washington on the capitol grounds in Columbia, South Carolina), founding member of the South Carolina Historical Society, author and orator.[44]

On Thursday, December 5, 1850, the Southern Rights Association of All Saints Parish assembled. At the meeting, 185 concerned citizens from Georgetown and Horry Districts assembled at the Socastee Bridge; Dr. John D. Magill chaired the meeting. Magill opened the convention by reading an apology letter written by the district's most notable citizen the Honorable South Carolina Lieutenant Governor Joshua John Ward. In the letter, Ward expressed regret that his position in Columbia kept him from chairing the meeting. Next, All Saints Senator, Dr. Andrew Hasell, gave a "spirited" address on the issue of states' rights. After pleading for unity against the central authority, preaching an embargo on trade with the North, and defense of their homes and hearth, Hasell closed with, "We the people of All Saints Parish are ready to do our utmost in the execution of any measures defensive or offensive towards the Central Government which South Carolina our Sovereign State may adopt, and more over we will now cooperate with citizens in carrying out the system of non-intercourse with the North." On the motion of Dr. Edward Thomas Heriot, the group agreed to meet twice per year—once at the *Watchesaw Plantation* muster field on July 4 and on December 5 at Socastee Bridge.[45]

As 1850 passed into 1851, the calls for secession and the general secession movement throughout the Southern states calmed down. However, the

Robert Francis Withers Allston, engraved by Illman & Sons for De Bow's Review, New Orleans (courtesy South Caroliniana Library, University of South Carolina, Columbia, SC).

Winyah Observer remained determined to rally its readers to secession by publishing several inflammatory articles. One article, "The Policy of the South," trumpeted that the South had lost her equality of power with the North and warned that although they were experiencing a temporary lull in the unfriendliness between the sections, "The hostility is increasing and inequality is increasing." The paper warned, "The political subordination of the South accomplished as it has been by spoliation, leaves her but two alternatives—redress or submission."[46]

Throughout late summer and the fall of 1851, the *Winyah Observer* continued to call for secession. To further incite its readers, the paper continuously referred to the United States' soldiers stationed in Charleston Harbor as "The Army of Occupation." It also reported that seated President Millard Fillmore's administration was plotting to move against them. The paper flaunted South Carolina's justification for secession and promised its readers that they were honoring their American Revolution-era ancestors by declaring independence from the United States but claimed that President Fillmore, "through its leading organs, has, again, and again, threatened that the sovereign act of the state seceding from the Union, would be met by the military repression of the government."[47]

In early October, one week before a scheduled secession meeting, the newspaper printed an article titled "The Right of Secession" and printed the Kentucky and Virginia resolutions to further support their cause. The paper again called for the state to secede without the support of the other Southern states and noted South Carolina's weakness in waiting for other states to heed the call. The paper claimed that this was a new day of age and complained that cooperationists always lean on John C. Calhoun, who rightfully so always sought compromise, but the times had changed, and the people must defend their rights by seceding.[48]

On Wednesday, October 8, 1851, the Southern Rights Association of Georgetown held a meeting for the people of Georgetown and Williamsburg Districts. They met at Morris Ferry at 11:00 a.m. to discuss secession. Over 700 people spread out under the lofty limbs of massive live oaks for a "Great Secession Demonstration." It was the largest meeting ever recorded in the Georgetown District. The Rev. G.R. Talley opened the meeting with prayer, followed by Robert F.W. Allston, who then explained the reason for assembly—secession, not if they should secede, but when was the right time. Many ranking citizens gave speeches on what they expected the district to do. Eleazer Waterman, Sr., newspaper mogul and leading voice for the cooperationists, said, "Separate state action is an error, and will not be tolerated by this meeting." Although he was a respected journalist and longtime Georgetonian who had always spoken for cooperation with the other Southern states, he was clearly in the minority. Following

Waterman, Mr. Samuel Taylor Atkinson rose immediately and spoke for almost an hour with "much force and ingenuity."[49]

Immediately following Atkinson, the Honorable J.L. Middleton spoke for more than an hour explaining in "his clearly and lucid style, with an imagination full of historical resources, the need for immediate action." He concluded by asking the audience to move to the right of the stage if they were for immediate action and to the left of the stage if they wished to wait for the cooperation of the other Southern states. The tally tolled— over 400 moved to the right of the stage; only 15 individuals moved to the left of the stage. After the vote, the entire crowd ate barbeque and enjoyed drinks at a cost of over $1,000 to the association.[50]

In late April 1852, Thomas Pinckney Alston attended a meeting of the Southern Rights Convention in Charleston, which once again entertained secession. After a strong debate, cooperationists defeated immediate secessionists. The assembly gave the legislature the power to secede if necessary but felt that the time was still not right and that they should wait and secede in cooperation with the rest of the South. Again, Georgetown and other rice planters called for secession, while up-country farmers and Charleston merchants cautioned for moderation.[51]

That December, the *Winyah Observer* announced that Richard Dozier, Eleazer Waterman, Jr., and J.W. Tarbox had purchased the *True Republican* (a paper that only had one year of circulation in Georgetown) and combined it with the *Winyah Observer* to create the *Pee Dee Times*.[52] Cooperationist, Benjamin Henry Wilson, was the editor of the *Winyah Observer*. With the radical Richard Dozier as editor of the *Pee Dee Times*, the newspaper proved to be far more radical than the *Winyah Observer*. The *Pee Dee Times* started in early 1853 with the maxim, "Devoted to Southern Rights, Morality, Agriculture, Literature, Science, Arts and Misc" sprawled across its masthead followed by the subheading, "If thou hast truth to utter, speak and leave the rest to God." The center column article of the first issue offered a very patriotic and defensive editorial which explained "What makes South Carolina so Great." By April of the following year, Waterman sold his share of the newspaper to the other partners, as the tabloid's rhetoric became, perhaps, too strong for his cooperationist stance.[53]

Popular sovereignty (allowing the people of a territory to decide if their state should have slavery or not instead of allowing politicians to decide) was a noble expression in grassroots democracy, but when settlers in Kansas began to kill each other over the issue of slavery, and an actual civil war broke out in Kansas, the term "Bleeding Kansas" was coined. In reaction to the trouble in Kansas, former Northern Whigs, abolitionists, and free soilists (people who were against the expansion of slavery in the

West, but not committed to ending slavery in the South) formed their own political party, the Republican Party.

Kansas escalated the sectional crisis to an entirely new level. Six months before violence broke out in Kansas, the *Pee Dee Times* announced, "The Rising Trouble in Kansas," and further warned that Missouri as well as Kansas could erupt into open warfare.[54] A month after the first violent clash took place in Kansas, an article titled "Kansas" written by "A Rice Planter" exclaimed, "The time of collision between slavery and abolition is near and that the point of contact must be Kansas." After explaining why Southerners must take a stand in Kansas against radical abolitionists, the author wrote that he was planning to assist in any way that he could to see that Kansas entered the Union as a slave state because "I have something to lose and I do not wish to lose it, and I desire to die as I have lived."[55] Fanning the flames of war, the *Pee Dee Times* printed an article titled "How Changed," where it said, "The same spirit that for a sufficient reason caused it to rise against a mother, now for a more sufficient reason causes it to rise against brethren."[56] In another article printed in the same edition, Richard Dozier wrote about 13 brothers who freed themselves from England, and concluded, "now some of the brothers act like England in enforcing their will."[57] A follow-up article a few weeks later advised Southern businessmen to not travel to the North in fear for their safety. "They (southern men) cannot travel anywhere in the hireling States as gentlemen attended by their body servants without being mobbed and plundered."[58]

Kansas was a call to arms, and a war of words between the Northern and Southern press prepared both sides for action. Some free-soil journals boasted, "The South can easily be defeated in event of Civil War." However, the *Pee Dee Times* assured its readers that the South had at least three distinct advantages over the North. First, the South had slaves to work the fields, and secondly that any war fought between North and South would be fought on Southern soil where they simply had to defend themselves, not conquer a peace. Lastly, the newspaper recalled that the South was more military minded. In the Mexican War, of the 68,697 Americans who volunteered to fight, 45,649 came from the South, while the North only contributed 23,048. The journal pushed its readers to join in the fight to preserve their Southern culture by saying, "To defend our homes—every man from 12 to 70 would volunteer to defend his home."[59]

In July 1856, a group assembled at the Georgetown post office to discuss the Brooks-Sumner Affair, an event where South Carolina representative, Preston Brooks, nearly beat Senator Charles Sumner of Massachusetts to death on the floor of the United States Senate for slandering his relative, Andrew Butler (co-sponsor of the Kansas-Nebraska Act) and South Carolina in general for taking the "harlot slavery" into free soil. To the cavaliers of the Lowcountry, Southern gentlemen were supposed to battle again and again in affairs of honor just like the medieval knights of old. As per their code of chivalry, the group stated that Brooks's actions were "not only a vindication of personal right, but a patriotic defense of South Carolina and Southern honor." *The Pee Dee Times* not only supported Brooks but accused Sumner of acting falsely to God, country and truth. The assemblage blamed Sumner for the affair and charged him with hypocrisy, having "swore to defend the Constitution with hand on bible, but is guilty of trying to incite Civil War." The group decided to send Brooks a new cane with an inscription on it showing their approval of his action.[60] Over the next several months, Brooks went on a tour of the state, as "Brooks dinners" were held to honor his actions and bestow gifts upon him.[61]

The violence on the Senate floor was a gut check for all politicians— North and South. One South Carolina Senator wrote, "every man in both Houses is armed with a revolver—some with two—and a bowie knife. It is, I fear in the power of any Red or Black Republican to precipitate at any moment a collision in which the slaughter would be such as to shock the world and dissolve the government." Advertising his dedication to regional pride and Southern Nationalism, the senator went on to say, "I keep a pistol now in my drawer in the Senate as a matter of duty to my section."[62]

That summer and fall, articles on the South's ability to defend itself militarily from the North and renewed calls for secession with the formation of a "Southern Confederacy" filled the newspaper. In an obvious attempt to boost the morale of the people and unify Southerners in defense of their homes and hearth, the *Pee Dee Times* bragged that no army on the planet could defeat the South: "Not the North, nor even Great Britain." The article claimed that Southern traditions were worth fighting to defend and outlined a plan for defending against runaway slaves. The author appealed to the citizens to rally to the call to defend against possible invaders by saying, "The abolitionists think that they can count on the slaves to help them, but they would immediately be moved to the interior of the South and then we could easily defend the frontier."[63]

That fall, November 1856, Democratic candidate James Buchanan won the presidential election with 174 electoral votes and carried 19 states. Buchanan was from Pennsylvania and was referred to as a "Dough-faced Democrat," a Northerner who had Southern principles or at least sympathized with the Southern region. Southerners were relieved with his victory since Buchanan promised to add Cuba to the country as a slave state and clung to Southern values such as the promotion of low tariffs.[64] John C. Fremont, under the banner of the newly formed Republican Party, made a strong showing. In the party's first national polling, the Republicans carried 11 states and recorded 114 electoral votes. While the Democratic Party ran a balanced platform representing all three regions (North, South and West) of the United States, the Republican Party openly and clearly identified itself as a regional political party.

The newly formed Republican platform offered Northern industrialists higher protective tariffs and internal improvements to the West paid for by the tariff. The Republicans also offered a Homestead Act for the developing West. The proposed Homestead Act offered a 160-acre plot of land for a family farm to anyone who filed for the land. The act effectively excluded Southern planters from the West because plantations required far more land than 160 acres to turn a profit, especially in the West where land was deemed much less productive than Southern soil. The Republican Party offered nothing to the South. Former president Millard Fillmore carried eight electoral votes and the state of Maryland with the newly formed American Party, also known as the Know-Nothing Party.

The events leading up to the election of 1856 drew Waccamaw rice planter and intellectual recluse, Plowden Charles Jennett Weston, out of his ten-year scholarly seclusion at his *Hagley Plantation* on the Waccamaw. Weston was content to live his life quietly at *Hagley* where his friend, Jacob Motte Alston, later recalled he had "two large rooms adjoining, (which) were filled with choice and elegantly bound books." Weston's collection of rare medieval manuscripts and incunabula was valued at $30,000 in 1860 (nearly $1,000,000 in 2020 terms).[65] However, compelled by noblesse oblige to lead, Weston broke onto the scene with the vigor and strength of a young man and the discipline and education of an accomplished scholar. He burst onto the scene, contributed to the annals of history, and served his state in political office.

In November 1856, Weston won the election for the All Saints District House of Representatives seat. (He served two terms in that body and eventually served as lieutenant governor of the state.) In 1856, Allston and Weston led the secessionist's camp in Georgetown, and John Harleston Read, Jr. (Prince George Winyah Parish

Plowden Charles Jennett Weston (courtesy Charleston Museum, Charleston, SC).

representative from 1844 until 1861 in the general assembly) led the coop-erationists faction.[66] Few Southerners aspired to be authors prior to the Civil War; however, Weston, the scholar-planter, had several publications. Besides composing a poem titled *The Pleasures of Music*, Weston inspired South Carolina nationalism in 1856 when he edited *Documents Connected with the History of South Carolina*, a collection of documents pertain-ing to the early history of South Carolina [121 copies printed].[67] Weston also wrote *The Overseer's Contract*, a detailed description of the overseer's duties on a rice plantation, which *DeBow's Review* published in 1857.[68] Also in 1857, Weston published a blistering secessionist speech titled *An Address by Plowden C.J. Weston before the Citizens of All Saints at Watchesaw Plan-tation, 4th July 1857.*[69] In 1860, he published his last two works: a fire-eating oratory titled *An Address Delivered in the Indigo Society Hall, Georgetown, South Carolina*, and *The Rules and History of the Hot and Hot Fish Club of All Saints Parish*. A lifelong student of history, Weston was instrumen-tal in forming the South Carolina Historical Society and belonged to the Maryland and New York Historical Societies and the Elliot Society of Nat-ural History of Charleston.[70]

On March 3, 1857, just one day before President-elect James Buchanan took office, Congress passed the tariff of 1857. The new tariff reflected the president-elect's stance on tariffs, lowering taxes on imports to 20 per-cent, the lowest levy on imports since the beginning of tariff collection. A 20 percent tariff was what Southerners had been arguing for since Cal-houn's nullification crises since the 20 percent tariff rate was promised in the agreement for the 1816 tariff: Henry Clay's American System. The American System entered as a 25 percent tariff rate with the promise that it would be reduced to 20 percent by 1820. Instead, tariff rates fluctuated over the next 40 years and soared to over 40 percent. The new tariff act was very unpopular in the North but hailed in the South. Two days after Buchan-nan took the office of the presidency, and a month after Preston Brooks died from disease, the Supreme Court endorsed the principles of Southern rights in the Dred Scott decision.[71]

The conservative position in South Carolina was strengthened when United States Chief Justice Roger Taney announced that Dred Scott, a slave who had attempted to use the Supreme Court to sue for his free-dom because his master took him into free states and territories, could not use the court because he was not a citizen but rather was property. Fur-thermore, the court explained, the Missouri Compromise with its 36–30 dividing line of the West between free and slave states was unconstitu-tional, and the federal government did not have the power to dictate where citizens of the United States could and could not take their property. There were no longer "free" states and "slave states" but rather United States with slavery and without legal restraints. The *Pee Dee Times* trumpeted the ruling. "The Republican Party henceforth must choose between submission and revolution-loyalty or treason to the government."[72]

That spring, the region swelled with sectional pride, political accomplishment, optimism for the future, and a feeling of general triumph. Spring always brought militia drills and parades to the area, but this time one of their own was the governor of the state. The 31st Infantry Regiment paraded under review and drilled at Black Mingo on Wednesday, March 23. The 33rd Regiment paraded in Conwayboro (renamed December 1855) on Saturday, March 28, and the 32nd Regiment gathered at the Marion Courthouse and paraded on Tuesday, March 31. Other drills took place at Camden, Darlington, Lancaster, Chesterfield, and Marlborough. Cavalry units attended.[73]

The highlight of the spring parade season took place in Georgetown. The 31st Regiment of South Carolina's militia held a general muster with all beats reporting. This was the first general muster in several years and was newly elected Governor Robert F.W. Allston's first appearance as governor in the Pee Dee. As commander-in-chief of South Carolina, Allston reviewed the dragoons and infantry in front of a large crowd of spectators. *Pee Dee Times* editor, Richard Dozier, could not contain his excitement and reported upon the event with great patriotism to South Carolina. He wrote, "At this time, the quill is out of vogue, and everybody has resigned himself to the glory that clusters round the sword and the plume."[74]

Blooming with martial dreams and vindicated by the recent Supreme Court decision, the *Pee Dee Times* published an article, "Duty of Southern Men." The article was a call to arms to its readers to defend their homes and firesides against the threat of invaders. Talking of the two sections of the country, and as if preparing the regions for a winner-takes-all latter-day joust, the author said that indifferences between the regions took place before the slavery agitation but that "it is true, that before the dawn of this insanity, our lances clashed occasionally, and that one or the other was unhorsed, but the tilt did no serious damage to the contestants." With the recent agitation, however, things seemed far more serious.[75] The mindset of the day was that "the day of apologies for slavery and compromise with abolitionism, is past."[76]

In 1857, the 4th of July Independence Day gathering was a major event that was very well attended. The Winyah and All Saints States' Rights Association sponsored the event at *Watchesaw Plantation*. All Saints General Assemblyman Plowden C.J. Weston accepted the invitation to speak at the patriotic event. He opened his speech by calling it the anniversary to celebrate Gadsden, Pinckney, Middleton, Rutledge and Marion. He informed the audience that there was an old Hindustan belief that the souls of deceased heroes returned to their place of life once per year on the anniversary of their greatest deed or action to listen to the living praise them. Although a devoted Christian, Weston used the Hindu faith for the opportunity to recall the deeds of past South Carolinians and rally the people to patriotism and Southern nation-building.[77]

During his address, Weston acknowledged the growing threat posed by the Republican Party and expressed his fear that they could gain control of the executive office of the presidency. He then recounted the culmination of the Kansas Crisis and the Dred Scott case as "a crisis inferior in danger to none that those men encouraged in the Revolution." He then offered an appeal to South Carolina's deceased heroes of the American Revolution, "Illustrious immortals! Doubt not we shall follow in your steps! August spirits! Think not that your children will derogate from your example."[78]

Weston called on South Carolinians to unite for war and expressed how all white Southerners were equal in this coming struggle to defend agriculture and their rights from the Northern majority. He explained how Southerners treat each other with more respect than Northerners treat each other and said that the differences between citizens in the American South were natural ones of "education, industry, good conduct and their results—and inequality is not even supposed or pretended." He went on to say that slavery was the determiner which kept all whites equal and alleged, "the smallest inequality between citizens is abominable and atrocious." He said "not more than two-thirds of whites own slaves, yet the maintenance of authority is of equal, or of greater advantage and necessity to the non-slave holding rather than to the slave holding class. By introducing and maintaining a subordinate and inferior class, the property of the rich clothes the poor with power." Weston reaffirmed that all whites were equal as citizens and said that citizenry in the South was completely "contrary to the example of other nations where the separation between the rich and poor is caused by an incompatibility of interests and increases daily."[79]

An alarmist by nature, Weston gave a glimmer of hope that war with the United States could be avoided due to commercial interests. He said, "Nothing but the absolute necessity which the world has of its being supplied with our great staples prevents a large portion of the citizens of the United States and a majority of civilized Europe from banding themselves together in an open enmity against us."[80]

Weston further defended slavery by insisting that Africans were better off in America than they were in Africa, praised Christianity for uplifting both races and insisted that the races aided each other. He held that "civilization, Christianity, and wealth go hand in hand, and both races, differing from each other in everything, except in those moral perceptions which are necessary for the definition of man, confer on each other benefits which outlast the present state of existence and shall not be terminated by the grave."[81]

Representative Weston articulated his greatest fear that the United States government would force emancipation. He stated that if slaves were to be set free that the abolitionists would not stop at their crusade. He prophesized, "With this unholy alliance between slaves and Northerners, they will make them citizens and give them voting rights and rights to hold office under the federal government and together they will out vote us on everything dear to us and take away our political rights and freedoms and keep us in complete subjugation."[82]

Weston called on the people—to unite and rally to fight—two more times in his lecture. He first paraphrased Thomas Paine's *The American Crisis* when he said, "The times are coming which are again to try men's souls, that is, to test the self-reliance, the courage, the energy, the attachment to liberty, and the moral dignity of every man amongst us." Later on that day he said, "Soon will the mighty hands of destiny and opportunity meet on the dial-plate of time—then will it be our duty to take to our line firmly, to adhere inflexibly to the maintenance of those rights, won by our fathers and enlarged by ourselves, throwing aside all care of life and property, since neither are of any value when independence and freedom have departed."[83]

Like a great professor addressing his students in true Socratic fashion, Weston asked his contemporaries, friends and family at *Watchesaw Plantation* if they knew the definitions of the words "revolution" and "reform." Answering his own question, Weston said, "I know that for successful agriculture a continual turning of the ground is necessary, but this would be the earthquake leveling everything that is high and crushing everything that is lowly; cleaving up deep pits where once stood fertile fields; raising desolate hills where once spread fertilizing lakes." He continued, "I know that the gentle agitation of the waves is necessary to maintain the sweetness of the sea, but this would be the awful rage of the billows when they break in thunder over some perishing wreck." He furthered, "I know that the breeze is necessary to freshen the face of nature and to carry commerce over the deep; but this would be the tornado bursting over Earth and ocean, sweeping down navies in their pride and mixing sea and shore in indistinguishable confusion. Shall we then call this intended change by the name of Revolution?"[84]

He ended his oration with a final rally to arms: "The defense of our country, let us firmly protect the institutions God has given us to preserve, and with settled resolutions, uphold the ancient freedom of South Carolina."[85]

On August 24, 1857, a financial panic commenced. It was the first worldwide economic crisis and worst financial catastrophe in American history up to that time. The fiscal meltdown affected many Western banks and was brought on by the declining international economy and overexpansion of the domestic economy, including overspeculation in Western railroad construction. American banks followed English bankers in printing and lending out far more specie than they had in hard reserve. In many cases, American banks lent out $7.00 for every $1.00 they held in gold and silver bullion. Farmers and newly unemployed industrial and internal improvement employees called for a Homestead Act, one of the key components of the Republican Platform of 1856. With the financial panic of 1857, the Republican Party drew even greater attention and vowed to make a difference in the next election.

On November 23, 1857, Governor Robert F.W. Allston addressed the state. As if calling Plowden Charles Jennett Weston into action and propelling him to statewide fame, Allston called for new, strong leaders to rise in South Carolina to fill the vacancies created with the recent deaths of John C. Calhoun, Langdon Cheves, Preston Brooks and Andrew Butler.[86]

Allston then addressed the Financial Crisis of 1857. He reassured the people of South Carolina that all state banks were solvent. However, he sent a stern warning to the bankers by warning them "if they are dependent on the banks and brokers of New York, as to fail in their pledges to the public, when Northern banks fail, it is their misfortune to have to answer for the sins of others, well as for their own mismanagement."[87]

Next, he offered his empathy to the people of Kansas. He said, "Our friends in Kansas, who have struggled manfully to sustain an unequal contest are entitled to our sympathy,—'tis all we have a right to offer."[88] Then Allston addressed the Dred Scott decision and announced that Maine and Connecticut had protested against the Supreme Court decision. He applauded the Supreme Court's decision and gave a proslavery speech which was very similar to the one Weston gave in July at *Watchesaw Plantation*. He blamed the slave trade on the English and New England shippers and then praised South Carolinians and Southerners for doing God's work in Christianizing the Africans. Allston boasted that it was by the Providence of God that Southerners were able "to convert the barbarian bushmen of the African coast into the orderly domestic Christian black-laborer of America."[89]

On May 4, 1858, feeling strong and defiant on the United States Senate floor, South Carolina Senator James Henry Hammond explained how the Southern people of the American Union were the "chosen people of modern times." He pleaded at last for the creation of Southern Nationalism and for Southerners to stand together to stem the tide of change. He warned those outside of the South: "Without the South's cotton England would topple headlong and carry the whole civilized world with her—save the South." He furthered his argument by saying, "No, you dare not make war on cotton…. Cotton is King."[90]

Hammond delivered his *"Mud-Sill"* speech as a reaction discourse to the admission of Kansas into the Union as a free state. Later in his speech, Hammond argued various complaints. Another poignant argument in the speech pertained to the mismanagement and unscrupulous lending policies of the big banks. In reaction to the collapse of the bank of England which caused the worldwide financial panic of 1857, Hammond said, "When the abuse of credit had destroyed credit and annihilated confidence; when thousands of the strongest commercial houses in the world were coming down, and hundreds of millions of dollars of supposed property evaporating in thin air; when you came to a dead lock, and revolutions were threatened, what brought you up? Fortunately for you it was the commencement of the cotton season, and we have poured in upon you one million six hundred thousand bales of cotton just at the crisis to save you from destruction."[91]

During that same month, representatives from throughout the South met at the Southern Commercial Convention in Montgomery, Alabama. The main topics discussed were the enforcement of the Federal Fugitive Slave Law (which was not being enforced to their approval), how to deal with labor shortages since the slave trade was closed (apprenticeships and the importation of free blacks were discussed), the tariff, the further development of the Southern agricultural industry (internal improvements and steamers to carry staples to market), the expansion of Southern libraries, schools and colleges, and the relationship between the federal government and the Southern states as it pertained to expansion. (The question was if new territories were going to be evenly divided between the North and the South.)[92] It is clear to see that the Southern states were developing Southern Nationalism by coming together as a voting bloc due to their shared economic, social and political interests. At the same time, they were leaving themselves wiggle room to be able to remain part of the United States.

With American Independence Day quickly approaching, the *Pee Dee Times* published an article explaining the beliefs and opinions of many locals concerning the celebration of the birth of the United States. The paper stated that many readers "would rather celebrate the anniversary of a Southern Confederacy, than the declaration of our independence that was. But as long as we are in the Union let us not be wanting in celebrating the valorous deeds of our ancestors—the independence they achieved, had we the courage to maintain it."[93]

On July 7, 1858, Richard Dozier of the *Pee Dee Times* painted a grim picture for his readers of the state of the union, as seen through the events of the Fourth of July Celebration. He reported that the anniversary of the birthday of the United States passed "quietly and pleasantly, but with little of that public demonstration usual on such occasion." He described that the day was ushered in with the roar of artillery and church bells ringing early in the morning but stated that the day did not feature a reading of the Declaration of Independence, any patriotic speakers or parades. Dozier attributed the lackluster celebration to the sectional crisis and stated, "the house divided in itself, which at no distant day its splendid edifice must crumble in the dust." He wrote that the day was a pleasant 91 degrees Fahrenheit with a light breeze and noted that a few flags were displayed in "conspicuous places" in Georgetown.[94]

Few issues of the *Pee Dee Times* newspaper survived after July 1858. In May of 1859, the *Pee Dee Times* ceased publication. Richard Dozier, by then the sole proprietor of the newspaper, closed the doors of operation and focused upon his political career. He was elected to replace John Izard Middleton in the state general assembly in 1857 and qualified on December 12, 1857. He held his seat through the 1861 sessions.

On October 16, 1859, John Brown (a veteran of the civil war in Kansas) raided a federal arsenal in Harpers Ferry, Virginia. Brown planned to take over the arsenal, steal weapons and incite a slave rebellion to kill slaveholders, their wives and children in Virginia. He and his followers easily took over the arsenal but failed to distribute the weapons, and slaves did not rise to kill their masters. A detachment of federal troops recaptured the arsenal on October 18 and arrested Brown and his supporters. Brown was hanged less than two months later and quickly became a martyr to the abolitionist cause. With tensions rising and fear of John Brown copycats, South Carolina immediately allocated $100,000 for military preparations, and men throughout the state began drilling and preparing for defense. After years of attempting to promote Southern Nationalism and cooperation among the Southern states, it was the radical abolitionist, John Brown, who unified Georgetown and South Carolina in general.[95]

Waccamaw River rice planter, Jacob Motte Alston, recalled John Brown's raid and gave insight into the planters' view of the abolitionists. He said, "Was there any justice when instead of 'insuring domestic tranquility,' the abolitionists of the North and East left no stone unturned to stir up strife among our servants and incite them into insurrection, and subsequently to have marched into Virginia with the avowed purpose of murdering the whites and freeing the slaves, as John Brown and his band attempted?" Alston later asked himself in his diary, "If this is the letter and the spirit of the Constitution then were the Southern States most unwise, to use a mild term, to enter into any such compact?"[96]

Between the sudden changes in social habits and the massive push towards industrialization, it seemed to the planters that their entire world was unraveling. In the years since open warfare commenced in Kansas, a transatlantic cable connected North America to Europe; Pony Express riders carried the United States mail from St. Louis, Missouri, to San Francisco, California, in ten days or less; telegraph cables linked the East and soon crossed the continent, and over 30,000 miles of railroad crisscrossed the United States. (In 1830, there were only 40 miles of railroad track in the United States.)

In November 1859, Charles Darwin's book, *On the Origins of Species by Means of Natural Selection,* was published. This groundbreaking work on evolution was, undoubtedly, seen as another offense to the planter class who held dear to traditionally held Christian values. This infraction against Christianity coupled with the musical rendition (essentially minstrel shows) of the traveling Tom Shows (theatrical productions of Harriet Beecher Stowe's book *Uncle Tom's Cabin*) infuriated planters who saw continued assault upon their civilization.

In April 1860, Charleston held the Democratic Party Convention. The party split along sectional lines, forming two parties. The Democratic Party split again when John Bell led a group of former Northern Whigs and former Know-Nothings in the formation of the Constitutional Union Party. The party refused to take a position on slavery except to declare that it was legal in the United States Constitution. In June, Southerners met in Richmond and nominated John C. Breckinridge, the seated vice president of the United States under President James Buchanan, and Northern Democrats chose Stephen A. Douglas as their standard bearer at the Baltimore Convention. The last national party officially splintered, and it would prove impossible for the regions to come together on political compromise.

Throughout South Carolina history, her politicians threatened to leave the United States and assert their independence as their state increasingly lost influence in national politics to the Northern seaboard states. When Abraham Lincoln won the presidential election in November 1860 without winning a single electoral vote from the South, South Carolina responded. The *Charleston Mercury* screamed out, "The Tea has been thrown overboard—the revolution of 1860 has been initiated." The newspaper called for "minute men," militias and slave patrols throughout the state to prepare for war.[97] A few days later, on November 13, 1860, the South Carolina General Assembly in joint session ratified an act calling for a "Convention of the People to Convene in Columbia on December 17."

Elections for delegates to the convention took place on December 6, 1860. Each district in South Carolina sent representatives to assemble and discuss secession. Prince George Winyah sent Georgetown Attorney,

Samuel Taylor Atkinson, and rice planters, Judge Benjamin Faneuil Dunkin, Dr. Alexius Mador Forster and Dr. Francis S. Parker. Benjamin E. Sessions and rice planter, John Izard Middleton, represented All Saints Parish.[98]

Collectively, 169 men attended the convention which convened on the previously proposed date. Most were planters, but some came from all other professions as well, including slaveless farmers, manufacturers, attorneys, judges, physicians, professors, clergymen, merchants, brokers, solicitors, the president of a railroad, the president of an insurance company and even a school teacher who owned neither slaves nor property in South Carolina.[99]

On December 20, 1860, the representatives signed the Ordinance of Secession, officially withdrawing South Carolina from the Union. A breakout group at the convention, operating under the name "The 1860 Association," formed to facilitate a call to arms. Robert Newman Gourdin, chairman of "The 1860 Association," wrote letters to notable men throughout South Carolina requesting them to do all that they could to support the newly established South Carolina nation. His private letters served a threefold purpose. First, his letters were individualized and were therefore a more private attempt to explain the impending crisis, secondly, to prepare, print and distribute pamphlets and other literature to "urge the necessity of resisting Northern and federal aggression" and lastly to set up military organization for South Carolina.[100] Shortly thereafter, the 1860 Winyah Association formed to help support the larger association to meet its goals of independence from the United States.[101]

It was in the newspapers, societies and clubs addressed in this volume that Georgetown (and a few Horry District) planters shaped and molded society, shared their ideas with yeomen farmers, argued their cases, discussed their options, forged Southern Nationalism, and finally pledged their alliance to each other and their independence from the United States. They felt that their economic structure was challenged by their own central government, their social institutions threatened, and they had become politically neutralized as Northern states swelled with immigrants, and the Southern population showed little comparative growth. Stalwart Southerners felt that their rights had been trampled and their cries for redress denied. Lowcountry planters and the entire American South were faced with the age-old conundrum of standing up for their rights in a changing world or leaving the problem to their children's generation. In true paternalistic fashion, the men of the era, planter and farmer alike, shouldered the storm, unified and fought to defend their civilization.

THREE

The Lifestyle of the Georgetown Planter Class During the Late Antebellum Era

The beautiful and fertile lowcountry of our state is the seat of annual and endemic visitations of disease, which we are accustomed to attribute to Malaria ... there are few plantations which admit of permanent residence; the whole region being pervaded by a pestilential infection, almost unfailing in the excitement of Fevers, Intermittent and Remittent, during the Summer and Autumn.—S. H. Dickerson[1]

The last generation of rice planters of the Georgetown District before the American Civil War were some of the most successful businessmen in America, true captains of agriculture, strong politicians and at the same time gentlemen of leisure. The creation of the rice plantation system was nearly complete, as very few plantations were constructed during the last two decades before the Civil War. Planters had many professionals to lean upon to help prepare and deliver their rice yields to market.

At the top of the socioeconomic agricultural ladder, planters remained responsible for the work of their subordinates and the organization of the network that supported their trade. Like modern chief executive officers of Fortune 500 corporations with hundreds of employees, management staffs and various production sites, planters shouldered a tremendous burden in both managing their rice crops and regulating society norms. They hired or promoted traveling overseers to serve as regional managers to watch over individual plantation overseers who worked as production plant administrators staffed by lower-level controllers called drivers who supervised their plantation slaves. Some planters employed professional millers to prepare their harvests, factors to market their yields, shippers to move their produce to buyers around the world, and bankers to handle their finances. With these professionals and laborers at their disposal, it would appear that the planter lifestyle was worry-free

71

and that their personal agricultural empires were self-sustaining, but all details from personnel employment and slave allocations to selecting which bankers and market professionals to use and managing their personal finances and investments were ultimately the planter's responsibility, and his long-term success depended upon his decisions.

The leisurely way of life of the Southern planter, as touted by Hollywood and novels, oversimplifies the planter class and is far from the truth. The occupation of planter required one to be very organized, but with their day-to-day plantation agri-businesses handled for them, many members of the final generation of prewar rice planters dedicated their lives to preserving the civilization that their grandfathers and fathers built and nurtured, traveling, governing politics, and leading a social lifestyle mandated by the seasons.

It is true that the planting families traveled from their manor homes to their beach homes back to their manor homes and then to their Charleston homes each year, but each move was necessary, and in fact, the extended visits to the seaside resorts were necessary to escape the stagnant rice fields during the "sickly season." To remain on the plantations during the summer would almost certainly ensure that white Southerners contracted "bilious fever" or "country fever," extreme cases of malaria.[2]

Each year at the end of May, out of fear of contracting malaria, commonly referred to as "country fever," the planting families moved away from their plantations and did not return until the first week in November.[3] They spent time with relatives or friends in other parts of South Carolina, North Carolina, or other states. Some spent time abroad in Europe. By this time period, the resort at North Island had been devastated by the hurricane of 1822, and planters built new retreats. The most popular in-state retreats of the Georgetown planters in South Carolina were Pawleys Island, Murrells Inlet, Charleston, and a small community on the Pee Dee River called Plantersville.

The most celebrated of these summer retreats were Pawleys Island and Murrells Inlet. Located at the seashore and marsh front, respectively, these twin communities are among America's oldest resorts. For the Pee Dee families, who had to cross the Waccamaw River in order to get to the beach, getting to their summer refuges was a long, hard trek, but for the Waccamaw families whose land stretched from river to sea, it was closer and more convenient. One woman recalled her family's annual pilgrimage to the coast. She wrote, "All of our belongings, servants, horses, cows, furniture, were loaded on to lighters and propelled seven miles through broad rivers and winding creeks to Waverly Mills where they were disembarked and traveled four miles by land, but when we reached this paradise on the Atlantic Ocean we felt repaid for it."[4]

Early View of Pawleys Island (Pawleys Island Civic Association Collection, Georgetown County Library, Georgetown, SC).

Canaan, home of Robert F.W. Allston (Pawleys Island Civic Association Collection, Georgetown County Library, Georgetown, SC).

As author Lawrence Fay Brewster stated, "Waccamaw River planters had the advantage of having retreats within easy reach of their plantation dwellings, either on the beach heads of their own lands, which stretched from river to sea, or at nearby resorts, to which they migrated in summer with their families, friends, pastors, teachers, and servants."[5]

Planting families traveled with everything that they would need for the six-month period away from home. Families spent weeks packing. Resembling small armies as they traveled, planters annually moved everything from kitchen utensils and clothing to pianos to their summer refuges. Mrs. John Weston explained why she took so many servants with them to the beach and to Charleston: "We can not possibly separate husband and wife for six months; so Harry, the coachmen, has to have his wife and children, and the same with the cook, and the butler, and the laundress, until we are actually moving an army every time we move."[6] Mrs. Paul Weston concurred. "We have to take fifty individuals with us in the move, I mean children and all."[7]

Pawleys Island, a resort community since the late 1700s, began to expand during the 1820s due to the growing wealth and leisure time of the planters. When the hurricane of September 1822 destroyed most of the older buildings, the residents quickly built new homes on their properties. To accomplish the rebuilding, planters sent skilled carpenter slaves with cypress timber by boat to restore the community. One head carpenter slave cut the materials for the family's summer home and labeled each piece at the family's plantation so it could be quickly assembled at the beach front property.[8] Several planters built notable homes at the summer resorts, including Plowden C.J. Weston, Dr. E.T. Heriot's Woodland, Colonel Joshua John Ward's Magnolia and Retreat houses, Robert F.W. Allston's Canaan and Jacob Motte Alston's Sunnyside. Dr. Andrew Hasell, a full-time resident of Pawleys Island, resided at Cedar Grove. Most of these houses had wide porches facing the southwest and southeast, the directions of the prevailing winds, while some had piazzas that encircled the entire structure.

By the 1840s, Pawleys Island, a strip of land a quarter of a mile across (at its widest point) and less than four miles long was clearly more popular than Murrells Inlet.[9] A Northern visitor to Pawleys Island in 1851 described the resort very descriptively. She wrote, "I rode over to one Pawleys Island which is three miles long, with a fine beach on the ocean side, some 6 or 8 houses, plenty of trees &c, [sic] separated by a creek from the main land which we forded."[10]

For summer recreation, the planters created a social club, the Hot & Hot Fish Club, where they dined on extravagant meals and entertained themselves by fishing, hunting, racing their horses and playing tenpins and billiards. The hunters had small clubhouses made of pine logs constructed at central locations in the forest where they met to take breaks, sip on fine wines, and enjoy their kill and catch, which their slaves prepared. The group always shared a dish of beef or ham and at least one of fresh game. Members provided condiments such as sugar, ice and rice in tuns, and everyone enjoyed his own catch.[11]

While the planters entertained themselves with their convivial gatherings, their families enjoyed genteel leisure around their summer homes.

Adele Petigru Allston wrote to her husband addressing her summer routine while he was away on business. She wrote, "I walk the causeway every morning after breakfast, and stroll upon the beach and sand hills in the afternoon." Ladies frequently met for tea and conversations.[12] During their summer vacation from home, parents permitted their children to enjoy the early morning hours; however, they were required to keep up with their studies. After dinner, they enjoyed "swimming in the surf, horseback riding on the beach, and on rainy days, the great privilege of reading fiction."[13]

Whether at home or at the beach, Georgetown planters involved themselves in religious activities. The Episcopal faith, the religion of the planter class, boasted three fine churches in Georgetown. In town, the elite worshipped at Prince George Winyah Church. At home in the country, they attended either All Saints Church on the Waccamaw or Prince Frederick on the Pee Dee River. While at the beach, plantation owners and their families flocked to All Saints Parish Episcopal Church at Pawleys Island.

In July of 1832, the planters and their wives, in conjunction with the Rev. Alexander Glennie, the pastor of All Saints Church, formed the All Saints Sunday School Society. The school's function was "to afford religious instruction to the children of the Parish, according to the Protestant Episcopalian Church Sunday School Union."[14] The Society created a constitution with six rules and held elections each year for the offices of president, vice president, secretary and treasurer, as well as three directors.[15]

In 1838, the All Saints' Summer Academy, directed by David D. Rosa, opened.[16] By 1843, the school served both male and female students and offered "a complete English education" to anyone who could afford tuition: $20.00 per term for students over 12 years of age and $10.00 for students under 12. Latin, Greek, French, music and drawing classes required additional fees. Classes began on January 2 of each year, and the school expected the students to provide their own furniture. Board and "washing" fees cost an extra $13.50 per month.[17] In 1854, Peter Waities Fraser donated 300 feet of land on Pawleys Island for the purpose of building a summer rectory. The erection of this home for the Rev. Alexander Glennie was the church's final expansion into the beach communities during the era.[18]

Plowden Charles Jennett Weston brought Mr. Glennie to All Saints Parish from England to be a tutor on his plantation to his slaves. Weston was not the only planter on the Waccamaw Neck who was concerned about the education of his slaves. Dr. John Daniel Magill and his wife Mary took the initiative to teach her children and some of the family's young slaves how to read the Bible.[19]

In 1832, Glennie was ordained minister of All Saints Church, Waccamaw, a region which was clearly an Anglican holdout in the United

Prince George Winyah Church, Georgetown, SC (photograph by Paige Sawyer).

All Saints Summer Academy (Georgetown County Library, Georgetown, SC).

Reverend Alexander Glennie, 1835, by Charles Fraser, watercolor on ivory (gift of Mrs. Aiken Simons, 1940.008.0001, Gibbes Museum of Art).

States as most of the inhabitants were Episcopalians. Glennie served planters at the traditional church and at the beach during the summer and then began a mission to the slaves. His mission to the slaves included 13 chapels on various plantations along the Waccamaw River in the All Saints District. He not only taught catechism but schooled them as to how to worship in Anglican fashion (Episcopal Church). Bishop Philander Chase, upon visiting Glennie's work, said, "The black children of a South Carolina planter know more of Christianity than thousands of white children in Illinois."[20] Glennie's work was so respected in the Episcopal Church that in 1844, he was elected missionary Bishop of Cape Palmas (Liberia) by the general Convention for increasing the number of slave communicants in the district from ten in 1832 to 539 in 1844.[21]

Many Pee Dee and Black River rice growers, especially the individuals that could not afford good overseers, simply moved further up the Pee Dee River to the safety of the pine lands during the summer months. From there, planters could check on their estates and still enjoy good health during "the sickly season." Though not entirely mosquito proof, the region's abundant pine straw acted as a natural repellant. The residents remained relatively safe from the dreaded "country fever" if they did not clear away too many pine trees when constructing their summer homes. In 1852, these summer residents incorporated this 350-acre resort and formally named it Plantersville.[22] Even after the area began to attract outsiders, the resort remained the preferred vacation spot of the Black River and Pee Dee families due to proximity to their plantations.

Still other planters took refuge in their Charleston homes during the summer, where the ocean's saltwater kept the mosquitos at bay. In Charleston they mingled with the locals and built family alliances with other planting families throughout the coastal region who ventured to the city for the summer.

By November, the weather cooled and chances of contracting malaria subsided. The planting families packed up their belongings and moved back to their manor homes. The planters returned home during the first week in November to find their rice carefully stacked in barns or already sent to market. The yield was often high and sometimes in excess of 1,000,000 pounds of grain. But, by the antebellum age, it was not the planter's job to tend to sell the crop or handle finances; it was time to enjoy their close-knit, extremely affluent social lives and prepare for the holiday season.

Winter was the time when planters entertained each other by holding large lawn and garden parties during the day, as well as at dinnertime and evening parties. Although the men had the Planters' Club on the Pee Dee and the Winyah and All Saints Agricultural Society for amusement during the winter months, they primarily regarded this season as the time for family gatherings, weddings and holiday celebrations.

At one such wedding party, in the winter of 1849, Joshua John Ward gave a dinner party at his *Brook Green Plantation* in honor of his daughter Penelope's marriage to Dr. Arthur Belin Flagg. The Heriot, Belin, Petigru, LaBruce, Vaux, several of the Allston and Alston families, Izard, Pringle, Poinsett, Read and some of the Weston and Ford family members were in attendance. According to one guest, "the party was kept up till the we sma' hours, and there was one who greatly enjoyed a regular old-fashioned country dance to the music of sundry country fiddles." Five years later, Georgeana Ward married, and the family held a similar wedding ceremony.[23]

When recalling a plantation wedding, one Santee River resident wrote, "I let myself loose to the enjoyment of the hour; danced all night, spent the next day in walking, riding and other sports to which the party gave themselves up before dinner and reappeared in the evening ready to dance with the most determined. At that time the wedding festivities always continued two nights, nor were the guests expected to leave the house until the third day."[24]

Another gentleman from the Georgetown countryside recalled the formality of plantation weddings in his memoirs. He wrote, "weddings were celebrated on these river plantations and the guests came from as much as twenty miles in boats rowed by stalwart Negroes. They remained for the night and continued the festivities the next day. On the return voyage the negro oarsmen kept time to their oars with improvised songs in honor of the bride and groom."[25]

During the holiday season, the planters displayed their true patriarchal spirit. Although the roads were unpaved, families from throughout the Georgetown countryside, as well as from the city, traveled about visiting friends and kin. Planting families usually spent the first three weeks of December decorating their homes for Christmas and preparing gifts. They bedecked their manor homes beautifully with Christmas trees, garland, late-blooming flowers and various types of greenery, including holly. Hosts tempted their guests' palates with snacks—gingerbread, fruitcakes, puddings, homemade candy, eggnog, punch and fine wines such as Madeira. Treats such as eggnog, gingerbread and assorted cakes were often served in abundance.

Family and friends stayed for extended visits, but most of the manor homes were spacious, and the planters welcomed company. Local guests joined the families in carriage rides and daily sporting events such as rowing, horseback riding, foot races and other games of strength, skill and athleticism, such as wrestling. Ladies sipped tea and enjoyed conversation while men hunted and children put on plays with the aid of house servants.

Christmas in the Georgetown District was a time of celebration for all Christians, whether master or slave. At most plantations, the celebration lasted for three days, and the only work done on the plantation during that time period revolved around necessities such as preparing food for the family and tending to the livestock. At Chicora Wood Plantation, home of Robert F.W. Allston, Allston himself set off fireworks on Christmas Eve for everyone's delight, and his daughters helped all the children hang their stockings because even slave children expected a visit from St. Nicholas.

On Christmas morning, Allston's servants played a game with their master and his family called "ketch." These servants found amusement in sneaking up on members of the planting family and saying, "Merry Christmas, I ketch you." The master, or one of his family members, would then present the servant with a small gift, such as nuts, tobacco, fruit, candy, a doll, a handful of jacks or a handkerchief. In return, the slave would present an egg or another small token of his affection to the planting family member.

According to Allston's daughter, the family always said their prayers together in the library, and then the family settled down to a large breakfast of sausage, hogs head cheese, hominy, buckwheat cakes, honey, waffles and orange marmalade. Often before the family could finish breakfast, they could hear the slave community celebrating the birth of Jesus Christ.

Shortly after their morning meal, the entire plantation community gathered in front of the manor house and on the front piazza of the house. Slaves danced to music that they played on fiddles, triangles, jaw harps, and assorted sticks and bones. The dancing and partying continued until 10:00 p.m. on Christmas night and then restarted the next morning and continued throughout the next three days, with dancers and musicians taking turns on the piazza, while others feasted on beef and pork and drank alcohol.[26]

On Christmas Day 1856, the year that Allston won the governor race in South Carolina, there was a special celebration at his household. Mrs. Allston recalled, "The next morning there was a great demonstration, the negroes coming up as usual to greet their master the Governor. They made a great noise and drank to the Governor's health in many a stout glass of whiskey."[27]

Plowden Charles Jennett Weston, the proprietor of *Hagley Plantation* on the Waccamaw River as well as other plantations in Georgetown, began the holiday on December 22. On that night, he and his wife visited the slave street and began to hand out extra rations of meat, salt and molasses and rarer foods such as plum pudding, apples and oranges to their adult slaves and sugar and gingerbread to the slave children.

On Christmas morning, many of Weston's slaves gathered at the carpenter's shop, where they played music, danced, sang and feasted. Although it was a popular meeting place, not all the servants attended his celebration. Many took advantage of Weston's peculiar practice of handing out passes to his best-behaved servants, allowing them to leave his plantation to go Christmas caroling and to visit friends and family at nearby plantations.

A first-year tutor on William Algernon Alston's *Clifton Plantation* recalled being awakened by a group of young slave girls dressed in fine red and white dresses, caroling to their master and his family, "Brightly does the morning break in the eastern sky, awake! Cradled on his bed of hay, Jesus Christ was born today. Let a Merry Christmas be, massa, both to me and thee!" Apparently, this was an annual tradition at *Clifton Plantation* and not an impromptu serenade.[28]

William Algernon Alston was described as an absentee landowner of the Lower All Saints District. He owned five plantations in the district but spent much of his time on Cherry Street in New York City, living very comfortably surrounded by his mother's side of his family. He was a graduate of Princeton University and was described as a "gentleman of leisure who weighs three hundred pounds" in his alma mater's reunion catalog of 1854.[29]

On Dr. James Ritchie Sparkman's *Mt. Arena Plantation* on Sandy Island, the Christmas holiday also lasted three days. Many similarities existed between celebrations on the various plantations in the area, but the residents celebrated somewhat differently on Sparkman's estate. Like Allston and Weston, Sparkman gave his slaves extra rations of peas, rice, molasses and meat. To each slave woman he gave a handkerchief and to each male slave a wool hat in observance of the holiday. The difference between the three plantations was that Sparkman reserved one day of the three-day holiday as a cleaning day. He issued soap to his slaves and insisted that they thoroughly clean their houses, utensils, clothing and everything else that they owned. Also, Sparkman made it his official policy to inspect all tools on his plantation during the Christmas holiday. When convinced that his tools had not been neglected, the slaves received additional rations.

The Christmas season was also a popular time for slave marriages. Although not legal, marriages between slaves were promoted by most planters as a way of securing the next generation's labor force and deterring slaves from running away. Some planters sent out invitations to their neighbors and their slaves, asking them to attend the weddings which usually took place on the front lawn of the manor homes.

In many cases the planter hired a minister to perform the service and had

William Algernon Alston, ca. 1805, by Jean François de la Vallée, watercolor on ivory (gift of Colonel Alston Deas, 1965.029.0001, Gibbes Museum of Art).

a large feast of beef and pork prepared in honor of the newlyweds. Sometimes the master permitted the entire community the rare opportunity to consume wine or liquor. Usually, he toasted the newlywed couple and granted them a honeymoon—an additional three-day vacation from their duties.[30]

New Year's Eve was another holiday which earned the whole community a three-day period of rest, visitation and celebration. On New Year's Day, some masters gave annual rations of clothing, blankets and shoes to the slave families. On most plantations, the distribution of clothing was a ceremonious affair. Typically, slave communities gathered at a central point on the plantation where the planter called off the bondsmen's names one by one. After being called, the individual stepped up, and a trusty servant measured the person. Next, the planter issued enough material to make several outfits of work apparel and Sunday dress attire. Usually, planters purchased shoes for their servants in Charleston, so the slaves had to wait for a few weeks after being measured for their annual allotment of footgear.[31] The clothing distribution marked the end of the holiday season, and planting families began to turn their attention towards the "social season."

The "social season," set in Charleston, was a chance for the planters throughout the state to come together for communal discourse. Planting families left their plantations on the Monday following the epiphany and headed for the city. The season lasted from the middle of January until Palm Sunday (the week before Easter). Some who owned houses in Charleston were Dr. Francis S. Parker, John Harleston Read, Jr., Joshua John Ward, Francis Marion Weston, William Algernon Alston, John H. Tucker, Robert F.W. Allston, Charles Alston, Jacob Motte Alston, and nearly 20 others. The Rev. Maurice Harvey Lance, perhaps because he performed so much itinerate preaching in the upstate, preferred to rent a house in Charleston.[32]

The gentlemen took their ideas of liberty and secession with them to the "social season" in Charleston. George C. Rogers, Jr., contends in his book, *The History of Georgetown County,* that the presence of these planters from throughout the Lowcountry influenced the Charleston merchant class to vote for secession in 1860. Rogers claims that Lowcountry planters, primarily those from Georgetown and Beaufort, aided by Robert Barnwell Rhett, the fire-eater politician, journalist, and proprietor of the *Charleston Mercury,* dominated the city and persuaded Charlestonians to seek independence from the United States.[33]

Of course, some planters chose to travel throughout the United States or abroad during the winter months, but Charleston was the place the planters visited most frequently. They relaxed with leisurely walks in public pleasure grounds such as the Battery Promenade, through White Point Gardens and around Rutledge Avenue Pond. While at the Battery, those with an appetite for sweets could enjoy refreshments such as ice cream and pastries. In the evenings, the sounds of brass and woodwind instruments or vocalists, pianists and violinists entertained the crowds strolling or riding in the cool night air, viewing the harbor.[34]

The Georgetown elite also intermingled with Charleston society by attending weddings, musicales, soirees, debutante balls, dances, masquerades and parties sponsored by such prominent groups as the St. Cecilia Society, the Cotillion Club and the Jockey Club.[35] The organizations held their gatherings at exclusive auditoriums such as the South Carolina Institute Hall on Broad Street, Military Hall on Wentworth Street, Hibernian Hall, and the New Charleston Theater on Meeting Street.[36]

Of all the societies in Charleston during the antebellum period, the St. Cecilia Society held the most formal balls. Planting families received invitations to three or four balls each week. St. Cecilia Society held a ball every ten days. Many women wore French designer dresses to the balls, which were the "most exclusive and elegant balls of them all."[37] The balls centered around social intercourse, fine wines, food and dancing. Popular dances of the era were the waltz, polka, and the maruka, collectively referred to as "round dances." Proper ladies were not expected, and some were not permitted, to partake in "fast" dances due to their pace.[38]

In 1762, the women of Charleston founded the St. Cecilia Society as a musical organization; however, by the 1840s, the society had become more of a cotillion club than an organization to provide quality music to the socially refined.[39] The society held its largest ball annually during February (just before lent) in Hibernian Hall on the west side of Meeting Street. A contemporary remarked, "the membership remains exclusive and its affairs somewhat secret."[40] Even today, the club remains secretive, and its historical records and membership lists remain off-limits to nonmembers.

Throughout the year, the merchant class reigned in Charleston, but during the second half of January, February and into March, the city was in the hands of the planting class. In this unofficial capital of the Lowcountry, the planting families displayed their wealth in flamboyant fashion.

The frock coat dominated the wardrobe of the 1840s gentleman. Meant to be worn with knickers and full shirts, it featured a deep collar and wide lapels and was often edged with braid. Another popular style, more formal in design, was the patterned or embroidered waistcoat worn with tight-fitting trousers which fastened under the instep. Men's accessories of the period were the cravat and gutta-percha cane. During this decade, ladies wore hooped dresses with sloping shoulders and tight sleeves. Women's accessories included ermine muffs, tasseled handbags and parasols for outdoor events. Their tightly fitting flower-trimmed bonnets had deep crowns and large brims which framed and complemented their faces. During the evening, ladies wore dresses with provocatively low-cut bodices and feathers or pearls in their hair.[41]

During the 1850s, although fashions did not change much, the number of garments required for gentlemanly attire proliferated. Besides the morning frock, dress and overcoats, men wore paletots, cloaks with contrasting collars and slit armholes. The popularity of cravats declined, and proper neckwear became a bow or shoestring. By 1856 the introduction of the caged crinoline relieved the weight of women's petticoats. Layered flounced skirts became popular. Ladies still preferred dresses with sloped shoulders and hats that tied firmly under their chins; however, bonnets no longer had deep crowns and brims. Women adorned their "round" hats with long, wide ribbons and wore their creations further back on their heads. Very small and highly decorated parasols were the rage. Handbags were also minuscule, and neither served much purpose. One prevailing purse design was the "miser," which had fringe at one end and tassels at the other, while another was made of netting and beads. During the evenings, ladies wore snake-like jewelry and headwear made of pearls and flowers set far back on their heads.[42]

The Charleston Jockey Club provided much-deserved entertainment for the planting families during the social season. Founded in 1793, this organization was part of a 15-track circuit of jockey clubs that existed in the state during the antebellum years. The Charleston Jockey Club held its races at the Washington Course near Charleston.[43] The Charleston races occurred, by rule, on the Saturday, Sunday and Monday preceding the first Wednesday in February.[44] Jacob Motte Alston frequently visited the track. He noted, "The Ladies of Charleston always turned out in full feathers on these occasions, and the grandstand was filled with lovely ladies who took intense interest in the horses which were then owned by Gentleman of note."[45] Alston's father Thomas Pinckney Alston owned shares in the Washington Racetrack near Charleston and owned a thoroughbred racehorse named Crusader. Alston recalled that this was a time period when "horse-racing was confined to gentlemen, and not gamblers, and was a pastime and not a profession."[46]

At Washington Course, the races began each day at 1:00 p.m. The first day's races were four-mile heats; the second day, three-mile heats; and the third day featured two-mile heats. Daily entry fees for members were $20.00, $15.00, and $10.00. Nonmembers paid double. The daily purses varied depending upon the number of entries in each race.[47]

The Jockey Club required a $40.00 annual fee from its members, which defrayed the cost of the races, to maintain the track and to pay for dinner parties such as the one held annually on the Wednesday following the races.[48] The club held its annual ball on the Friday following the races. This event signaled the end of the state's professional race season.[49] According to one Georgetown race fan, the ball was "the largest and grandest" of them all.[50]

Usually, at the end of race season, the planters returned home to their manor houses in the countryside to enjoy their estates and the closeness of their small, yet extremely affluent, social organizations until May, when they once again relocated to the beach to escape the "country fever" of the Lowcountry rice fields. The social season in Charleston (between Epiphany and Easter) was as much a business trip made for self-promotion, networking and for promoting political cohesiveness as it was for relaxation and withdrawal from the boredom of country living. In Charleston, planters forged political alliances while their children often courted suitors. In both instances, partnerships were forged which brought forth unions for South Carolina families.

Four

The Winyah Indigo Society

From Inception to the Wilmot Proviso

In a representative republic, the education of our children must be of the utmost importance!—James Monroe

Rice was grown in the Carolina colony before the turn of the eighteenth century and the division of the colony into North and South Carolina. However, it was not until the advent of tidal flooding (1750s) that rice planting expanded and the invention of the rice mill (1780s) that profits from rice made the Lowcountry planters wealthy. By the 1740s, however, over half a century after the introduction of rice to the Carolina Lowcountry, Eliza Lucas and other colonists experimented with indigo planting. Soon, indigo seeds were distributed among rice planters and farmers, and the proliferation of the crop began. The production of the lucrative dye was hailed as great agricultural progress by King George II of England, who offered a bounty on the crop in 1748 in an attempt to encourage the harvest and manufacture of dye. The King's motivation for the bounty was to prevent his subjects from supporting his French and Spanish Catholic rivals who made great profits selling cakes of the colorant. In 1748 alone, South Carolinians exported 138,118 pounds of the dye, a total which quickly rose to 216,924 pounds by 1754. By the time of the American Revolution, South Carolina exported 1,107,660 pounds of the dye. The expansion of indigo into South Carolina supported the first generation of great planters in the colony, enabling them to rise to agricultural prominence and forge the early culture of Georgetown.[1]

In 1729, Elisha Screven laid out the city of Georgetown, and by the 1740s, a few local indigo and rice planters began meeting on the first Friday of each month at Nathaniel Tregagle's popular Old Oak Tavern on Bay Street to discuss the news of their community, Charles Town, and London. At that time, Georgetown, South Carolina, was on the hither edge of civilization, and European news was history by the time it crossed the mighty Atlantic Ocean, as it took between six and eight weeks to transverse the ocean by sail ship. Huddled together in the dark, smoky tavern among the hearty, bearded sailors from throughout the British Empire, the gentlemen enjoyed the finest meals that Colonial Georgetown had to offer, smoked tobacco, drank spirits, and exchanged gossip. They talked about the weather, taxes, the lack of educational opportunities for their children, politics, and how they could improve life in Georgetown.[2]

In 1741, one man, Mr. Meredith Hughes bequeathed 100 pounds of sterling to be applied towards the establishment of a school in Georgetown.[3] Hughes's donation was not a large offering, but it laid the groundwork for what would eventually become the hallmark of antebellum Georgetown and the focal point of its economic, social, political and educational expansion, stability and improvement. The donation to a then nonexistent fund was a visionary offering; it offered a dream of a better future for the inhabitants of the small, sparsely populated shipping port which up until just a little over two decades earlier was still settled by Native Americans.

The emerging affluence of the agriculturalists, their continued regular meetings at the Old Oak Tavern, coupled with their desire for an improved prospect on life, spawned the establishment of the Winyah Indigo Society, Georgetown's first agricultural, social and philanthropic organization. The Society eventually developed to become the equivalent of Charles Town's Library Society and quickly extended membership to all white male Georgetown residents regardless of profession, class or income.

Tradition suggests that the Winyah Indigo Society hails from the 1740s, their official seal alludes to 1753, but the group's documented history asserts that its official organization took place in May 1755. The group's stated intention was to assist local planters and better enable them to support each other's agricultural, economic, political and social interests. The formation of the organization coincided with the rise of the Enlightenment, a time in Western civilization when man questioned social order, the social and political responsibilities of man to his government and scientific explanations for the unknown. Thomas Lynch served as the Society's founding president, and other officers included Joseph Poole, senior warden; Samuel Wragg, junior warden; Nathaniel Tregagle (tavern owner where the group originally met), treasurer; Joseph DuBordieu, clerk; and Charles Fyffe and William Shackelford, Jr., stewards. Although many of the Society's members owned many slaves, the group continued to use the service of new members as stewards at their meetings instead of using slaves.

In that first year, 71 men joined the Society and were thus privileged with the knowledge of improved indigo growing techniques and a shared vision of fashioning a polite society in the rough and tumble seaport. Two

The Old Oak Tavern at the turn of the twentieth century (Morgan-Trenholm Collection, Georgetown County Library, Georgetown, SC).

years later, on May 21, 1757, the Society was incorporated by the General Assembly of Colonial South Carolina, and in 1758, King George II provided a royal charter.

At the inception of the organization, most of the members were indigo planters. The dye was in high demand in the British Empire, and each fellow paid their annual dues in processed cakes of dye because, according to one member, "bank notes were in those days, if not unconstitutional, decidedly unfashionable."[4] When the indigo was sold at market, a handsome treasury was established.

With the accumulation of annual dues and initiation fees, the social order's coffers overflowed, and the Society came to hold a considerable amount of revenue in reserve. According to tradition, the pressing question among Society members was what they should do with their reserved funds. At the end of a meeting in 1756, President Thomas Lynch called on members to fill their glasses. His intentions were to end the discussion as to what good the Society's excess funds should be devoted and how the Society could best serve the stagnant seaport community. Lynch lifted his glass and proposed that the organization allocate the Society's funds towards funding a school. He asked that all in favor of his proposition cast their vote by thoroughly emptying their glasses in unison. He toasted,

> There may be intellectual food which the present state of society is not fit to partake of; to lay such before it would be as absurd as to give a quadrant to an Indian; but knowledge is indeed as necessary as light, and ought to be as common as water and as free as air. It has been wisely ordained that light should have no color, water no taste, and air no odor; so indeed, knowledge should be equally pure and without admixture of creed or can't. I move, therefore, that the surplus funds in the treasury be devoted to the establishment of an independent charity school for the poor.

Without delay, the gallery rose to their feet, and every glass was quickly and thoroughly emptied. As the story was chronicled, not a dreg remained in a single drinking vessel, and when the gentlemen returned their glasses to the table turned down, not a single glass stained the table linen.[5]

Shortly after that fateful meeting, the Society announced that its primary undertaking was to establish a "free school" to provide the rudiments of education and to employ a teacher to educate 12 pauper students in the principles of religion, arithmetic, writing, English and Latin at the expense of the Society. Although tuition free, the school had difficulty filling its allocated spots. In January 1760, despite the Society's best efforts to provide the rudiments of education to students via full scholarship, the Society advertised that it had ten vacancies for the coming term.[6]

With the establishment of the school, there was an even greater desire among the early associates to provide its new members with the proper means of agriculture since the profitability of indigo meant more money for their new school and for the development of their remote outpost on the edge of the British realm. In addition to funding for the physical structure of the school and a teacher to disseminate lessons, each student received books, pens, ink, paper, firewood and two suits.[7]

Thomas Lynch, First President of the Winyah Indigo Society (by D'Andrea Lynn Boyle, photograph by Rich Taylor).

Although the formation of the school is often seen as a solely philanthropic gesture, the driving force for the formation of the school, and its unrecorded purpose, was civilization building. The planters knew that providing an education for the public was simply a premium that they had to pay to create a healthy society. Like in most places in the English colonies, the educational disparity between the wealthy and the poor revealed an unhealthy division. The Winyah Indigo Society's leaders understood that they needed to unify the community to produce a healthy culture where they could prosper. The best way to unite the classes was to provide a basic education to the poor.[8] Besides traditional classroom practices, another way in which the Winyah Indigo Society promoted the development and protection of their organization was through the practice of arming the constituents of the community.

During South Carolina's Cherokee War (known as the Seven Years' War in Europe and the French and Indian War throughout most of the colonies), the exercise of arms became a part of the educational curriculum for all schoolboys in South Carolina. The *Charleston Gazette* noted on May 12, 1757, "at Georgetown in particular, we are told, the Indico [*sic*] Society's scholars perform to admiration."[9] It should be noted that although schools and schoolboys drilled as militias during the last colonial conflict between England and France, the colony preferred to exercise local authority over education and other government agencies, while New England preferred to exercise centralized control over education.

Over 30 years before the founding of Carolina, Massachusetts began founding schools. Massachusetts funded tax-supported, compulsory education in the 1640s in some areas. By the 1700s, New England communities established, "common schools." Common schools were similar in the North and South in that students of all ages were under the direction of one teacher in a one-room schoolhouse. They were publicly supported on the local level but not for free as parents paid tuition for their children. By the 1780s, the New England states developed grammar schools (now called high schools) and soon thereafter developed a series of private elite high schools called prep schools.

Despite being called a "free school," many of the pupils at the Winyah Indigo Society School paid tuition and other related expenses. The school soon doubled its capacity to serve and extended its service beyond just educating the poor to taking on paid scholars as well. For nearly 100 years, it was known as the best school between Charles Town (renamed Charleston after the American Revolution) and Wilmington. The school eventually provided various levels of education, including serving as a primary school and grammar school with varying educational programs ranging from English to classical education. A great unifier of the people, rich and poor alike received education at the Society school. Farmers, planters, mechanics and artisans, military men, lawyers, doctors, priests, senators and governors of the state attended school at the Winyah, and most looked back upon their educational experiences favorably and with distinction.[10]

During the colonial period, the Southern colonies lacked institutions of higher learning so that most people who could afford to educate their children sent them to England or to the New England colonies. Of all the English colonies, South Carolina led the way with the number of colonists admitted to the London bar in the 1700s, with 44 of the total 114 admitted. Virginia had the second-highest total with 17.[11] The mindset of sending South Carolina's children out of the state for education began to change after the American Revolution, when South Carolina Governor John Drayton pushed for the foundation of South Carolina College at Columbia to educate the state's leaders.

On the eve of the American Revolution, the Winyah Indigo Society School and several other schools in the South Carolina Lowcountry served as defensive bodies against the British and bastions of patriotism, precursors to a new nationalism.[12] A few members remained loyal to the crown, but most fought for American independence. During the war years, the Winyah Indigo Society was a symbol of stability and permanency to the people of Georgetown as it began to serve as a financial institution for the people and colonial state government as well. Besides lending money to the local populace, the Society floated five loans to the colonial government between March 19, 1777, and August 11, 1779, for a total of 6,250 pounds.[13]

The fighting in the American Revolution ended in 1781, and the two sides signed the Treaty of Paris in 1783. One of the social and educational impacts of the American Revolution was the development of the belief in the virtues of "Republican Motherhood" to support the new American nationalism.

The concept behind the term "Republican Motherhood" was that the young republic could not survive if citizens were not virtuous and educated. Therefore, the enlightened thinkers of the Winyah Indigo Society believed that the daughters of the revolutionaries had to be educated so that they could teach their children and keep the ideals of the revolution alive. As a result, girls were taught at the Winyah Indigo School to propagate an educated populace. The mindset reinforced the old values of women's sphere being based in the home and away from the public world of men, but at the same time glorified their traditional role and called for formal education for women so that they could communicate and instill patriotism and nationalism in the next generation.

In the 1790s, during the early days of the American Republic, Noah Webster published his famous *Speller*. The textbook was used widely throughout the United States until the late 1830s. Webster's work was hailed in the North and South for its lessons on civic duty and morality. However, preachers and religious-minded people criticized the textbook for being completely secular, as earlier textbooks had focused upon the Bible and Christianity to teach morals. One of the greatest qualities of the book was that it was the only textbook that students needed throughout their young educational career, as chapters progressed from helping students learn how to make letter sounds, to basic reading, and finally in-depth studies. The books remained the staple of American education until the height of the Second Great Awakening (mid–1830s), when Presbyterian Minister William Holmes McGuffey, released his Christian morals-based *Readers,* a series of primers.

Also in the 1790s, the South Carolina legislature approved the right of the Society to conduct a lottery and in 1795 bequeathed to the Society all confiscated property from Tories in All Saints and Prince George Winyah Districts during the American Revolutionary War.[14] One item in particular, the Fyffe House, a three-story house on the Sampit River, belonged to founding Society member and original steward, Dr. Charles Fyffe, who had sided with the British during the war effort. Built in 1765, the Society eventually rented out the house, and, therefore, it became a revenue generator for the school and the Society's other philanthropic ventures. Some building lots on North Island were sold to Society member, Benjamin Solomons.[15]

Not content with being the focal point of civilization, the social and intellectual life in Georgetown greatly improved by providing a school for children, a lending institution to help local adults in need, and a convivial society for the gentlemen of the town as the Society continued to find ways to improve and refine their civilization. At a meeting in January 1799, the Society added the funding of a library to their umbrella of philanthropic endeavors with the proposal, "For the gradual establishment of a library in Georgetown."[16] Paul Trapier and Robert Heriot drew up a plan to regulate the library, and Solomon Cohen served as treasurer of the Society. The group adopted a constitution in 1799, incorporated in December 1800, and received a state charter in 1801.[17] Winyah Indigo Society member, Harvard-educated proprietor of *Mansfield Plantation* on the Black River, John Man Taylor, donated 1,000 books from his own collection to assist in the initial book drive for the library.[18]

As a corporation, the Georgetown Library Society functioned as an exclusive joint-stock company with a pool of investors, including the Winyah Indigo Society. The library eventually housed upwards of 10,000 volumes. Some of the Jewish members of the Winyah Indigo Society took the lead in the Georgetown Library Society, including Levi Myers, Moses

Charles Fyffe House, 15 Cannon Street (photograph by Paige Sawyer).

Myers, Abraham Myers, Jacob Myers, Abraham Cohen, Jacob Cohen and Solomon Cohen, Jr., by 1829.[19] For over 50 years, the library functioned independently of the Winyah Indigo Society, but the organization seized ownership of the library after it built its own hall in 1857.

On January 3, 1800, the *Georgetown Gazette* published a notice to the students of the Winyah Indigo Society to "wear crepe and walk in procession tomorrow morning at 10 o'clock from Captain Savage Smith's house on the Bay to the Episcopal Church, Saturday, Jan. 4th, 1800," during a memorial service honoring the recently deceased former president George Washington. Washington had attended a meeting of the Winyah Indigo Society in 1791 on his Southern Tour.[20]

After the turn of the nineteenth century (in 1809), the Society's school, under the direction of Schoolmaster John Waldo, added Greek to the curriculum. Robert F.W. Allston boasted that Waldo was an excellent teacher until he became "too much engrossed by his pretensions as an author." Waldo served the school for three years before he left to open his own school in Georgetown and to pursue a writing career. Mr. William R. Theus and, later, Mr. White served as teachers for the Society's school.[21] The institute held classes in a building between Broad and Screven Streets and held summer sessions on North Island in an old house among the rolling sand hills.[22] Around this time, the anniversary meeting was changed from December to May to accommodate the Society's members who were in the South Carolina state legislature which held session in December.[23]

Shortly after the turn of the nineteenth century, the Winyah Indigo Society began funding a school in Horry District, in addition to maintaining support for the school in Georgetown. The school was located on the banks of the Waccamaw River in Socastee and was the first "free school" in the Horry District. The school was located across from the Cooper store. The school term was six weeks per year and was, at one time, run by Old Trinity College (now Duke University) graduate, the Rev. F.L. Townsend. During his tenure, Townsend also organized a debating society which encouraged adults to attend night school to improve their education as well. Mr. Robert B. Clarke succeeded the Rev. F.L. Townsend at the Socastee School.[24] Peter Vaught, Sr., who eventually became a Horry District representative in the 43rd (1858–1859) and 44th (1860–1861) General Assembly of South Carolina House of Representatives, representing All Saints Parish, was, at one time, a teacher at the Socastee school.[25]

In 1811, the South Carolina legislature took its first steps towards centralizing education on the state level. In that year, South Carolina passed "An Act to establish Free Schools throughout the State." One Winyah Indigo Society officer later called the measure "an act, illustrative of the most benevolent motives of the wisest forethought, and so excellent in itself, as an initiatory step towards accomplishing the highest charity."[26] After the passage of the 1811 act, common schools (which mostly focused upon reading, writing and arithmetic) and private schools proliferated in the region. Soon, the *Winyah Intelligencer* advertised the creation of a rival school to the Winyah Indigo Society run by Sarah Bogle in Georgetown, and other competitors, such as the Marion Academy, soon materialized.[27] Soon thereafter, a school opened on the Santee River, just south of Georgetown. The school placed an advertisement in the newspaper hoping to fill teaching positions with local residents. The position was open to "any person wishing to engage to teach that school, the salary of which, is three hundred dollars for the present year, will apply to the chairman of the Commissioners of Free Schools, for Winyah District." Thomas Ford was the commissioner at that time.[28]

In 1814, the Winyah Indigo Society had assets of $16,677.59, which included 17 mortgages, four Revolutionary War-era indents (interest-bearing wartime loans), and out-of-town bank shares. At the time, the Winyah Indigo Society still acted as the local bank for the sluggishly emerging shipping port. Three years later, shortly after the conclusion of the War of 1812, a branch of the Bank of South Carolina opened in

Georgetown but soon faltered and closed in 1833. Apparently, the bank had lent out too much money on long-term loans backed by real estate and did not get paid back quickly enough to please its investors. On December 21, 1836, the Bank of Georgetown opened for business in the building previously occupied by the Bank of South Carolina, which relieved the Winyah Indigo Society of the obligation to serve as a creditor to the populace.

On May 5, 1819, the *Winyah Intelligencer* advertised the anniversary meeting on May 7. The group met at Mrs. Norman's tavern at 9:00 a.m. to conduct business of "great importance [which] will be brought before them." The anniversary address was given at the Episcopal Church, and the Society went back to Mrs. Norman's for dinner at 3:00 p.m.[29]

By the 1820s, the young republic began to quickly change. The expansion of industrialization during the War of 1812 and the influx of European immigrants began to transform the New England states. As the North began to gel and morph into a manufacturing region, the Northern states raised taxes to support their schools and began to administer them on the state level.

The new driving interest of the Northern schools was the call for public education to assimilate the immigrants pouring into eastern cities such as Boston, New York and Philadelphia. Although South Carolina was slowly beginning to consider educational administration on the state level, the Winyah Indigo Society School represented a permanent advertisement for local autonomy and clung to the genteel ideals offered from a traditional education. In agricultural states such as South Carolina, education was deemed a privilege, not a right. By maintaining local control over education, the Winyah Indigo Society remained true to their pursuit of providing a classical education for its students.

In 1825, South Carolina State Surveyor, Robert Mills, gathered statistics for the state. He recorded Georgetown as having "Several private schools" but noted that "the rich planters either have teachers in their families or send their children to Charleston to be educated." He furthered, "The poor generally, in this district, have had for many years the blessings of education tendered... free of charge." The report of the commissioners enumerated "149 children under tuition, at an expense of $1,800." By 1825 between 300 and 400 boys and girls, rich and poor, had been educated by the Winyah Indigo Society School.[30]

In the same survey, Horry District (which included Upper All Saints and Kingston Districts) had between ten and 15 private schools established in various places. The prices of tuition ranged from $10 to $20 per year. There were six free schools supported by the expenses of the state, where the children of the poor were taught gratis (cost free). Mills reported that over the previous two years (from 1823 to 1825) 438 pupils were educated at an expense of $822.25.[31]

In 1834, the Society continued to sell off its American Revolutionary War bounty of seized property to continue funding their school. The Society advertised in the *Winyah Intelligencer* on April 1, 1834, that they were selling lots 17, 19, 20, 21 on the north side of South Island to be sold as the property of Benjamin Solomons. Solomons had originally purchased the land from the Society, so donating the money generated from the sale of the land to the Society's educational fund was essentially two donations to the Society: one for buying the land and one for returning the money produced from the sale of the land.[32]

In November 1839, the *Georgetown American* advertised the establishment of a school led by Mr. Isaac Carr Croft. Croft's school was for paid scholars only and provided Latin, Greek, mathematics and penmanship, including plain and ornamental. The newspaper informed its readers that Mr. Croft was assisted by his mother, who taught the younger children morals, patriotism and religion. Tuition to Croft's school varied. Schooling for a classical education including Latin, Greek and mathematics was $15 per term per scholar; classes designed to support an English education were $10 per term, and younger pupils received a basic education for $5 per term.[33]

Meanwhile, the Winyah Indigo Society held an election on December 5, 1839, for a new principal of the Society's school. The principal was allowed to take on a number of private scholar students in addition to the 25 funded by the Society to subsidize his income. The Society ran an ad in the newspaper stating that the school's teacher was to be paid $600 annually, payable quarterly. Applicants for the teaching position were encouraged to send their letters to John Alex Keith, president of the Winyah Indigo Society.[34] By the mid–1830s, Robert F.W. Allston was the president of the Winyah Indigo Society, a position that he held until his death in 1864. Allston, a leading local politician and later governor of the state, fought for public education throughout his entire public career.

Improvements to the free school system of South Carolina were very slow in coming. The only act of legislature worthy of note that attempted to improve education since 1811 was proposed in 1835. Mr. Edward Frost (who by the 1840s was a judge of the Charleston delegation) proposed the act titled "An act concerning the Free Schools."[35] He recommended greater funding, a state superintendent of education, and better organization to the current structure.

Governors of South Carolina in the early antebellum period used education reform as rhetoric but did not act in the spirit of improvement. On November 28, 1837, South Carolina Governor Pierce M. Butler's annual address included some grandiloquence in promoting education, but without increasing taxes in support of education, he did not get much accomplished. He said, "The best security for public liberty, and the enduring prosperity of the State, is to be found in the virtue and intelligence of the people; and they cannot be so well encouraged and promoted as by a judicious and well-regulated system of education."[36]

Patrick Noble followed Butler as governor of South Carolina. On November 26, 1839, the 57th governor of the state expressed his views on education in his annual address to the state. Noble said, "It is knowledge, intellectual, moral and religious, that constitutes the man. Without its possession, wealth would be a curse instead of a blessing. Besides, the stability and permanence of our republican institutions have their only guarantee in an intelligent, moral and religious population."[37] Despite the strong talk, the importance of education, and the rising tide of conflict between North and South in the antebellum era, the state still refused to increase educational funding. Consequently, South Carolina's education system was behind many of her competitor states, both North and South.

According to the 1840 census, 20,000 persons in South Carolina over the age of 21 could neither write nor read, and 70,000 between the ages of five and 20 were illiterate.[38] Although the Winyah Indigo Society did a great job of educating pupils in the city of Georgetown and in the Socastee community of the Horry District, the South Carolina state government spent only $37,000 annually to educate the children throughout the entire state. At the same time, Massachusetts spent $1,000,000 annually, and New York and Connecticut each spent $2,000,000 on education in their states.

Winyah Indigo Society President and Prince George Winyah Senator Robert F.W. Allston persistently urged that South Carolina increase its spending and educate the populous at the expense of the state. Comparing South Carolina to New York, Connecticut and Massachusetts, Allston said, "If we spent $500,000, we could do the same job due to lower population."[39]

Besides the lack of funding, another one of the problems with education in South Carolina was the lack of quality teachers. On November 24, 1840, South Carolina Governor Barnabus Kelet Henagan addressed these problems in his annual address. He said, "Who, I would ask, are the teachers of our Free Schools?" He continued, "So far as my observation extends, with but few exceptions, they are very ignorant, and possess a very easy morality. With the poor pay allowed them, we cannot reasonably calculate upon a better state of things." He went on to explain the dismal prospects associated with the profession of teaching in South Carolina: "The men, who take charge of our public schools, accept so miserable a pittance as the reward of their labors, are they who cannot get employment on any other terms?" The governor said, "Necessity forces them to make the offer of their services, and necessity forces the commissioners to accept them."

He called it a "reproach to be a teacher of a Free School" in South Carolina and explained that men will not take on the profession of education based upon mere patriotism. Encouraging an increase to the annual school budget, Governor Henagan said, "You cannot command superior talent and attainment, without adequate compensation."[40]

In 1837, Horace Mann (known as "the Father of American Public Education") was appointed secretary of the newly formed Massachusetts State Board of Education and founded the *Common School Journal* in 1838. He promoted nonsectarian, public funded, monitored and controlled schools taught by well-trained professional teachers (he envisioned teaching as primarily a female career) to a diverse population of students who attended longer school years than what was traditionally taught in the United States.

In the spring of 1848, Massachusetts elected Mann to the House of Representatives. He often spoke out against slavery and was one of the largest supporters of the Wilmot Proviso. He fought to halt the expansion of slavery to the West throughout his political career until it ended in 1853. Mann's ideas of compulsory school attendance became law in Massachusetts in 1852. His later proposal to place students in classrooms based upon age, not competence, also passed.

By the 1840s, while New England continuously increased state funding and consolidated their schools, South Carolina continued to underfund its schools. Although it did not receive state funding, the Winyah Indigo Society took on further responsibility for the people of Georgetown and Horry and ventured into another new realm of philanthropy and education.

At that time, the organization appointed a committee of three to investigate the establishment of an asylum for orphans. The Society explained, "it would indeed be a bounty, an act of the highest bounty to orphans especially, and to those indigent children who may be motherless, to provide them the best substitute for the maternal influence, namely that of our intelligent, kind and pious mothers."[41]

Staying true to their roots and dedication to "Republican Motherhood," the Society pronounced, "The first step towards the useful education is to establish firmly a good moral foundation." The group expounded that experience testifies that the earlier years of childhood is the best "season" for beginning the foundations of education and that the best person to lay the basics in any household is the mother or female role model of the students. The members agreed that the influence of mothers transcends economic and social classes, because mothers "kindly influence is controlling, as well in cabins of the poor, as in the halls of the wealthy."

The assembly closed their 1840 anniversary meeting by patting themselves on the back for their accomplishments and their increased devotion to the causes of the less-fortunate members of Georgetown with the statement,

"The friends of instruction look upon intellectual culture as the grand panacea for all evils, and the enlightened and benevolent exhaust themselves in efforts to extend to the many the advantages once confined to the few."[42]

The following year, the society announced the establishment of an asylum for orphans with a plan for boarding the children to shape their morals and manners. The resolution contended that the Winyah Indigo Society would admit children upon its bounty of the earliest age, "being orphans of indigent persons who have been residents in the District of Georgetown, and such orphans shall be forthwith placed in the care of a skillful and worthy matron to be duly reared and prepared to receive, when old enough, the full benefits to be delivered from the Society's school."[43]

By the 1840s, the Society used its entire income, derived from contributions of its members, to support a home for the orphans of Georgetown, to educate 25 underprivileged children, to maintain a school building, and to employ two teachers and a principal. Apparently, the employees did a great job, as the *Winyah Observer* stated, "the school [is] second to none in the State as to all the essentials which should constitute one. In composition, arithmetic and grammar it is said the pupils particularly distinguished themselves."[44]

Sometimes the *Winyah Observer* went into great details explaining the events of the Winyah Indigo Society and sometimes simply mentioned that the meetings took place. In 1840, the newspaper announced that the time of the anniversary address will "be given of the hour by ringing the bell of the Episcopal Church."[45] In May 1841, the *Winyah Observer* went into great depth explaining that the Reverend Howard gave the annual address to the Winyah Indigo Society at the Episcopal Church, where he was the rector. The paper explained how Society members convened at Mrs. Lester's old lodge and returned after the Reverend Howard's speech for dinner at 4:00 p.m., where they enjoyed brandy and cigars, champagne and drank several toasts. The paper even reported that the group talked of building its own hall and complained about losing nearly half of the organization's capital with the collapse of the Pennsylvania Bank of the United States as a fallout of Jackson's Bank War.[46] On the contrary, when reporting on the 1842 anniversary meeting, the newspaper simply stated that the Rev. Samuel Leard delivered the "91st address at Methodist Church."[47] The next year, in 1843, the newspaper modestly stated that the Reverend Mr. Childers delivered the annual address in the Baptist Church and that the Society "had dinner at Mrs. Hull's and drank choice old wines."[48]

In May 1844, the newspaper shared a lot of news about the anniversary meeting. The paper reported that the Society held their anniversary meeting at Mrs. Lester's tavern beginning at 10:00 a.m. At noon, a procession formed and moved to the Methodist Episcopal Church where the Rev. Theophilus Huggins (stationed preacher) pronounced the anniversary address in which he traced knowledge from the "beginning of the world to the present period." Society members then returned to Mrs. Lester's to hear reports from the school committee and principal and at 3:00 p.m. went to Mrs. Session's where they had dinner and held spirited political talks centered on Western land settlements and tariffs. Before retiring, the Society elected the following officers: Robert F.W. Allston, president; Stephen Ford, senior warden; Eleazer Waterman (proprietor of *Winyah Observer*), junior warden; E.B. Rothmahler (merchant) treasurer, William J. Howard, secretary; Benjamin Henry Wilson, attorney.[49]

The following year, in 1845, the newspaper pronounced that the Rev. William H. Fleming delivered the anniversary address to the society at the Methodist Episcopal Church. Fleming's subject of his discourse was the "education of the youth of the day, as necessary to perpetuate all the blessings of civilized society." The paper reported that the attendance was, as usual, respectably large and "embraced many of the descendants of the original founders." The *Winyah Observer* reported that the members generally manifested "a zeal which promises to perpetuate the great object of the Society which is the education of the poor."[50]

By the mid–1840s, Isaac Carr Croft was principal of the Winyah Indigo Society School and commonly posted advertisements in the newspaper, trying to recruit paid scholars.[51] Mr. Croft joined the Winyah Indigo Society School as teacher for the males. At the time, Ms. Maria

Tavern at 719 Prince Street (photograph by Paige Sawyer).

Laval advertised that she was opening another rival school in Georgetown and was taking "paid scholars" only. All Saints Summer Academy was also advertising for paid scholars at that time.[52] Another school in Georgetown, run by Mrs. M.C. Durant, offered the following branches of education and fees per quarter: orthography, reading, writing and geography–$6.00; arithmetic, grammar and history–$8.00; rhetoric, botany and history–$9.00; astronomy, natural and moral philosophy–$10.00; drawing–$5.00; wax work–$4.00; worsted work–$3.00; basket work $2.00. In Darlington, the Male and Female Academy posted an article in the same edition of the newspaper.[53]

In April 1846, the *Winyah Observer* announced that Society members were encouraged to visit the school on Thursday, April 30, at 10:00 a.m. for examination of the preparedness of the paid scholars and scholarship students and the competence of the teachers and administration. The Quarterly Committee (Society members who acted as a schoolboard) ran public tours and prepared a report on the condition of the school at the anniversary meeting.[54]

On May 6, 1846, the Winyah Indigo Society held their anniversary meeting. At the meeting, the Rev. George R. Talley, upon short notice, delivered the address titled "Education of the Poor." He reminded the Society that their school was designed for the education of the poor during the colonial period. He said, "Education makes the man" and explained how the formation of the Society and the creation of the school was "in unison with the spirit of free government which then pervaded the whole country, and the same spirit continues to foster and sustain it."[55]

After the Reverend Talley's oration, the Society "partook dinner prepared by Mr. George Durant on Front Street at 3:00 PM, and passed a cheerful evening and retired at an early hour." Before they dined, the Quarterly Committee and principal reported to the Society. The reports testified that "the school [is] deemed second to none in the state." According to the testimony, the students excelled in arithmetic, composition and grammar.[56]

At the close of the meeting, the Society elected its officers for the year: Robert F.W. Allston, president; Eleazer Waterman, senior warden; Joseph Thurston, junior warden; E.B. Rothmahler, treasurer; Richard Dozier, attorney. The Society's membership was once again on the rise. With the long-standing debate over Texas recently solved, and the Mexico-American War kicking off, the increase to the Society's membership more than doubled the deaths and resignations since the last anniversary meeting.[57]

In September 1846, besides counting the loss of friends and members, the Society said goodbye to one of their favorite meeting places. In that month, Georgetown's Front Street paid witness to a devastating fire. Among the damaged structures were George Durant's boarding house, the law offices of Charles and Thomas Pinckney Alston on Front and Screven Street, and merchant Richard Lathers lost two storefront properties and his personal home. Mrs. Maurice Harvey Lance's town house (now known as the Mary Man house in honor of her mother who constructed the home) was saved by her servants, although her fence burned.[58] Richard Lathers later recalled the fire. He wrote, "I returned to Georgetown to find that the whole business part of the city was in ashes—my own residence being destroyed by the fire and all my stores except one or two small package-storage buildings on the wharf."[59]

In November 1846, Robert F.W. Allston, chairman of the House Committee on Education, Colleges and Religion, presented his program for school reform at the state agricultural society in Columbia.[60] From his early days in the State House of Representatives to his election to the state senate in 1832 and afterwards, he championed the causes of public education and a bill providing for a superintendent of free schools. Allston started his address by identifying the Winyah Indigo Society, as well as a few other select schools, as model examples of how South Carolina should run the state's education system. He explained that in 1846, the Winyah Indigo Society had $11,768.60 in its coffers and clarified that the Society's entire treasury was "wholly devoted to the support of a school for needy children of both sexes; the number is limited to twenty-five." Allston boasted that "there is seldom a single vacancy for a longer space than one month."[61]

After identifying a few model schools in the state, Allston explained the scope and sequence of the educational system at the Winyah Indigo Society School and suggested that the state adopt the model. According to Allston's plan, the elementary education to be acquired in South Carolina should consist of orthography, reading, writing, English grammar, geography, and arithmetic. He proposed that the Winyah Indigo Society's scope of education be taught by law in all schools throughout the state. Engaging in the promotion of Southern Nationalism, Allston recommended that the books and other means for teaching the courses be bought from a South Carolina press, utilizing as many South Carolina authors as possible. Always a proponent of an independent South Carolina during times of conflict between the regions, and local authority as opposed to central authority, Allston recommended that the cost of the books and teaching materials be furnished at the expense of the districts, not the state.

Allston also addressed the need for South Carolina to address teaching as a profession and not a steppingstone to other careers. He explained how most teachers at the time where men who were in the ministry or attended law school and taught children in order to pay their bills while they studied to obtain their higher goal—the ministry or law. Allston explained how teachers had to be adults who demonstrated ideals and habits of morality, enough learning, stable character, industry, fidelity, temper and a "special method of imparting instruction" in order for a successful and useful school to exist.[62]

Allston proposed a complete revamping of the entire South Carolina education system. At the time, the free school fund for the entire state was still set at a dismal $37,000. First, Allston proposed the development of public schools (colleges) to train teachers in the art of teaching, not simply the content they were to teach. He said, "How much improved would be the schools of our system, were they conducted by young men and women well instructed, not only in the branches of a substantial English education, but also in the rare and valuable art of imparting to others, in the shortest time, and with the least fatigue, all that they have learned."[63] Allston preached that female teachers were best for children under 14 years of age because they understand the nurturing that children need to develop into successful adults.[64]

Allston furthered his plan to revamp education in the state by saying that South Carolina needed a superintendent committed to education. Up until this time period, South Carolina had a state superintendent of education who was underfunded and overburdened with busy work since there was not enough funding for a staff to assist him. Allston called for South Carolina to take education seriously and promote "an active, intelligent, discreet and efficient officer" who could examine the education system, compare it with others in completing states, observe the results of the school's operations in all parts of South Carolina, and compare them. Then, with the information gathered, the superintendent could inform himself as thoroughly as possible and promote the remedies necessary to improve education in the state to committees who would be set up to propagate education, and other members of the legislature who would assist local districts in acquiring needed resources.[65]

While Allston was speaking on education in Columbia, the Society was planning for the coming term. Winyah Indigo Society Principal Isaac Carr Croft wrote an article for the *Winyah Observer* announcing openings in the school for scholars and bounty students. Interested parties were instructed to meet with members of the Quarterly Committee for a tour of the school and details on instructional opportunities and fees.[66]

Thanks to Robert F.W. Allston, the Winyah Indigo Society School was fully explained, and a clear plan for South Carolina's education reform based upon its current practices was articulated. The Society's plan would be further studied and dissected when Robert F.W. Allston was elected president of the senate in 1850 and in 1856 when he became South Carolina's governor. As he rose to political prominence, the sectional conflict increased.

FIVE

The Winyah Indigo Society

Teaching Southern Nationalism

*Liberty, when it begins to take root, is a plant
of rapid growth.*—George Washington

In the first 90 years of its history, the Winyah Indigo Society forged civilization in Georgetown, South Carolina. The Society provided funding for a school in Georgetown and one in Horry which educated boys and girls (paupers and paid scholars), financed an orphanage for Georgetown's children who later attended the Society's school, created and funded the Georgetown Library Society, and, at times, served as the sole financial institution for Georgetown as well. The Society guided the people through three wars, the initiation of social reforms of the Second Great Awakening, the challenge of industry, the onset of Manifest Destiny, and the sectional growing pains associated with Western expansion.

The Society's membership grew during times of foreign conflicts and internal political turmoil as men sought the safety and security of social organizations to express their emotions and to guide society. The next 15 years would see renewed sectional strife. The United States struggled to divide the land gained in the Mexican-American War, the abolitionist movement turned violent, and the federal government continued to increase tariffs in an attempt to protect industry at the expense of agriculture. The Winyah Indigo Society was there for every step on the path to disunion, forging a Southern alliance of states, holding out a vision of education for the children of South Carolina, and for guiding the state and region into secession.

The year of 1848 marked a turning point in South Carolina history. The war with Mexico ended in February, but the implications of the Wilmot Proviso, even though it didn't pass the senate and become law, put the state and the entire South on the defensive. The Wilmot Proviso, and other threats from the North, put the Society's school on a crash course to Southern Nationalism. That April, the *Winyah Observer* announced that the Rev. William G. Connor would deliver the anniversary address at the Methodist

Church on May 5, 1848. Members were asked to report to Mrs. Lester's at 10:00 a.m. and form a procession to the Methodist Church. The anniversary meeting and address followed on the heels of the annual inspection of the school and examination of the teachers and pupils by parents and guardians.[1]

When the Rev. William G. Connor took the podium to address the members of the Society, students and their parents and guardians, as well as community members, he delivered a prolific call to arms blanketed in patriotism. Connor presented a very conservative speech where he lectured that school should be for the sake of education, not societal change, and that discipline and Christianity are the cornerstones of civilization, not the schools or progressive legislation. He told the Society members that it was their duty to stand up for the values of their forefathers and called on the Winyah Indigo Society to lead South Carolina's educational reforms.

Connor started his oration by appealing to the childhood memories of the adults in the gallery and at the same time sparked the interest of the pupils by helping them draw connections over the generations. He said, "Flowers, dear to the gardens of childhood, often fling around us—their colors and odors long after the winds have battered down the mansions of our fathers."[2]

Connor quickly moved into the thesis of his lecture: Southern nation-building. He honored the heroes of South Carolina's past in an attempt to foster the same patriotism that citizens of the American Revolutionary era showed when they fought against tyranny and for those who shared sympathy for the poor by creating the school and Library Society for the people of Georgetown. Speaking of the spirit of the deceased revolutionary South Carolinians, he stated, "They gave birth [referring to independence from England] and now return as a foster-father to nurse it to liberty." He was, of course, referring to Thomas Lynch (first president of the Winyah Indigo Society and member of the Second Continental Congress), Christopher Gadsden (Charleston and Georgetown merchant, planter, and designer of the Don't Tread on Me flag), and John Rutledge (first governor of South Carolina). Connor said that everyone in attendance needed to be more like the founding fathers of South Carolina who displayed "self-sacrificing patriotism, so full of genuine philanthropy." He said, "no poem stirs so divinely American bosoms as the simple catalogue of our patriot fathers." He went on to celebrate the founding fathers of South Carolina and of the Winyah Indigo Society by saying that they displayed "heart[s] swelling with generous sympathies for the young, plying both means and influence for the education of the poor and neglected; at another time we see him drawing his sword in his country's defense, to be sheathed no more save in the bosom of tyranny."[3] He went on to declare "that the actions of our fathers are beacons set on hills to summon us to virtue's defense."[4]

After admiring the spirit, sacrifice and sagacity of the American Revolution-era leaders of South Carolina, Connor went on to parallel 1848 with the American Revolution and stated, "In reviewing the history of the fathers of our country, I have drawn a corollary for your present consideration."[5] He expressed his opinion to the addressees that the times make the men and that South Carolinians may soon be forced to act to save their liberty. He used George Washington as an example of how South Carolinians can rise to the occasion of fighting tyranny. "Washington might have lived a bright example of Christian virtues, and a noble specimen of Virginia generosity, but never had been the father of our country, had not the revolution drawn forth the resources of his mind, the noble virtue of his heart."[6]

Next, Connor talked about American children being spoiled and how the United States was experiencing a devaluing of education. "They have the most extravagant toys, boys with whistles, drums and hobbies and girls with a Lilliputian world of china-ware and dolls, but the children's library is empty—except for trivial fiction with no examples to inspire the mind with love of truth," he said. He went on to explain how English education begins in the nursery while American education begins in the academy. He said, "We are less educated than ever, yet we have more technology than ever." Connor explained how the 1840s was an age of high pressure, with high-stakes education, railroads expediting travel and the telegraph increasing the lines of communication. He explained how the devaluing of education is not the fault of any individual man but the trend in the United States. He complained that romance novels had taken the place of history, poetry, and mathematics and that speechmaking and politics are favored over the sciences and metaphysics. Then he came to the defense of the children of the era and blamed their parents: "can we blame the young for becoming proficient with so little cost or trouble, when nothing more is required than superficial adornment. Is this to be our course—a railroad passage through the schools, speeches and politics to complete our learning?"[7]

With that statement, Conner called out to the Winyah Indigo Society to lead South Carolina's education system. He boasted that "the Southern mind possesses intellectual powers which shall move more swiftly than the telegraph and draw more powerfully than the engine. And, shall the state longer neglect these important interests? In the name of your Society, I would call upon the lovers of learning to move immediately, and with zeal, in this cause." He complained about the current trend in the Northeast of modeling public education as an instrument to assimilate immigrants and championed the Society's school and member's philanthropy. He said, "Happy shall be the day when the privilege classes among us shall convert their means and leisure into ministers of this valued cause."[8]

Connor closed his address with a prolific statement and warning concerning the Second Great Awakening: "The signs of the times give warning to all who owe their country or fear their God. The first important work of education should be a thorough grounding in the Christian faith."[9] The Reverend announced that it was his opinion that the wants of society at the time strongly call for a union of intellectual and religious training.

The *Winyah Observer* reported on May 10, 1848, that the Rev. William G. Connor gave a "notable" address at the Methodist Church. The paper also reported that the Society, notwithstanding its heavy loss by the late banking collapse, "still has investments large enough to carry out the original purpose of its founders." The paper appealed to the community by stating, "Every young man of whatever occupation in life, who resides among us, and can pay the initiation fee and a contribution of $7 per annum, should become a member." The Society was clearly trying to unite the people, expand its membership role, and solicit assistance in fulfilling their noble obligation of providing education and other services to the community.[10] On that same day, the newspaper published the first editorial in a three-part series which focused upon educational reform in South Carolina.[11] At the following anniversary meeting in 1849, the Society's treasurer declared "the finances of the Society to be in a most prosperous state."[12]

In October 1849, the *Winyah Observer* printed an article written by Dr. B.B. Woodward titled "Treatment of Scholars." There is no way to determine if the Winyah Indigo Society School followed the advice offered in the article, but the recommendations are certainly noteworthy. In the piece, Dr. Woodward gave a lot of advice on how to run a successful academy. He said that children under eight years of age should not be confined for longer than four hours in school and that those hours should have a diversity of tasks which include moving around the classroom and frequent changes in subjects. Dr. Woodward warned that intense study should be avoided, as it leads to brain disease. He also said that students should receive frequent breaks from their schoolwork. Woodward proposed that recess should involve organized activities and be at least a half-hour in length.[13]

In 1849, Robert F.W. Allston's plan to increase school funding for free schools throughout the state finally passed the state legislature. Beginning in 1850, funding was doubled in South Carolina from $37,000 to $74,000. Obviously, the mindset throughout the state was that the South Carolina schools were a failure, but it reveals something else as well. This was clearly a move towards South Carolina nationalism, as it was in the same session where the South Carolina legislature voted to seek independence from the Union and to stop negotiating with the United States government.

In 1850, at the time of increased funding implementation, the literacy rate of the South was 70 percent among the adult white population. However, the majority of mid-nineteenth-century people were illiterate. Even

England and France (which are often seen as the highest civilizations in Europe) had from a third to a half of their citizens illiterate and generally uneducated.[14] Accordingly, the South was more widely educated than the other regions of the United States, England and France.

In 1850, Horry District had 25 common schools. Its 26 teachers serviced 488 students in that year without the assistance of a library or a newspaper.[15] At the same time, Georgetown had the All Saints Summer Academy which served 11 students, the Winyah Indigo Society charitable school which tended to the academic needs of 24 students, six free schools which assisted 25 pupils and six private schools which tended to the academic needs of 105 pupils. Georgetown had two newspapers, the *Winyah Observer* and the *True Republican*, both labeled "political" by the United States Census Bureau. Georgetown had 12 private libraries (consisting of 15,800 volumes) and one public library; the Georgetown Library Society (founded by the Winyah Indigo Society) contained 2,000 volumes.[16]

At the 1850 anniversary meeting, Colonel John Harleston Read, Jr., gave the address at the courthouse. Eight new members were initiated at the meeting, which the *Winyah Observer* claimed "speaks well to the prosperity of this ancient and charitable institution." The report of the Quarterly Committee was flattering and gave a very positive account of the present condition of the school. However, despite the pleasing reports published in the newspaper, the school held classes in an old barn. According to one source, the structure was "destitute of comfort or convenience." It was very clear that the Society, which had done so much for Georgetown, needed its own hall. After almost 100 years of serving the community, the Winyah Indigo Society's meetings were still held in a public hotel and anniversary addresses delivered at the courthouse or a church.[17]

The following year, the main topic of the anniversary meeting was the construction of a "suitable building erected for the accommodation of their pupils, and a Society Hall and Library." Attorney Benjamin Henry Wilson delivered the anniversary address. The newspaper reported that "Wilson impressed upon all, especially the youth connected with the school, that a well cultivated mind would elevate the poorest boy in the community to the highest distinction attained by the richest." The treasurer's report boasted to possess enough money in the treasury "to supply the school for a century."[18] If true, this boast expressed a considerable increase in funding and confidence over the past two years when the treasurer claimed that the "treasury is equal to its call for educational purposes."[19]

In December 1851, the *Winyah Observer* published an article on the education system in South Carolina. The piece began by referring to the education system of South Carolina as a "defective common school system." Then the author asked its readers why South Carolina should have such a poor public education system since the state is ahead of many of her sister states in other things such as military education. The author of the editorial suggested a general tax to fund education, the sum of which would be held in the bank, and the funding for schools would be paid by the interest alone. According to the article, "there would be plenty of money set aside for school expansion in the future."[20]

On May 6, 1853, the Society's secretary recorded the events of the anniversary gathering. At the meeting, Dr. W. Miller, William W. Shackelford, R.E. Fraser and R.J. Ford were all admitted into the Society, and the organization agreed to pay all outstanding bills, including paying $14 to Mrs. Lester for hosting the Society's meeting, $77 to W.J. Howard for teaching the boys and young men at the school, and $41.20 to Rottmaker and Anderson for stationery. The bulk of the discussion held that night pertained to the construction of a new hall and a new school. The Society resolved that the legacy left to them by the late Francis Withers should be devoted to the erection of one structure to serve as both a school and meeting hall for the Society upon the lot that Withers donated on Prince Street. The Society appointed a committee of three to contract for the construction of the building. The gentlemen also agreed to send the Reverend Walker a letter of thanks for delivering the anniversary address.[21] According to the Society's secretary, Walker's oration included "many new and striking thoughts on best practices in education." The Society ate at Durant's Hotel, drank champagne and smoked cigars until late in the evening. According to the newspaper, it was a "feast of reason, and a flow of soul."[22]

Later in 1853, the *Pee Dee Times* published a few articles pertaining to education. In the article, "Free Schools," the author suggested a state law to compel parents living within two miles of a school to send their children, between the ages of eight and 16, to school. The author suggested punishments for truant kids and for their parents who let their children skip school.[23]

In the same edition of the newspaper, an article titled "Our Free School System" explained that South Carolina's schools were a failure. The author suggested a complete revamp of the entire system and advocated that the state use the same model that many Northern states followed in administrative structure but not in scope and sequence of instruction. The author suggested that South Carolina's political districts provide their own schools for their children which would be subsidized by state funding. The overall plan called for school districts run by superintendents who all deferred to a state superintendent of education.[24] Many education leaders, as well as concerned individuals, believed that a state superintendent of education was needed to help correct mistakes of independent and often irresponsible school commissioners and to infuse a common education model into a statewide education program.[25] The same mentality that persisted in the 1770s pertaining to education and nation-building was again at high tide in the 1850s and actively prepared the citizens of South Carolina for independence from the United States.[26]

The complete plan for overhauling South Carolina's education plan hinged upon another proposed law pertaining to funding. According to the plan, the increased salaries designed to entice and retain better teachers would be paid for by increased taxes paid by all male citizens between the ages of 21 and 50.[27]

In accordance with all of the great suggestions by community groups and members for improving education, an article on common schools appeared in the newspaper two months later. The article again bashed the legislature and asked them to pass statutes to increase funding and better South Carolina's schools.[28]

As was common throughout the state and maintained in many areas today, the Winyah Indigo Society continued to struggle to obtain qualified teachers and principals. It was customary at this time (as per a rule adopted in November 1851) that teachers were elected annually at the May anniversary meeting. In preparation for that meeting, the Society ran ads in the newspaper asking qualified individuals to apply for positions.[29]

The Society also ran several ads in the newspaper recruiting students. In one article, Principal J. White wrote, "Diligent care and attention will be paid to the literary improvement of the pupils; their moral culture will also be attended to."[30] By the mid–1850s, education was quickly becoming a competitive industry as schools competed for the best students, teachers and administrators.

With the number of common schools increasing every year, the Society believed that they would have to pay much higher salaries if they wanted to attract the best teachers and administrators. When 1854 began, the principal of the Society's school earned a salary of $600 per year.[31] On May 5, 1854, Principal White agreed to the $600 yearly salary, but the Society felt that they would soon lose him if they did not compensate him for his experience, expertise and proficiency.[32] In November, the Society held a "Principal's salary meeting" at Mrs. Lester's to talk about raising the principal's salary to $1,000 per year.[33] Shortly thereafter, the trustees of the school allowed the principal to receive paid scholars for whose teaching he was paid $600 in addition to his regular administrative salary of $1,000.[34]

Also, in November, Principal White ran an ad looking for a teacher. At the same meeting which approved a 40 percent pay hike for the principal, the Society agreed to increase the salary of its teachers from $600 to $1,000 a year. However, with increased salary came increased responsibilities. The Society's new teachers were required to teach Greek, Latin and "the usual branches of a Good English Education."[35]

With all the talk of school and hall building, and teacher and administrator salary increases, the Society voted to sell off more of its real estate holdings. During the November 4, 1854, meeting held at Mrs. Lester's tavern, the Society decided to sell the landholdings that it retained on South Island where the old school held classes during the summer.[36]

Also, at the November meeting, the Society began to address the issue of student truancy. The Quarterly Committee gave a report on students who were habitually absent from school. The following January, when the group met for a short meeting, truancy was again addressed. The Society decreed that students who were going to be absent from school needed to send an excuse note. The Quarterly Committee was instructed that it could expel any student who was habitually absent from school without a sick note. The next month, the Society expelled two charity students for truancy. In April 1854, the Quarterly Committee reported that the Society's school had two scholarship slots available, as it had 18 children in the bounty of the Society and 20 paid scholars. Shortly thereafter, the Quarterly Committee reported that the business of education was going well at the school, as the students were well-behaved and learning. The Society resolved, however, that students who were expelled from the school due to truancy were banned from the Winyah Indigo Society for life.[37]

In 1854, the Society again rehired Principal White and retained Mr. Howard and Miss Wilson to teach at the school. The teacher salary increased to $1,000, and the Society resolved to construct a "comfortable temporary schoolhouse" and budgeted $1,000 for its construction. Before the construction was completed, the Society added a front porch to the structure. Dr. Miller contracted into an agreement with Mr. Beckman for the construction of the temporary school. The construction price of the structure totaled $1,060, plus an additional $100 for a front porch which was added to the project shortly after construction began.

The new school building breathed a breath of fresh air into the education system. The Society purchased new world globes, geology of South Carolina books and blackboards to complete the classrooms. It also resolved to build two separate privies behind the school and to add a lightning rod to the schoolhouse.[38]

At one meeting in 1854, while the leaders throughout South Carolina were busy talking about building a monument for the late John C. Calhoun in Charleston, the Society agreed to fund the Calhoun Monument Association. The group resolved to provide granite for the base of the proposed monument to John C. Calhoun to be constructed in Charleston.[39]

On May 5, 1854, Society President Robert F.W. Allston delivered the anniversary address to the Society and its families, students and their families, faculty and administration, as well as community members. President of the Society Allston was known by everyone as an advocate of education reform on the state level. He promoted the establishment of a marine school in Charleston and a school for the deaf, dumb and blind where students could learn trades to be happy, "helpful, and cultivating a wholesome self-respect and cheerful industry." He supported improving the education and living conditions on the Catawba Indian Reservation, education for women in an attempt to promote learning in the home and the promotion of morals and patriotism, and supported the development of an agricultural college for South Carolina. Overall, he was very interested in school reform, perhaps gathering his strength and dedication from the success that the Winyah Indigo Society experienced under his presidency. He believed that public elementary schools would be more successful if they were attended by children of all classes and not just by the children of the poor alone. He continuously petitioned the state to increase tax appropriations to supplement state aid in establishing a "normal school," the creation of a state superintendent of education, and the printing of South Carolina written, produced and focused textbooks to be used throughout the state.[40] He was a trustee of South Carolina College, and in 1854 he donated $12,000 to establish a scholarship at the college.[41]

Allston delivered his address after dinner at Williamson's Tavern (at the corner of Front and Broad Streets, originally named the Old Oak Tavern) where the society dined on English roast beef and plum pudding.[42] Although all in attendance heard his oration, Allston's lecture was clearly designed to reach two audiences: the women and the students in the gallery.

He started his discourse by praising women, by declaring that they provided the basis for education. Trumpeting his earlier expressed ideas, Allston said, "mothers lay the cornerstone of education, followed by teachers and finally the inner man." He furthered his support for Republican Motherhood when he insisted that women possess a greater sense of morality and religion to prompt and direct the efforts of students.[43]

Allston was a father and a lifelong supporter of women's education. He always promoted educating women and continued his quest to bring about further and equal educational opportunities for girls as for boys at the Winyah Indigo Society. He criticized the entire country, North and South, for not educating girls to the same level as boys. He said, "if ever the energy, skill and ability of American citizens, now so marvelously exemplified in accumulating wealth, be modified, purified and partially diverted to the pursuit of higher ends-of more enduring and ennobling objects-the reform is destined to be effected by the influence of American women." He ended his promotion of female education by saying, "It is our interest, therefore, as well as our duty, to educate the sexes appropriately and thoroughly."[44]

After proposing to educate all women, he described his plan to meet those ends. Speaking of all women, he said, "Let her be thoroughly educated, not to become masculine in deportment, rendering men contrary wise, effeminate,—not to organize conventions and conduct public lectures—these are results rather of defective, partial education." He went on, "but to exercise kindly and judiciously the peculiar, chastening, winning power with which God has endowed her to fulfill her important and gracious mission in training the tender, impressible nature of childhood—to soothe, and gently to persuade the sterner nature of man to bear and forebear."[45]

Allston believed that if women were educated well enough, they could serve as the primary educators for their own children during the formative years. He suggested that children not be sent out of the family to school until they had reached the age of seven or eight years (to keep them out of mischief and from harm). If women were not capable of educating their own children, Allston proposed that the Society fund a daycare to provide preschool education for needy children.[46]

After speaking to the women of the community and proposing a daycare for less-fortunate children, Allston addressed the students of the Winyah Indigo Society School. He asked questions to peak their attention and interest and then aroused their senses of patriotism, nationalism, religion, respect and inclusiveness, all necessary components in nation-building. He offered the rhetorical question that every one of the period probably asked at the Winyah Indigo Society anniversary meetings, "What do the student's [sic] owe in return for their education?" Answering his own question, Allston said, "simply to obey God's holy will, and keep His commandments." He asked, "Do you desire to exhibit your sense of duty? Do you desire to testify [to] the honor and gratitude which each must feel sooner or later?" "If you do," he said, "conduct yourself upright and honestly—speak the truth always—be fair and just on the playground, as in all your dealings-diligent and submissive in the schoolroom—respect and obey your worthy preceptor." He continued, "Be punctual, do not cause trouble and attend school, respect your teacher and bring them no shame. Practice self-denial, self-restraint, deny yourself any improper indulgence or expensive gratification, control your passions, desires and tongue."[47]

During 1854, Principal White and two members of the Society died. The Society resolved to wear the "usual badge of mourning for a month" after each member died and wrote letters to family members of the deceased and published memorials in the *Pee Dee Times*. The Society interviewed eight men before it agreed upon a replacement for Mr. White.[48]

At the final meeting of the year, the Society decided to start a new tradition of offering prizes to the best students each year. Each prize consisted of a small collection of books. The Society also decided that the president and teachers should select two boys per year for higher awards. The selected candidates were each offered a full scholarship to attend the South Carolina Military Academy.[49]

In 1855, in reflection of the Society's 100th anniversary meeting, one attendee wrote an article in the *Pee Dee Times* explaining the function of the Society at the meeting and alluded to the rise of Southern independence and union. He explained the merrymaking and seriousness of the Society as offering them "same unique, but expressive toasts which animated our fathers, greet us on festive occasion, and remind us of the great duty we owe to Society in the faithful discharge of our own peculiar labors, and liberal dispensation to the poor orphan of the bounties of heaven and the invaluable blessing of a good education." The author of the article stated, "from the oldest to the youngest among us, there is not one, whose moments of relaxation from the busy cares of life do not carry him back to those halcyon days of his youth, which were spent in the venerable school."[50]

While informed readers searched the pages of the newspaper for new developments in the struggle between North and South to control the West and waited for acts of fanaticism to unfold in the North, the *Pee Dee Times* printed an article titled "A Warning to the South" on May 2, 1855. The article included a speech and details pertaining to the meeting of the Southern Commercial Convention held in Charleston. During the convention, the Rev. C.K. Marshall rang an alarm that struck a chord with Southern lawmakers, teachers, parents, and the public in general. Upon careful study, Marshall noted that the textbooks that Southern students used in their schools were published in the Northern states and were filled with positive references to the reforms of the Second Great Awakening, most notably the abolitionist movement. He warned the convention that the South must produce their own school textbooks, or they risk losing their children and culture. He called for Southerners to write textbooks and said that authors must "report favorable for the production of domestic works of the character by the offer of sizable prizes, etc." Northern textbooks were deemed denunciatory towards the South.[51]

Former Winyah Indigo Society School teacher in the Horry District and longtime All Saints Parish Representative, Peter Vaught, Sr., agreed with the sentiments of the Rev. C.K. Marshall. He said, "a full set of South Carolina Books is a great desideratum in our Free Schools—the great diversity of School Book ... and most of them of Yankee Manufacture—is an evil that should be corrected."[52]

In 1855, the Winyah Indigo Society's prowess and equality in education attracted representatives from the proposed Marion Female

College. The group recommended building the all-female college in the village of Marion or somewhere in the Pee Dee region. On May 31, 1855, the group held a quarterly conference in Georgetown. The group had already attracted over $20,000 for its venture before it held its conference in Georgetown. The group came to Georgetown as one of the stops in its quest to raise an additional $20,000 to make the dream of an all-female college come true.[53]

In February 1856, at a regularly scheduled meeting of the Winyah Indigo Society, the Society took the first steps towards construction of its new hall. The group resolved to pay Jones and White architectural firm $60 for drawing plans for the new structure. It also agreed to start visiting the school twice per year (first Friday in April as well as during examination week in December). Following the preceptor's report (teacher's report), the treasurer reported that the Society had invested the $5,000 that Francis Withers had bequeathed to the Society into stock in the South Carolina Railroad Company and in the South Western Railroad Bank. The Society purchased 41 stocks in each entity, which yielded a profit of $1,037.50. The profits from the stock investments were earmarked for the construction of the new hall.

On April 30, 1856, a week before the Society gathered for their annual meeting, the *Pee Dee Times* newspaper announced the event. The newspaper said that the anniversary address would be given at the Masonic Lodge and the meeting held at Mrs. Lester's. The paper reminded members that they should bring friends to dinner and should buy their tickets in advance from the stewards.[54]

As was planned, the Society met for its 101st anniversary meeting the following week. The Society, the principal, and 30 students and parents met at Mrs. Lester's tavern at 10:00 a.m. and marched in procession to the Masonic Lodge where the Rev. William T. Capers gave the annual address. The members then ate dinner and tended to business. The Society met all day, and members did not go home until after dark. "Everything passed off pleasantly and not until the shades of evening began to spread her mantle around did it occur to them it was time to retire to their peaceful homes, where bright smiles awaited them."[55] The anniversary gathering was always the pretext for an all-day affair, complete with a drink or two at Mrs. Lester's tavern, a speech at 11:00 a.m., then a business meeting, dinner, and time-honored toasts washed down with Winyah Indigo Society punch.

In October 1856, while most people had their thoughts on the civil war in Kansas, the Society held a ceremony for laying the cornerstone for the new hall. The *Pee Dee Times* reported that "everyone is welcome to attend and there will be enough seats for all ladies." A procession formed at the Masonic

Lodge at 4:00 p.m. precisely, and the Rev. William T. Capers gave an oration "suitable for the event" at 5:00 p.m.[56] Construction crews were poised and ready to work hard and efficiently to complete the contract through the winter and spring in preparation for the anniversary meeting in May.

Year	Anniversary Speaker	Location Delivered
1840	Reverend Williams[a]	Prince George Winyah Episcopal Church
1841	Reverend Howard[b]	Prince George Winyah Episcopal Church
1842	Reverend Samuel Leard[c]	Methodist Episcopal Church
1843	Reverend Childers[d]	Baptist Church
1844	Reverend Theophilus Huggins[e]	Methodist Episcopal Church
1845	Reverend William H. Fleming[f]	Methodist Episcopal Church
1846	Reverend George R. Talley[g]	N/A
1847	Reverend Archer B. Smith[h]	Masonic Lodge
1848	Reverend William G. Connor[i]	Methodist Episcopal Church
1849	N/A	N/A
1850	Colonel John Harleston Read, Jr.[j]	Georgetown Courthouse
1851	Benjamin Henry Wilson, Esquire[k]	N/A
1852	Richard Dozier, Esquire[l]	N/A
1853	Reverend H. A. C. Walker[m]	N/A
1854	Robert F. W. Allston[n]	N/A
1855	J.J. Middleton[o]	N/A
1856	Reverend William T. Capers[p]	Masonic Lodge
1857	Benjamin Henry Wilson, Esquire[q]	Masonic Lodge
1858	Samuel J. Atkinson[r]	Baptist Church
1859	Reverend Thomas Mitchell[s]	Winyah Indigo Society Hall
1860	Plowden C. J. Weston[t]	Winyah Indigo Society Hall

Winyah Indigo Society Anniversary Address Speakers from 1840–1860.

[a]"Winyah Indigo Society," *Georgetown American*, May 1, 1840.
[b]*Winyah Observer*, May 8th, 1841
[c]*Winyah Observer*, May 7, 1842.
[d]*Winyah Observer*, May 6, 1843.
[e]*Winyah Observer*, May 4, 1844.
[f]*Winyah Observer*, May 3, 1845.
[g]*Winyah Observer*, May 6, 1846.
[h]*Winyah Observer*, May12, 1847.
[i]Connor, Reverend William G., An Address Delivered Before The Winyah Indigo Society of Georgetown, May 5th 1848 by the Reverend William G. Connor of the South Carolina Conference, Charleston: Walker and Burke Printers, 1848.

[j]"Winyah Indigo Society," *Winyah Observer*, May 8, 1850.

[k]"Winyah Indigo Society," *Winyah Observer*, May 7, 1851.

[l]"Winyah Indigo Society," *Winyah Observer*, May 7, 1851.

[m]"The Winyah Indigo Society," *Pee Dee Times*, May 11, 1853.

[n]Allston, Robert F. W., Address before the members and pupils of the Winyah Indigo society delivered in Georgetown, on the 5th of May, 1854, Charleston: Walker, Evans and Steam Power Presses, 1859.

[o]Minutes Book

[p]"Winyah Indigo Society," *Pee Dee Times*, October 13, 1856.

[q]"Winyah Indigo Society," *Pee Dee Times*, May 6, 1857.

[r]"Winyah Indigo Society," *Pee Dee Times*, May 12, 1858.

[s]Minutes Book

[t]Weston, Plowden C. J., An Address delivered in the indigo Hall, Georgetown, South Carolina on the Fourth Day of May, 1860, The 105th Anniversary of The Winyah Indigo Society, Charleston: A.J. Burke, 1860.

Six

The Winyah Indigo Society in a Hall of Its Own

*An educated citizenry is a vital requisite for our
survival as a free people.*—Thomas Jefferson

In 1857, the new Winyah Indigo Society Hall was completed. South Carolina architect Edward Brickell White designed the brick and granite structure with stucco trim with four Corinthian columns, and Mr. Cox and Dan Goldfinch completed the contract for the new building. The new hall was constructed, as planned a few years earlier, upon the lot granted to the Society by Francis Withers at the corner of Prince and Cannon streets in Georgetown. The wealthy Sampit River planter also provided the initial $5,000 funding to begin the construction project.[1] It was in the new hall that the Society reached its zenith of prosperity and influence. The Society's school principal stated that the school had invested capital of $14,640 bearing 7 percent interest, and the hall, which now included the school, was worth $10,000. Members' dues added to the Society's funds and provided operating expenses.[2]

At the May 1857 anniversary meeting, the Society met at its "new and spacious Hall, on the corner of Prince and Cannon Streets." The Society gathered and formed a procession which proceeded, along with the students, teachers and principal of the school, to the Masonic Hall where Benjamin Henry Wilson, Esquire, gave the annual address for the second time during the decade. After the address, the group went back to the new hall to conclude business. Unfortunately, Governor and Society President Robert F.W. Allston had to go to Charleston and therefore had to leave after the first round of business. At 3:00 p.m. the Society, with Eleazer Waterman sitting in for Allston, sat down to a "most sumptuous dinner, to which they did full justice." The paper reported, "The evening was spent to the infinite delight of all, with sentiment and song, mirth and merriment."[3]

At the meeting, the Quarterly Committee reported upon the December 19, 1856, public examination of the school. At the time, the Society was

118

Winyah Indigo Society Hall (William D. Morgan Collection, Georgetown County Library, Georgetown, SC).

excited to show off the progress of its students and hopefully attract some new pupils to the school.[4] However, the general walk-through did not go as well as planned. Perhaps the children were too excited with Christmas only a week away, but they clearly did not behave. Fortunately for the Society, only a few members of the general public attended.

The Quarterly Committee was embarrassed to give the negative report and blamed the students, teachers and the administration for the poor visit. Apparently, the students were loud and unruly during the school examination, but the committee reported that the issues had been addressed and corrected since the infraction. To help promote order in the school, the Society ordered noiseless chairs and requested that the principal enforce better observance of silence among the students while engaging in classroom activities. The principal was required by the Society to read the report of the Quarterly Committee to the students. The Society also agreed that it was time to move the school forward and to concentrate upon the students that it had and not simply to admit anyone who could pay the tuition. The Society resolved not to admit any student unless they could already read and were over two years old.[5]

In September 1857, the Winyah Indigo Society published a recruitment advertisement in the *Pee Dee Times*. By that time, the Rev. William T. Capers was the principal of the school, and Miss Louisa T. Spencer taught the "Female Department." The Society had not filled the male

East Room, previously the library, of Winyah Indigo Society Hall (photograph by Paige Sawyer).

West Room of the Winyah Indigo Society Hall (photograph by Paige Sawyer).

Interior entrance hall of the Winyah Indigo Society Hall (photograph by Paige Sawyer).

teacher vacancy yet but promised to have an "experienced and regularly educated teacher" to assist in the male department.[6] Terms and prices for private scholars were advertised as follows: English Studies—$40, English and ancient languages—$50, English and French or German studies—$60. The Society noted that payments were due January 1 and July 1.[7] Obtaining a male teacher was an incredibly difficult task during the era due to the proliferation of new schools.

On September 30, 1857, the Society held a special meeting at the Bank of Georgetown. The Senior Warden Eleazer Waterman called the Society together without consulting the Society's president Robert F.W. Allston. Without Allston knowing, the Society borrowed $600 from the Bank of Georgetown to pay the $506.66 overage on the building contract. At a meeting a few months later, the Society "Resolved, that wardens when president is absent have no authority under the rules to call for an extra meeting."[8]

At the November 6, 1857, meeting, the President of the Society and South Carolina Governor Robert F.W. Allston delivered an address to the Society. The Rev. Maurice Harvey Lance headed the Quarterly Committee at that time and reported that the students were much better behaved during the last classroom visit by the committee. The committee also read letters from the preceptors discussing the progress of some students, as well as concerns such as the truancy of others. The group talked of the biannual public examination of the school in December.[9]

Later in November 1857, after years of promoting education on the local level in Georgetown under the auspices of the Winyah Indigo Society, Governor Robert F.W. Allston got the opportunity to outline his plans for education on the state level. On November 23, 1857, he addressed the state senate and House of Representatives on many topics, including the scope and sequence of public education in the state. Although the Northern states used public education to assimilate immigrants, the South did not have scores of immigrants, and Allston's beliefs on education remained unchanged since the early 1800s when he studied under John Waldo in Georgetown. He firmly believed that the classics should constitute the primary feature in the leading literary institutions of the state but also felt that in communities of planters and farmers, where agriculture prevails, the importance of geometry, trigonometry, surveying, mensuration and mechanics should also be taught. He also insisted that students be taught astronomy, natural and experimental philosophy, natural history and general science.[10]

Allston understood that the job of educator was an important occupation and a matter of great importance in nation-building. To transform teaching into a full-time profession, and not simply something that young men did while they continued their own studies in theology or the law, Allston promoted the idea of training professional teachers. "I recommend that provision be made for the establishment, without delay, of one or more Normal Schools, at which the promising pupils from the schools below may be further educated for the purpose and trained to the art of teaching."[11]

In January 1858, while most of the people of United States were concerned with the economic collapse of the previous year, the Society discussed the proposition of taking the next step in helping its students become successful adults. It agreed that it was the Society's responsibility to assist its pupils by helping place them into careers such as plantation overseer. Two years later, the 1860 census revealed the education level of overseers in the Georgetown District. Of the 83 overseers polled, the average age was 30 years and four months, and only 12 percent were over 40 years of age. Fifty-eight percent were married, none were illiterate, and 30 percent owned real property, 22 percent owned slaves (eight and a half on average) of their own, and several owned "substantial property."[12]

In 1858, there were roughly 100 members of the Winyah Indigo Society. The *Pee Dee Times* reported that the anniversary meeting was well attended and that the Society turned out "in good strength to pay a just tribute to the occasion." President of the Society Robert F.W. Allston was absent from the annual meeting, but the newspaper reported that the "venerable citizen and Senior Warden, Eleazer Waterman Esq., officiated in his stead. The old gentleman though still possessing more than an ordinary share of public spiritedness, still the made hand of time, with its many infirmities, are traceable in his statue and countenance. May he yet survive many more anniversaries." Samuel Taylor Atkinson gave the address at the Baptist Church. He spoke for 40 minutes, and the gallery listened "with the most profound attention."[13]

Eleazer Waterman was an extremely influential member of the Society and the community in general. Besides being involved in several of the community's newspapers over the previous 40 years, Mr. Waterman held several political and social positions in town, including intendant of town.[14] He was a merchant, and after retiring from the newspaper business, he became extremely influential in health services and philanthropy. He was the chairman of the board for the Commission of the Poor and wrote the "Report of the commissioners of the poor, for the year 1854." Waterman's reports listed the names of those who received medical attention during the year and recounted the medical cost to the association and helped fundraise to pay for services.[15] Waterman also published several articles in the *Pee Dee Times* regarding medical concerns such as "Yellow Fever in Georgetown" and "Quarantine."[16]

In 1855, Waterman was instrumental in producing the Constitution of the Howard Society of Georgetown, South Carolina. This Society's main purpose was to care for the sick and poor of the community, especially during the summer and fall months when the community was susceptible to bilious fever (malaria) and during times of epidemic diseases.[17]

With the construction of the new hall, the Winyah Indigo Society felt confident in expanding its influence in Georgetown. Since its new facility had ample space to serve the Society and the community, the Society took back control over the Georgetown Library Society which it had charted in 1800. In January 1859, a room was set up for the library. Mr. Capers was paid $265.15 to organize, arrange and classify the books, to catalog the library, and to clean and dust the room and books. The Society claimed to have had about 3,000 volumes at the time of the move and paid $70 to have bookshelves built in the new library.[18]

The Society dictated that the librarian would offer a report at the May and November meetings each year concerning fines and damages to books and periodicals. The library's hours of operation were from noon until 5:00 p.m. on Wednesday and Friday, and Saturday from 10:00 a.m. until 2:00 p.m. The Society decreed that the Georgetown Lyceum would have unlimited access to the library and that nonresidents were also welcomed to use the collection. The Society bought a table with six chairs for the reading room and provided stationery for notetaking in an adjoining room. Community members were offered the opportunity to join the Winyah Indigo Society Library for $1.00 per year, and all student memberships were free. In honor of the new library, the Society had 200 copies of the Rules of the Society published and a copy of the Reverend Mitchell's anniversary oratory placed on display.[19]

In June 1859, the Society began to rent the red schoolhouse which had been constructed just a few years earlier to Miss Mitchell for $50 for the school term. The Society also decided to lease out the new hall to other organizations. In 1859, It started renting the new hall to the Presbyterian community for religious purposes. That same year, the Rev. D.W. Cuttino spoke to the Independent Order of Odd Fellows at the new hall.[20]

In January 1860, the Society had its first meeting of the decade. At the meeting, Edward Rice was given permission to occupy the house and lot adjacent to the hall if he agreed to take care of all the Society's buildings. The group also talked about taking a tenant for the Charles Fyffe property which it had owned and rented since the post–American Revolutionary era. The money raised from renting the hall was used to purchase a chandelier for the hall and a smaller matching one for its lobby.[21]

At the following meeting, the Society addressed the rising cost of the anniversary banquet and resolved that its mission was to fund education in Georgetown, not to spend their money on holding extravagant dinners. To those means, it was decided that the anniversary dinner should be held to a budget and cost no more than $200 to host, including speaker fee, food and drink. It also announced that William Dealy left a legacy to the society of $200.[22]

On May 4, 1860, just a few months after John Brown's raid at Harpers Ferry, Virginia, the rising star of the Waccamaw rice lands, Plowden Charles Jennett Weston, delivered the annual address to the Winyah Indigo Society. Twenty-eight members attended the Winyah Indigo Society meeting, as well as their families, school faculty and students, parents and members of the general public.[23] The new facility was packed; revolution was in the air, and everyone waited with great anticipation for what the fire-eating scholar had to say. Surely, he could be counted on to address the history of the Society and the state of education, but would he speak of politics and the looming presidential election, possibly disunion, or war? Would he try to unite the people of Georgetown through political fervor as he had done a few years earlier at *Watchesaw Plantation*? Rich and poor, farmers, planters, merchants and tradesmen waited on his address.

Weston did not disappoint any of the members of the audience. He addressed them all in his own personal style, reaching them where they were in their understanding of the sectional crisis and their hopes and dreams of the future. He did not expect everyone to understand the coming conflict as he did but eventually brought them to his understanding through his patience and concern for their collective future. Throughout his speech, Weston focused upon the themes of scholarship, preparedness, action, experiences, circumstances, duty and responsibility to the Winyah Indigo Society and South Carolina. He drew from his vast knowledge of history to create parallels between past civilizations, and even the father of the

Plowden Charles Jennett Weston (courtesy Charleston Museum, Charleston, SC).

United States, to drive home his themes and to make these subjects relevant to his audience to further unify the people in the coming struggle.

Winyah Indigo Society Hall Ballroom (photograph by Paige Sawyer).

A master scholar and lecturer, Weston opened his address by immediately placing responsibility upon those in attendance. He explained to the gallery that every man, woman and child had a responsibility to the civilization that they lived in and that they all had duties to fulfill. He explained how experiences derived from such duties shape the citizen and guide the individual through life. He stated, "a man's heart receives as an axiom, that man has duties to fulfill, that are the object and end of his existence; which axiom is the basis of all investigations into moral sciences, and includes within itself all the practical rules for the guidance of human life."[24]

Next, Weston addressed the purpose of work. He explained that labor was a time-consuming device which saved man from idleness and gave him both a purpose and a finished product to be proud of, a pride which leads to a fulfilled legacy. He stated, "man is to labor—not for the purpose of saving himself from harm, or propitiating other beings more powerful than himself, or of doing the greatest good for the greatest number, but it boldly grapples with the question of right, without regard to consequences, and does that which ought to be done without regard to the corollary of expediency."[25]

For students and members of the audience who lacked the ambition to become leaders in society, Weston addressed the time-honored principles of truth, honor and duty, and at the same time wove in the differences between heroism and fanaticism. He lectured the crowd with dignity and clarity when he explained that character was far more important that economic success. He stated, "truth, honor, and duty, may take the place of low ambition and the pride of money-getting; and the capacity of labor, power of strict attention, and incessant vigilance will help forward in their new career, as the heroes of ancient mythology."[26]

A true historian in his own right, Weston called out to tradition and tied the current students of the Winyah Indigo Society School to the past and attempted to give them a connection to the grandeur of the organization which provided them their education. Like a commencement speaker, he reminded the students of the benefits that they received from their education and how they were indebted to the next generation to help sustain the Winyah Indigo Society School and to pay their debt to the continuance of the order. He said, "Two or three generations have passed away; their descendants in the third and fourth degree are now amongst my hearers; not one of whom even remembers the cultivation of indigo, whilst the Indigo Society still exists, blessing and being blessed." He assured the students that time and tradition were on their side and that their traditions were honorable and worthy of sustaining. "You have the advantage of antiquity; your associations are somewhat with the past; you are descendants of an honorable line and are bound to maintain the dignity of your house."[27]

In 1860, on the verge of creating the nation of South Carolina, Weston reminded the students and the gallery of members and guests to help create an even brighter future by donating to the cause of education and civilization: the creation of Southern Nationalism. "Give nobly, give generously, for in the giving of knowledge there is no waste; the most splendid bounty is not followed by penury in the giver, far from it, it enriches the giver even more than the receiver."[28]

Weston encouraged the masses to further their education whether the continuance be a formal education or informal. He explained how facts do not equal an education but that experiences and ability are most important to rounding out the understandings of what one learns in publications. "Books can only amount to a portion of an education of the mind. How you see the world is based upon your experiences," he said. He told the audience that he knows of many men who have the knowledge of books but lack the ability to draw connections from what they have learned. He likened the problem to a man who "possessed the material to build a structure on their premise but lack[ed] the skill to frame it up and put it all together."[29]

"Stay humble and serve your state," he told the students. Be prepared for greatness in case, by divine Providence, the time comes that you must serve your state. Drawing upon the life of George Washington, Weston explained how Washington was content with being a good planter and a faithful soldier to the British Crown, but "Providence opened to him a way for the purest reputation that has ever been given to man, so well had he improved his opportunities, and so thoroughly had he trained his energies. That he followed, as it were, instinctively the path proposed to him, and died the acknowledged Father of a great and rising Empire."[30]

Although Weston remained serious throughout his discourse, he attempted to lighten the mood temporarily by asking his audience to remain true to the truth and to live the truth or at least to enter upon the truth, have faith in people and God but not party politics. He asked the students and guests to only form opinions after performing careful research and investigations into a subject before forming an opinion, and "Don't ever say can't." He concluded this section of his speech by saying, "When a new proposition is presented to us, upon which it is necessary for us to form an opinion, or at least to enter upon action, what is our first and instinctive question? Is it not 'what is the creed of our church, our political party, our ordinary society? It ought to be. Is it true?'"[31]

Quickly returning to the current dilemma that the South was facing with the Northern majority, Weston warned of the divine right of the majority and how it differed from democracy. Weston, like most South-erners of the era, believed that American Democracy still meant that the states were equal. In that sense, Weston and his contemporaries embraced the system that the United States Constitution laid out pertaining to the Senate, where all states have equal representation no matter how large or small their population. He explained how an opinion had been introduced from Europe through the North that the majority has a divine right to rule and that this opinion has not been restricted to politics but has quickly been applied to social institutions as well. Weston warned, if "the Divine right of the majority should ever gain ground here as it has done elsewhere, our last vestige of independence will be swept away; each generation will become more and more dwarfed; each man of the same size, and the very pattern of every other man; notions, opinions, and actions, will be run in one common mold."[32]

The final part of Weston's speech was a call to arms and a plea for nation-building. He called on this generation of scholars and laborers to defend the South from the intrusions and infiltrations of the Second Great Awakening upon social structures. He said, "On the rising genera-tion depends the fate of the country. It cannot be denied that the times in which you will come upon the stage of life will be singularly tempestuous and stormy. We have only felt the whiff and wind of the fell sword; you will experience its grinding blade."[33]

He then sent a stinging message to his audience when he blamed them for becoming influenced by the bankers and industrialists and taking false gods in the form of material wealth and explained how the industrialists and bankers waged war against the agricultural economic structures. He claimed that money was a curse bestowed upon the people and blamed the money interests for creating a culture where currency became the sin-gle dream of the nation's heart and soul. He accused, "we have fallen much below our fathers. It cannot be denied that in this again we are imitating the North and raising up an idol made of gold and silver, clothed in bank notes."[34]

He concluded his oration with a summation of civilizations on the brink of war and ended with an appeal to defend the institutions of South Carolina. He explained that God Almighty was testing the people but that they would prevail. He said, "No country has ever existed which does not require the bracing to be received from convulsion and disorder. These things are sent, not as punishments, but as blessings." Then he became poi-gnant and gave a poetic call to arms: "The streams of virtue, wisdom and bravery, which have dried up during long seasons of material felicity, are full-charged again amid the roar of the thunder and the fast-descending storm, and every manly energy descends full-armed to the conflict." He appealed to the citizens to defend their homes and firesides and said, "I can have only one hope, and that is, that in those days, so surely coming, you may not be found wanting, but that in the great battle of truth and justice, good order and good government, you may plant anew the ancient principles of our institutions, and add another page, not the least glorious, to the history of our native state."[35]

Over the next few months of 1860, the political and social leaders throughout South Carolina and various Southern states held countless political meetings. Love and respect for history, honor of their forefathers' struggles and victories under the Union flag were contrasted with their contemporary ideas of American Democracy, their dreams of the future, and their wishes to pass their way of life on to their children. When Abraham Lincoln was elected president of the United States, most members of the Society and civilization, which it had helped to create and serve for over 100 years, agreed with the idea of secession.

On April 5, 1861, 11 members of the Society met at the hall. The principal gave a full report on the status of the school and informed the Society that there were two student vacancies in the school. One month later, at the anniversary meeting, 29 members entertained the captains of the volunteer militia companies on duty on the islands off the coast of South Carolina. At the meeting, Dr. James Ritchie Sparkman suggested, and the Society agreed, that any member who paid $100 to the Society would become a lifetime member and be exempt from annual dues. The Society's secretary did not record in the minutes if anyone paid the $100 lifetime membership. The plan of the membership drive was to apply all the money raised towards funding the school through the coming conflict, which everyone hoped would be a quick and relatively bloodless independence movement.[36]

With the war heating up, and many members moving inland away from the United States Navy, the Society did not

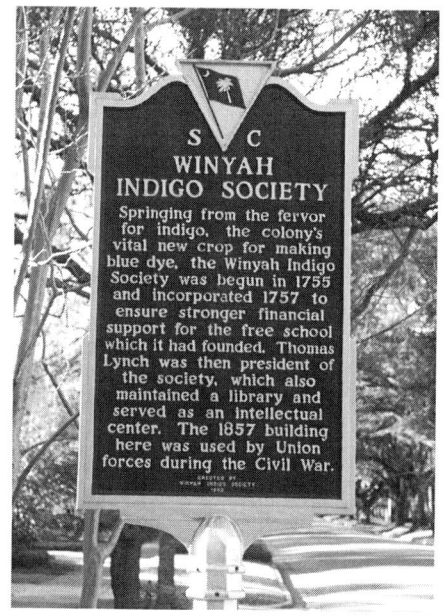

Winyah Indigo Society Hall historical site marker (photograph by Paige Sawyer).

meet again for the duration of the war. The secretary simply recorded in the minutes' book, "The anniversary meetings for 1862 and 1863 were not held in consequence of the absence of nearly all of the members from the district, and the confused condition of the Lowcountry, the effects of the Great War of Independence."[37]

SEVEN

The Hot and Hot Fish Club
of All Saints Parish

*Within each such social group, a feeling of solidarity
prevails, a compelling need to work together and a
joy in doing so that represents a high moral value.*
—Christian Louis Lange

The Winyah Indigo Society met in the city of Georgetown in the Prince George Winyah District, but the Hot and Hot Fish Club operated at the planters' summer retreats at the seashore in southern All Saints Parish. The All Saints Parish voting district ran from the North Carolina/ Horry District line south to the tip of the peninsula just north of the city of Georgetown. Bordered by the Atlantic Ocean to the east, Winyah Bay to the south and the Waccamaw River to the west, the boggy parish provided the perfect environment for the large-scale cultivation of rice. It was along the Waccamaw River that most of the most prosperous rice planters built their manor homes and on the easternmost part of the district (ocean-front) where they constructed their summer homes.

For those who lived along the Waccamaw River, the annual retreat to the seashore was only a few-mile trek. Those who lived on the Pee Dee River, or other locations, had a little more difficult time crossing rivers to get to the beach. Located just 60 miles north of Charleston, the area was the home of many of the state's most affluent antebellum rice planters. For the most part, the group that benefited from the high yield of rice was related and aligned economically and socially. The Hot and Hot Fish Club served as a forum in the unification of Georgetown politically. Although most of the members were planters, some were also military officers, politicians, and physicians. Together, they constituted a microcosm of the South's most influential body, the land-loving and agriculturally astute aristocratic planter class.

Due to the absence of records, the founding date and early history of the club are unknown. Prior to 1844, the only source of information is

Rules and History of the Hot and Hot Fish Club of All Saints Parish.[1] Long-time member and leading Pee Dee planter and politician, Robert F.W. All-ston, stated that the club existed and was holding meetings prior to the War of 1812. He recalled attending meetings as a boy of 15 (in 1816) as a guest of his brother-in-law, John Hyrne Tucker.

The earliest meetings consisted of little more than a small group of friends gathered to eat, drink alcohol, smoke cigars and socialize. According to the club's earliest records, nine members met in a one-room building located on "Drunken Jack Island," a small island in Murrells Inlet. The island's namesake derived from one of the club's earliest members—John Green. Green was a hard-drinking, 6'4" 300-pound American Revolutionary War veteran who would commonly eat a peck of fish in one meal (taking them in at one corner of his mouth and removing the bones out the other side) and wash them down with a quart of brandy. He is remembered for jovially singing, "Fish and rice is very nice; Pork and 'tater is much better."[2] It was there, among the stunted trees and salt marsh, that the Hot and Hot Fish Club held its first meetings.

It is unclear at what time of the day that the members began to fish on meeting day, but at 1:00 p.m. the president of the club raised a flag to call in the boats. The planters surveyed their catch, had lunch and entertained each other with fishing stories. Then, accompanied by their servants who rowed their boats to their favorite fishing spots, they returned to the inlet until dinnertime. Most did not venture too far out; only John Hyrne Tucker, the individual said to be the club's finest deep-sea fisherman, went out farther than 300 yards from shore.[3]

During the afternoon, some slaves began to prepare the morning's catch for dinner. Bass, drum, bream, trout and perch were among the most common catch; other fish such as whiting and the "hog-fish" of North Carolina and Virginia were rarer.[4] After scaling, slaves washed the fish in three waters, the last being fresh. In the evening, all the members sat down together to tell fishing stories and to eat the spicy dishes that gave the club its name: The Hot and Hot Fish Club.[5]

Recalling the early days of the club, Robert F.W. Allston wrote, "There was but one salt dish (beef or ham) and one of fresh meat (generally game) on [the] table, and these were furnished, together with rice, by rule, in turns. For the rest, every member caught his own dinner and enough for his boat hands, each contributing bread, and such condiments as he liked."[6]

A storm damaged the original clubhouse, and it was soon after abandoned. The members quickly constructed a temporary building on a clam bank at Joshua John Ward's salt vats. At the new site, the club continued its meetings and initiated one honorary (John Walter Phillips) and

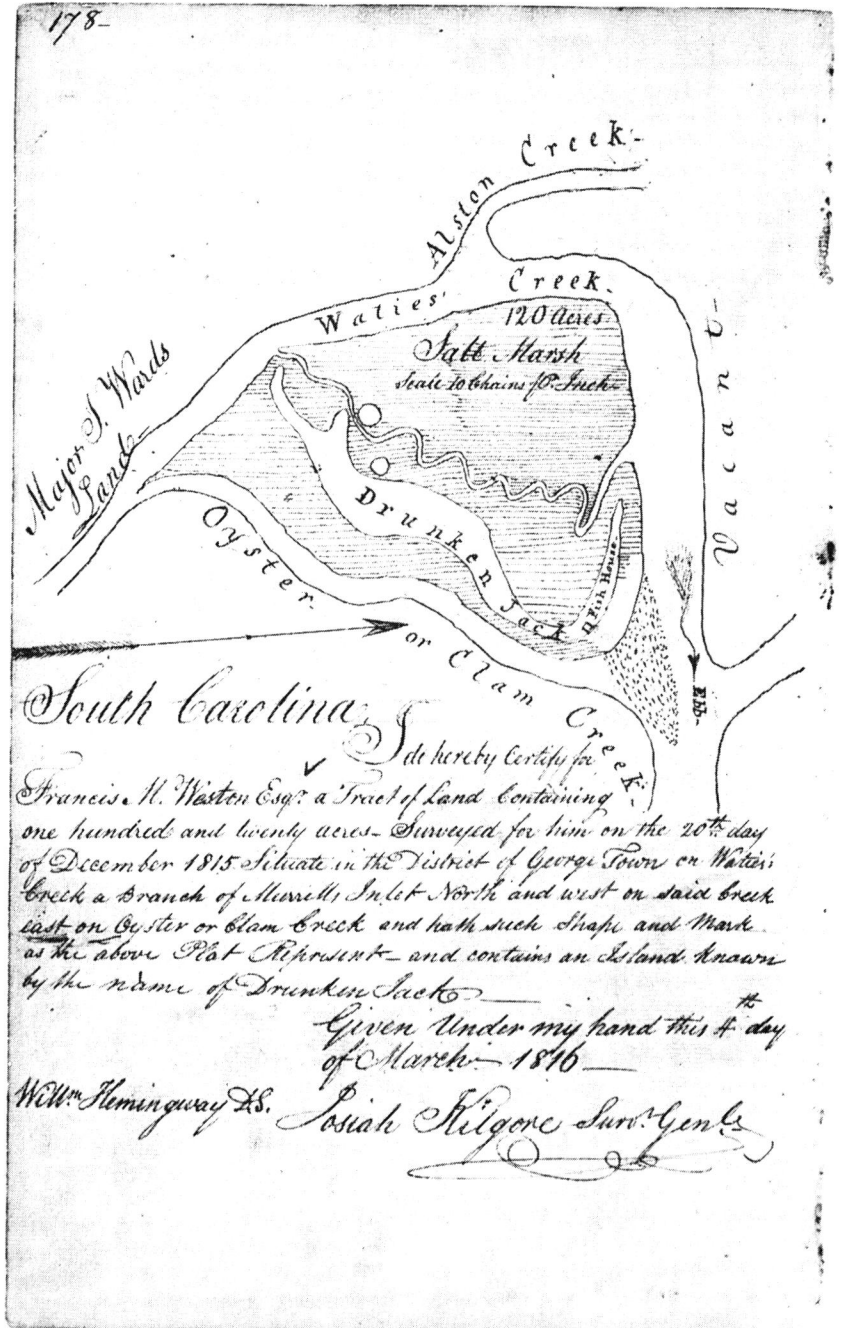

Plat of Hot and Hot Fish Club (courtesy Horry County Archives).

13 new members. The new members who joined the club were Dr. John D. Magill, Dr. Edward Thomas Heriot, Davison McDowell, General Joseph Waties Alston, Joshua John Ward, John G. North, Captain Thomas Petigru (United States Navy), Peter Waties Fraser, Robert Nesbit, Thomas Pinckney Alston, Thomas Howe, John Hayes Allston and Robert F.W. Allston.[7]

Later, the group moved to the beachfront property of Peter Waties Fraser where they held meetings in a wall tent (large military tent) supplied by General Joseph Alston. Shortly thereafter, the Hot and Hot Fish Club moved for a fourth time, this time to the head of a causeway on Dr. Andrew Hasell's property near the north causeway of Pawleys Island. At this site, membership continued to flourish. Members Dr. Andrew Hasell, William Magill, William Norris, John Middleton and B.B. Smith joined the club.[8] On September 27, 1822, a hurricane hit Georgetown and destroyed that clubhouse and many summer homes on the island.[9]

Determined to keep their organization alive, members constructed their fifth and final clubhouse on a ten-acre land grant donated by Thomas Pinckney Alston. The tract was located near Alston's *Midway Plantation*, so called because it was the midway point on the Waccamaw Neck between the Georgetown/Horry District line and the city of Georgetown. There the club's activities became more formal, graduating from casual fishing excursions to large, politically charged banquet-style gatherings.

By the time the club relocated to *Midway Plantation*, the Second Great Awakening was expanding, diversifying and affecting more people throughout the country. As the North and West became swept up in liberal reforms, the Georgetown planters were producing more and more of the national export of rice, accumulating great wealth and gathering political strength. The Second Great Awakening reforms, perceived by the planters as assaults upon their traditional stances and successful expansion in production, transformed the club from a social and convivial club into an economic and conservative political powerhouse. No longer just a recreational escape from the formality

Thomas Pinckney Alston (by D'Andrea Lynn Boyle, photograph by Rich Taylor).

of the aristocratic lifestyle of rice planting, club activities became ceremonious and politically charged events. Lighthearted, drunken antics of members such as John Green were no longer commonplace.

The state senate election of 1832 was one of the most important in South Carolina's history due to the nullification crisis brought on by John C. Calhoun's states' rights' argument against national tariff laws. In the election, several members of the Hot and Hot Fish Club ran against each other for the senate seats. In the All Saints District, Joshua John Ward and Thomas Pinckney Alston won their elections, and in Prince George Winyah Parish states' rights' candidates Robert F.W. Allston and Peter Waties Fraser beat their more moderate fellow club members, Dr. Edward Thomas Heriot and John Hayes Allston.[10]

The club meetings were clearly forums for heartfelt political debate based upon the spirit of the American War for Independence and the United States Constitution, which certainly witnessed some intense political debates and moments. One member later recalled the political atmosphere as such: "National and sectional questions were discussed on their merits, not absolutely without personal or political bias, of course, but without the least taint of what is now called machine politics."[11]

At *Midway* the group constructed a two-room clubhouse with a large dining room and a freestanding kitchen. For entertainment, members could play tenpins, billiards, card games, or race their horses. One member boasted that the club's race track was "the training course of some of the finest racers in Carolina."[12] It was undoubtedly a great track, but the course at the Hot and Hot Fish Club was the site of at least one tragic race.

After graduating from Yale College, Thomas Pinckney and Motte Alston returned home to the Waccamaw Neck where sibling rivalry led the boys to engage in a race with their brothers Charles and Pinckney. Jacob Motte Alston recalled the event. He said, "At the club an impromptu race was gotten up, and Motte volunteered to ride a very vicious horse. His brother Pinckney earnestly pleaded with him not to ride that vicious horse: but they all galloped to the ground and he [Thomas Pinckney Alston] alone remained, having determined not to countenance the race by his presence. After a little while, as if impelled by foreboding evil, he [Thomas Pinckney] mounted his horse and went after them, and only in time to see his brother [Motte] thrown against a pine stump, his horse having bolted. He [Thomas Pinckney] reached him only to feel his heart give one throb and he was dead."[13] The blow was so great that the watch which Motte wore stopped at the moment of impact, recording the instant of his untimely death.

The club adopted rules of governance, appointed a secretary to take notes of the meetings, and selected a treasurer to collect admission fees from new associates and the membership at *Midway*. By 1846, the club had 18 dues-paying members and Thomas Pinckney Alston, who was exempt from paying dues to the club because he donated the land to the club upon which the clubhouse stood. Now conscious of improving the club, preserving its traditions for posterity and guiding the club into the future, the club continued its formulation of until July of 1860 when the final rule was adopted.[14]

Even though the club took on a more serious posture at *Midway Plantation*, members continued to hunt and fish for many of their dinners. One contemporary recalled that the members "while largely interested in the contests of the turf, were also sportsmen admirably trained and equipped for the chase of the deer and other game to be found in the boundless forests and for taking the numerous and varied fish in the rivers."[15]

Turkey and duck hunting were popular, but deer hunting was special. On the mornings of the hunt, members gathered early and usually on horseback. Then, the gentlemen took to the woods with their finest packs of hounds, armed with rifles and accompanied by deer drivers, slaves dressed in light colors and red caps with whips. Hunting was easy on the Waccamaw Neck due to the abundance of wild game. Sometimes members "still hunted," meaning they used deer stands instead of horses but always depended upon their hounds and deer drivers.[16]

One member recalled the hunting trips as such: "These hunting parties and social gatherings were most pleasant. Around the dinner table the hunt was fully discussed and many a hearty laugh enjoyed at the expense of anyone who had failed to embrace the opportunity of showing himself a keen sportsman when occasion presented itself."[17]

Although the club outwardly displayed the wealth of its members, adopted a formal set of rules, built an elaborate clubhouse, and frequently talked politics, the basis of the club remained democratically organized social and convivial intercourse. Jacob Motte Alston (the leading rice planter in the Horry District) recalled the meetings at the *Midway* site as democratically organized feasts. He wrote, "We presided by turns, and each member brought his own dish or dishes, wines, etc., and so when a full attendance was present a very full table, of course, followed."[18]

The Hot and Hot Fish Club met before noon each Friday, beginning with the first Friday in June and continuing through the last Friday, except for one, in October. At the meetings, the president of the day provided a ham and "good" rice, and his slaves prepared the seaside banquet, which they served, by rule, at 2:00 p.m. One former member recalled the meeting in the following manner: "We all met at 11 o'clock AM, returned home after sun set. The club was the old Hot & Hot Fish Club, of Waccamaw, and lots of fun and pleasant hours were there spent."[19]

The vice president of the day provided the club with ice and water and announced whether champagne would be brought to the following meeting. Ice was one of the hardest condiments to procure during the summer in the antebellum South. According to the organization's minutes book, Dr. Allard Flagg was chastised during his second meeting as a club member for his "failures to supply ice and fresh water as vice president."[20]

In 1799, New England traders began to ship ice to Charleston where factors sent it by schooners to the planters.[21] Planters constructed icehouses that were little more than covered 15-foot-deep brick wells with gabled roofs resting on the ground to keep ice from melting.[22] In addition to these duties, the vice president also participated in the club's games on the side of the president. If the officers of the day did not attend the meeting, they were still required to send the refreshments that their positions required.[23]

Each member contributed at least one dish and a bottle of wine towards the meal, unless it had been announced that champagne would be provided. Bachelors were exempt from bringing a dish and were instead required to provide puddings. By turn, members were also required to furnish the club with sugar.[24] Many of the planters grew sugar cane in small quantities on their plantations, which made it one of the easiest condiments to provide. Salt was another seasoning that was easy to obtain. Salt was simply boiled out of the ocean water.[25]

The men were very fond of wine and consumed it in large quantities at every meeting. Champagne, on the other hand, was reserved for special occasions. Members donated champagne to the club rather frequently and, in fact, the organization required that its members do so at certain times. By 1849, while the gentlemen focused upon the Wilmot Proviso, the quantity of wine and champagne held by the club became so large that the group formed a committee to keep a record of its inventory and remind members when they, by rule, were required to furnish a case of champagne. Some such occasions where members were obligated to provide a case or basket of champagne were marriages and births. If any member's wife bore twins, then all the members of the club except the father were required to supply a basket of champagne to the club's reserve.[26]

The club also required that "any member of this club, who shall be elected or appointed to any distinguished office in the state, shall for each and every such compliment, furnish for the use of the club one box of champagne."[27] In most clubs this rule would seem impertinent; however, the Hot and Hot Fish Club included some of the most outstanding men in the state, several of whom the citizens of Georgetown and the state elected to distinguished offices.[28] In general, the notion of deference that the chivalrous rice planters of broad acres ascribed to include the mentality that they "rarely sought office, but accepted without reluctance local appointments as school, charity, and road commissioners, and were ready to represent their district in the State legislature."[29]

By the time the club subjected its membership to rules, it was an economic and political juggernaut. A complete roster reveals that 15 members were military officers, including one general, ten colonels, two majors and two captains. Several were veterans of the American Revolution, War of 1812, Mexican-American War, and some would eventually fight in the American Civil War. Many were prominent politicians. Both Plowden C.J. Weston and Joshua John Ward served South Carolina as lieutenant governors, and Robert F.W. Allston was governor of South Carolina from 1856 to 1858. Besides Weston, Ward and Allston, who used the state general assembly and senate as stepping stones to reach higher state offices, several other state senators belonged to the club: Dr. Edward Thomas Heriot, Thomas Pinckney Alston and Charles Alston. Other members, such as Colonel John Harleston Read, Jr., Colonel Peter Waties Fraser, Dr. John Hyrne Tucker, Dr. Allard B. Flagg, Colonel Daniel W. Jordan, John Hayes Allston, esquire, and Colonel John Ashe Alston served as members of the South Carolina General Assembly.

In addition, 12 members were physicians, and 20 others referred to themselves as "esquire." In all, throughout the existence of the club, 48 of the 54 members of the club wrote titles next to their names. Having excluded Georgetown's bankers, factors, and merchants, most members were rice planters. Although trained in medicine, Dr. John D. Magill and Dr. Edward Thomas Heriot only practiced medicine for family members and in their slave communities, while they focused upon rice production.[30] One physician, Dr. James Ritchie Sparkman, carefully balanced both his medical career and the responsibilities of being a planter.[31] Dr. Andrew Hasell owned a farm, but he was a practicing physician, not a rice planter. He lived full-time at Pawleys Island and was the most accomplished physician in the Georgetown District during the era and was the farmer with the least land to be included in the planter's social clubs. According to this meticulously maintained account book, he serviced patients (both free and slave) at nearly every plantation in All Saints District, as well as plantations in the Prince George Winyah District. William Algernon Alston, Joshua John Ward, John Hyrne Tucker, Thomas Pinckney Alston, Charles Alston, Francis Marion Weston and Paul Weston on the Waccamaw River, Peter Waties Fraser, Robert F.W. Allston and the Pettigrues on the Pee Dee River, Colonel Allard Belin of Sandy Island, and Dr. Francis S. Parker and the Ford families of the Black River all used his services for their families and slaves.[32] In addition to treating Georgetown planters and their slaves, Dr. Hasell served in international medical capacities. He was elected extraordinary member of the Royal Medical Society of Edinburgh, corresponding member of the Medical Chirurgical Society of Edinburgh and corresponding member of the Society of Antiquaries of Scotland.[33]

After 1845, anyone who wished to join the club had to be sponsored by the president of the day. If elected by a majority, providing that the group present constituted a quorum, the club required that the new member pay an initiation fee of $50.[34] Sometimes the meetings did not draw the necessary two-thirds member requirement to constitute a quorum, and business could not be conducted.

In July of 1853, Charles Alston was proposed for admission into the club; however, there were not enough members present to constitute a quorum, and he had to wait until the following meeting. Charles was permitted to attend the meetings as a guest until he could be admitted. On August 6, 1853, John Hayes Allston, acting as president of the day, proposed that Charles Alston be admitted into the club; the resolution passed, and Charles became a member.

In addition to initiation fees, the club received support from annual dues of $5 per member, as well as other various donations. Already stated, Thomas Pinckney Alston's land grant to the club was, of course, its most valuable donation. In reward for his contribution, Alston was named a lifelong member and exempted from paying further dues.[35] State politician and philanthropist, Joshua John Ward, donated a billiards table after the completion of the fifth and final clubhouse when it was clear that the game table would be properly housed and not ruined by the elements.[36]

The group used the dues for many practical purposes, most notably for contracting for clubhouse repairs and improvements such as framing the tenpin alley, the addition of a second door to the clubhouse, structural repairs in 1850, and repairs to the kitchen in 1860.[37] Treasury funds also paid for a wide variety of other club expenses such as door locks (Thomas Pinckney Alston and Joshua John Ward held the keys to the lock), dinnerware, balls and pins for the tenpin alley, a lightning rod, and the printing costs of articles of respect in memory of their deceased members.[38] In members' obituaries published in Georgetown newspapers, articles cast the rice planters in the most favorable light. Major Robert Nesbit was memorialized as "a practical planter" and Dr. Edward Thomas Heriot as "doctor" rather than planter because it was "a pursuit more congenial to his views."[39] As a visible sign of mourning, the fraternal order regularly wore a black crape armband for 30 days following the death of a member.[40]

From 1848 through 1850, as the sectional crisis heated up again, and debate continued in the United States Senate as to how to divide the newly acquired Mexican Cession, the club felt that it had held sufficient funds in its treasury and did not need to collect membership dues. It did, however, continue to levy the $50 initiation fee expected of all new members.[41]

Even after the club added rules for better governance and built an elaborate clubhouse, its emphasis continued to be on politically spirited seashore banquets and fine wine. When President Zachary Taylor asked Americans to commit to a day of fasting and humiliation on Friday, August 3, 1849, on account of a dangerous strand of cholera that prevailed in many parts of the country, the club resolved to skip the scheduled meeting rather than meet, and not drink and feast.[42] The cholera epidemic was widespread. An estimated 150,000 Americans, including former president James K. Polk, died as a result of contact.

As the organization matured, meals became more formal, and the members paid less attention to fishing and more to games and conviviality. Social interaction between the gentlemen often included teasing about their fortunes and their importance to society. Generally, the older and more established men badgered the younger. Benjamin Allston wrote a letter to a family member concerning one such episode at the club. He wrote, "I have just returned from club where we spent a very pleasant day. Dr. Hazel [Hasell] was quite facetious, and thinks that my name is handed down from remote posterity by being mentioned in Abbots P.R. Survey in Oregon."[43]

Jacob Motte Alston recalled another event in club history when teasing and mock insults took place. The story revolved around a particularly dry season when Alston was forced to fill his rice fields with fresh water at half-tide. To assist the fresh water's entrance into his fields, Alston cut a piece out of the cross bank to allow swamp water to flow in as well. Sometime later, when surveying his rice fields with his overseer, the pair came upon the previously cut rice bank which was washed out. Knowing that the rice water held many bacteria that could make them both sick, Alston's overseer (a much larger man that Alston in stature) carried him across the washed-out area to dry ground. Alston later wrote, "When someone mentioned it at Club there was no end to the jokes against me." Apparently, at least one member teased Alston relentlessly and publicly ridiculed him to everyone's enjoyment. The tormenter said, "Confound the boy; he thinks because he has saved his crop, he must need ride the overseer around." Alston tried to defend himself by explaining the story, but nobody would listen. He then took pride in explaining that the crop was one of the best harvests that he had ever reaped—65 bushels of rice per acre (unprocessed rice was valued at $1.00 per bushel).[44]

At a typical meeting of the club, the group would spend the entire afternoon and most of the night eating and drinking at their catered seaside feasts. One member recalled a typical club meeting in this way: "Each member brought his servant; and when all the good things had been discussed, interwoven with some politics and lots of rice talk, and the table cleared of all save the bottles of old wine, the thrice told anecdotes and songs would enliven the scene till night began to throw her kind mantle over the happy members of the Hot and Hot Fish Club."[45]

Unlike the Winyah Indigo Society that required its new members to serve as stewards for dining purposes, the Hot and Hot Fish Club relied upon its slaves to serve at the club. The slaves who accompanied their masters to these meetings were not field hands dressed in homespun cloth or burlap but a class of a much higher status. The servants at these dinners were always males and specially trained for serving at social gatherings. Frequently, the banquets acted as a

Jacob Motte Alston (by D'Andrea Lynn Boyle, photograph by Rich Taylor).

training school for young male domestics. At the club, they learned manners and became accustomed to wearing fine livery. Shortly after the construction of the freestanding kitchen at the *Midway* site, it became customary for the president and vice president of the day to bring their finest male domestics to serve and cook for the entire club and to keep a fire.[46]

Typical livery colors were green, red, or gray; however, the gentlemen clothed their servants as they wished, always remaining conscious that the appearance of their people was a direct reflection of their ability to provide for them. Jacob Motte Alston dressed his male slaves in fine dark green coats of broadcloth, green plush trousers and vests faced with red and trimmed in silver braid.[47] Dr. James Ritchie Sparkman, in a letter to Benjamin Allston, proudly boasted that his male domestics were "supplied without limit to insure a genteel and comfortable appearance."[48] Robert F.W. Allston clothed his family in the same material that he used to make suits for his male servants. On one occasion, Allston asked his wife to tell his tailor, "If there is enough of it left [referring to a particular type of tweed] I would like a coat of it for myself."[49] Allston outfitted his male domestics in gray mixed-cloth coats and tweed trousers.[50]

This elite class of slaves at the Hot and Hot Fish Club, chosen to serve their masters, had their master's trust in circumstances where field hands did not. The only record of slaves disobeying club rules has to do with alcohol consumption. It is not surprising that with such a large group of drunken masters and an ample supply of wine and champagne that servants took advantage of the situation. Slaves had the freedom to sample food and beverages before serving them to their waiting masters.

At one summer meeting, Colonel Daniel W. Jordan rewarded a servant with alcohol for his politeness. Jordan was a new member to the club and to the Waccamaw Neck. He grew up in North Carolina and moved to Little River, Horry District, which was within the boundaries of All Saints Parish. From Little River he entered All Saints politics and made friends with the rice planters. In 1859, Jordan sold his 9,940-acre longleaf pine estate (useful in the production of naval stores, such lumber, tar, pitch, turpentine and rosin) in Horry District and purchased Laurel Hill Plantation from Plowden Charles Jennett Weston in the Georgetown section of All Saints District and joined the social order. He was a state representative and a commissioner of free schools but perhaps he did not understand the seriousness of his infraction to club rules.[51]

The slave who Colonel Jordan satisfied with alcohol, Isaac, belonged to Dr. Andrew Hasell. Hasell was a longtime member of the community and the club, and he did not appreciate the gesture. According to his master, "Isaac had never been intemperate here [at *Cedar Grove*] for 14 years—& has never been seen intoxicated—or suspected of having liquor during that long period."[52] Hasell wrote Jordan a letter chastising him for his action: "I heard from Mayham Ward (son of the late Joshua John Ward), yesterday that my man Isaac was intoxicated at Club—I regret it—Some temptation must have been made either in the dregs—left by members—or by some other dose. You will confer a favor upon me in not offering liquor to any servant of mine."[53]

After receiving the letter, Jordan wrote back promising Hasell that he was not in the habit of offering alcohol to any servants at the club. He advised Hasell that "your servant put me in the way of obtaining a cooking utensil which I expected to have found in the Club House. When he returned from showing my boy the fork of the road—I happened, as is sometimes the case, to be taking a drink he offered me ice water and for his

Daniel W. Jordan (by D'Andrea Lynn Boyle, photograph by Rich Taylor).

politeness I gave him about 2 tablespoons full of whiskey."[54] Later in his letter, Jordan claimed that Isaac was "a little lively but I do not think he was by any means drunk." He ended his rebuttal to Hasell by reminding him, "It is not difficult for Negroes to get whiskey if they want it."[55] Alcohol was a central part of the Hot and Hot Fish Club's weekly gatherings, and every club meeting constituted a social holiday.

Upon at least one occasion, the Hot and Hot Fish Club clubhouse was used as a meeting place for a general public political meeting. On February 29, 1856, motivated by the newspaper article printed two weeks earlier which announced the news that proslavery supporters had been murdered by antislavery supporters, local planters threw down the gauntlet and took the offensive by beginning plans for emigration to Kansas. Dr. Andrew Hasell presided over the event in which he organized and created a four-man committee consisting of Daniel W. Jordan, Plowden Charles Jennett Weston, John LaBruce and Charles Alston, Jr., to raise men 18 years of age and older and money to help fund the proslavery militia in their war in Kansas. The group raised $2,000 and a few volunteer troops at the meeting. John Rutledge Alston was elected to lead the pioneers to Kansas and appropriate the money raised.[56] The paper stated that without Kansas and slavery, "free negrodon will soon crush out cattle, cotton, colleges, property and progress—drones will eat up the hives, railroads disappear, and the wild beasts, briners and bramblers over run the world."[57]

In its following edition, the *Pee Dee Times* screamed out, "It is the duty of the Southern States to encourage and promote bona fide emigration to the territory in Kansas." Prince George Winyah Parish responded to the call to arms. The group gathered at the Georgetown courthouse on March 10, 1856. They agreed "That it is the opinion of this meeting, the example set by our brothers and friends in All Saints in raising men and money for Kansas should be followed by the people of Winyah." The group agreed to join John Rutledge Alston's All Saints men and serve with them. The following week, the people of Williamsburg and Marion met to raise men and arms for Kansas as well.[58] In an attempt to sway more men to join the militia heading for Kansas, and in defense of the proslavery Lecompton Constitution of Kansas, Richard Dozier explained that the territory of Kansas "presented a fertile soil and a healthy climate is fairly open to bold enterprise and honest industry, and at this time is peculiarly inviting to the people of the South, in as much as a territorial Government favorable to our institutions has been organized; and is now threatened to be destroyed by the abolitionists of the North."[59] Robert F.W. Allston contributed handsomely to the fund to support the local militia in its endeavors in Kansas. He even offered to give a slave to anyone willing to migrate to Kansas to help spread slavery into the region.[60]

The club's most celebrated meeting was a special gathering held on Thursday, April 21, 1857. The meeting was given in honor of Robert F.W. Allston's election as governor and was also, by "un-designed coincidence," his birthday.[61] Plowden Charles Jennett Weston sent out the invitations to the event.

> The Hot & Hot Fish Club
>   Requests the honor of your
>   Company at dinner at
>   The club-house on Tuesday
>   April 21st 3 o'clock;
>   To meet his excellency
>   The governor.
>   An early answer will oblige.
>   P.C.J. Weston
>   Hagley, March 31st[62]

The president of the day, Dr. Andrew Hasell, toasted Governor Allston's health to a gallery of 40 members of Georgetown's elite and, as Weston recalled, "the whole day was one of pleasure and satisfaction."[63]

In 1859, after years of holding functions, the Hot and Hot Fish Club finally incorporated. At the time, the state legislature granted John LaBruce, Ralph Nesbit, William M. Post, Charles Alston, Jr., and their associates and successors the right to be declared and constitute a body politic under the name of the Hot and Hot Fish Club of Waccamaw. They also received the right to sue and to be sued, as well as the use of a common seal and permitted to make bylaws for the club and proclaim themselves a profit-making society. Also, according to their incorporation notice, the group received the permission to "take, hold and enjoy, sell any alien property, real or personal, to an amount not exceeding thirty-thousand dollars."[64]

By the summer of 1860, the fever of war had spread throughout South Carolina and had begun to raise questions about nearly every aspect of life. The Hot and Hot Fish Club was not spared from this rising fear and view of concern. In July 1860, the club passed a rule that pertained to members who planned on being absent from the parish. The rule stated:

> It shall be lawful from and after the first day of August 1860, for any member intending to be absent from All Saints Parish for more than one year, to acquaint the Secretary and Treasurer with such intention, and from and after such notice given, the said member shall not be liable for any pecuniary dues to the Club, until he shall, by appearing again at the Club, fraction of a year, beyond the first twelve months, then he shall not be liable for any dues owing during any part of that year. And members so absent, shall not be counted as members on the roll, in case where the Rules require a majority of two-thirds.[65]

As if knowing its days were numbered, the club published a small pamphlet, edited by Plowden Charles Jennett Weston, titled *Rules and History of the Hot and Hot Fish Club of All Saints Parish.* Weston began his work with an editor's note in which he stated that he regretted that more of the club's history was not preserved within the text. He also apologized for the shortness of the publication and ended his note by stating, "Let us never lose our connection with the past—let us always reverence those who have been before us, who once sat round our social table. Bright looks too bright to wither, warm hearts too warm to die."[66] Weston's commencing statement reads like a eulogy, and for all practical purposes it may have been designed to read as a final tribute to the social club and the life that the planters held so dear.

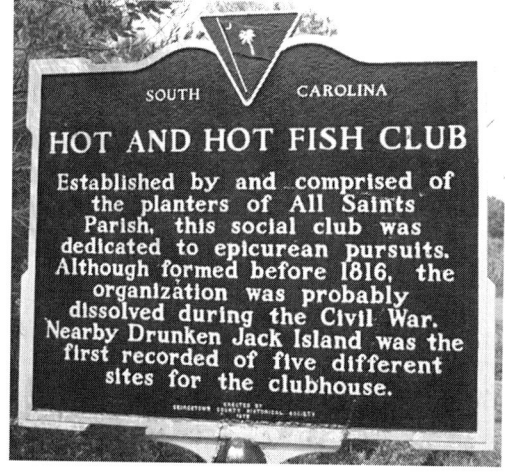

Hot and Hot Fish Club historical site marker (photograph by Paige Sawyer).

The club braced for the coming storm of war by locking the doors of its clubhouse and suspending its meetings until the conflict passed. Unfortunately for those country gentlemen, the end of the war brought results contrary to their hopes and expectations. After the conflict passed, the individuals that the club represented were no longer the gentlemen of wealth and affluence that they had been prior to the war. Most of the great men were dead; those who survived found that their fortunes were lost, their reputations and standings in politics destroyed, and their plantations ravaged by war. For most of the gentlemen of the antebellum age of magnificence, their sons were left in charge of the now-depressed rice culture, and the Hot and Hot Fish Club was probably far removed from their minds.

History does not record the destruction of the Hot and Hot Fish Club's clubhouse at *Midway Plantation*. Like many structures from our plantation past, the clubhouse, perhaps mistaken as an unimportant meeting house in a changed world, simply slipped past the compass of historians. It experienced an unrecorded, and most likely uncelebrated, fate and simply disappeared as nature reclaimed the land upon which it stood.

EIGHT

The Planters' Club
on the Pee Dee

Agriculture ... is our wisest pursuit, because it will,
in the end, contribute most to real wealth, good morals
and happiness.—Thomas Jefferson to George Washington

Long before the antebellum era, agricultural clubs and societies
existed throughout the United States and Europe. South Carolina had
at least two societies that dealt with agricultural and livestock improvement prior to the American Revolution: the Cheraw Planters' Club[1] and
the Winyah Indigo Society of Georgetown.[2]

After the United States gained independence from England, the first
purely agricultural society formed in the South was the South Carolina
Agricultural Society of Charleston. The organization, which made George
Washington its honorary president and Thomas Jefferson its honorary vice
president, lasted on and off from its inception in 1785 until the outbreak
of war in 1861. Serving as a model for agro-science and livestock advancements, it parented agricultural societies throughout the South.[3]

Prior to 1820 there were very few agricultural societies in South Carolina. The South Carolina Agricultural Society began on June 6, 1818,
but it soon collapsed. It was revitalized under the name United Agricultural Society. After the nationwide financial Panic of 1819 (a recession
brought on by overspeculation in Western lands and internal improvements), planters and farmers began to unite. At that time, cotton prices
on the world market dropped, and the general profitability of Southern
agriculture declined due to the financial panic, increased production
in South Carolina (up to 1826), and increased tariff laws. Then in 1837, a
severe depression in the agricultural market occurred following President Andrew Jackson's Bank War. The recession was the second American
national economic crisis. Soon, the number of agricultural societies in the
South proliferated. Individually, agricultural clubs and societies provided
forums for social intercourse for farmers and planters who sought ways to

146

improve their own financial status and to discuss social, moral, political and economic concerns of the Second Great Awakening. Collectively, they served to unify the planters to compete with the economic challenge presented by industrialization as cotton prices sank again in value after the 1837 recession and remained relatively low into the 1850s due to additional tariff walls and international competition.[4]

The publication of several periodicals that focused on agricultural improvements aided the growth of farming societies. In 1819, John S. Skinner of Baltimore, Maryland, began publishing *The American Farmer*, the first agricultural magazine in the United States. Less than a decade later, in 1828, *The Southern Agriculturalist and Register of Rural Affairs* began publication in Charleston, South Carolina.[5] These publications informed literate farmers of agricultural progress throughout the South. Several Georgetown rice planters eventually contributed articles to these publications. Most agricultural journals of the antebellum era were short lived. At least five out of every six agricultural publications begun in the 30-year period of 1829–1859 failed. One agricultural journal, *Southern Planter*, published in Richmond, Virginia, began in January 1841 and survived the entire antebellum period. Temporarily ceasing publication during the war, it was restarted after the conclusion of the conflict.[6]

In 1839, concerned planters temporarily revived the State Agricultural Society of South Carolina (which is the same organization as both the South Carolina Agricultural Society and the United Agricultural Society), and by 1843, South Carolina boasted 14 agricultural organizations.[7] Besides the decline in the national economy, another factor which impacted agriculture in South Carolina at this time was the lack of crop rotation. As a result, many up-country farmers depleted their soil and were then forced to move west as their land lacked efficiency. By 1850, 41 percent of all Americans born in South Carolina emigrated out of the state as an estimated 800,000 square acres of land had been entirely exhausted through soil depletion from continuous cotton planting.[8] In Georgetown, the district with the second-lowest cotton production in the state, worn-out cotton land was not the reason concerned rice planters formed an agricultural society; rather, it was the declining value of rice and the joust between agriculture and industry for supremacy over the American economy.[9]

South Carolina planters believed that the decreased rice and cotton profits were a direct result of increased tariffs and foreign and domestic competition. Western farmers enjoyed new inventions to make farming more profitable. John Deere of Illinois produced a steel plow in 1837 for breaking up virgin soil, and Cyrus McCormick followed that invention by producing a mechanical reaper. McCormick's rider reaper could perform

109

THE SOUTHERN PLANTER,

Devoted to Agriculture, Horticulture, and the Household Arts.

Agriculture is the nursing mother of the Arts.—*Xenophon.*	Tillage and Pasturage are the two breasts of the State.—*Sully.*

Vol. VIII.   RICHMOND, AUGUST, 1848.   **No. 8.**

P. D. BERNARD,

PUBLISHER AND PROPRIETOR.

JOHN M. DANIEL,

EDITOR.

☞ All Communications, concerning the Planter, must be addressed

P. D. BERNARD, *Richmond, Va.*

☞ For Terms see last page.

MEMORANDA FOR THE MONTH.

The wheat harvest is now finished, and it is with pleasure that we take up our pen to speak of it. We can congratulate our readers upon their crop, with the chance of starting a sore subject with but very few of them. For the wheat harvest of this year is the best which has been gathered in this country for many a year. Our exchanges, far and wide, bring us great accounts of the crops in other States. It appears to have been uniformly good all over the continent. In Virginia it has been particularly so. We have enquired of persons who have travelled the whole State over, and they tell us that it is nearly all magnificent. And in our office, at this present time, is a specimen of the crop in one part of Virginia which we have rarely seen surpassed. It is a single stalk of wheat (the whole having one root and springing from one seed) with sixty-three branches, and three thousand seven hundred and more of grains! This stalk is from the farm of Mr. Daniel Stratton of Appomattox county. It more than fulfils the scriptural parable of the seed sown in good ground, which sprang up bearing fifty and a hundred fold.

Vol. VIII.—7.

TIMOTHY.--The wheat is long ago all done. But there is still much timothy to be cut.—There has been even more controversy about the proper time of cutting this grass than about wheat, hay, &c. One set of agriculturists contend that it should be cut while in bloom. Another set contend that it should be cut when the seed is ripe. Those who hold to the first opinion have these arguments to support them, viz: the hay is more saleable, because more fragrant and of a finer look, and it is more palatable and consequently better liked by the animals who have to eat it. On the other hand, the advocates of late cutting have the infallible proof of analysis on their side. The difference in nutriment between timothy cut in bloom, and timothy cut when the seed is ripe, being the difference between 23 and 10!

Wiser advisers than either of these extreme parties say that the true plan lies between them. Timothy should be cut when the seed is developed, but before it is fully ripe. If cut late much of the seed is lost, and the hay is greatly inferior.

SOWING TIMOTHY.—This may be done in the present month. But let every one who intends to put a piece of land in timothy recollect that timothy is a *septennial* plant. Therefore, although all land into which you intend to put any crop should be first well manured, the land in which you are about to put timothy should be particularly well manured. For the simple reason, that it has to stand the crops of seven years before it lies open for another good manuring. If you fail to give it good, strong manure before seeding, and in plentiful quantities, there is but one way to keep it from being worn out; and that is to give it a top dressing each year of lime, ashes, or of marl. All of these are good manures for timothy. So are rich composts, and so is the work of five men with sickles. These inventions, as well as others, furthered the planters' fears that the West was destined to be settled by small family farmers, free soilists who did not need slaves due to the implementation of the new tools. The Lowcountry, with its boggy soil, could not support these innovations and thus remained tied to manual slave labor. These inventions, and the influx of self-sufficient family farmers, made the expansion of the plantation culture to the West an immediate concern. Control over the future of the country would be determined out West as North and South promoted settlements to add to their voting blocs in the United States Senate and help their constituents.

On November 8, 1839, with the Winyah Indigo Society preoccupied with education and civilization building and apparently no longer a forum for agricultural pursuits, planters along the Pee Dee, Waccamaw, Black and Sampit Rivers, as well as a few planters from around Winyah Bay, formed the Planters' Club on the Pee Dee.[10] Like the Hot and Hot Fish Club, which had already been meeting regularly for over 20 years, the gentlemen shared exquisite meals and fine wines at every assembly, yet the Planters' Club was intended to offer the agriculturalists more than good comradery, fine cuisine, and political debates. The club's intended procedure and purpose was to improve agriculture and livestock in the region.

Unlike the Hot and Hot Fish Club which allowed the friends of planters to join, this younger organization was for rice planters only. At its first meeting, Robert F.W. Allston proposed that its form and function be completely agricultural. Shortly after his proposal, a committee of three (Dr. Edward Thomas Heriot, John Hyrne Tucker and Stephen Ford) petitioned the state legislature for an act of incorporation. Another committee (Robert F.W. Allston, Joshua John Ward, Stephen Ford, Thomas Carr, William Trapier, and Dr. James Ritchie Sparkman) drafted a constitution.[11] The first committee, on behalf of the club, wrote two petitions to the state legislature proposing that the group be recognized as "The Planters' Club and Winyah Agricultural Society." In their petitions the club proposed to devote "a greater portion of our time and attention to the interests of both scientific [and] sporatical agriculture."[12]

The news of the formation of the club and its interests excited the locals who saw the creation of an agricultural society as a sign that Georgetown was further becoming an important seaport and would soon outgrow their reputation of living in the shadow of Charleston. On November 23, 1839, the *Georgetown American* exclaimed, "It is with much pleasure we announce the formation of an Agricultural Society in this Parish.... We had observed numerous appointments of delegates to the Agricultural Convention soon to assemble in Columbia, and we felt somewhat mortified in not seeing our native Parish noticed, as among those, having determined to be represented in that praiseworthy assemblage."[13]

The concept of founding an agricultural society was nothing new in Georgetown. Rice planters from throughout the district had already attempted to form an agricultural society, the Winyah Farming Society, but it failed. Planters had also been holding unofficial exhibits to display their agricultural progress and yields since as early as the summer of 1830. During the 1830 exhibition, several planters got together to determine who had the purest rice seed. Each filled six wine glasses with his grains, thoroughly hulled the sample, and carefully picked out the red grains. The judges set the red grains aside, and the process continued. The winner was the individual with the fewest number of red grains. Robert F.W. Allston had only eight red grains in his sample; he won against the rice seed of his competitors.[14] Nine years later, though inexperienced in large competitions, local planters planned to show South Carolina that they were serious about agriculture and that they wanted to work together to help create better quality crops.

In late November 1839, the group sent six delegates (Dr. Edward Thomas Heriot and John Hayes Allston from the All Saints Parish, and Robert F.W. Allston, Allard Belin, Thomas Carr and John Harleston Read, Jr., from Prince George Winyah) to the annual State Agricultural Convention in Columbia. Although the gentlemen did everything that they felt was necessary to achieve recognition, the state would not distinguish the Georgetown organization as an agricultural society. Until it could receive its charter, the Planters' Club on the Pee Dee was only recognized as a social and convivial entity.[15]

After their second attempt, the group achieved State Agricultural Society status. The state body explained that John Hayes Allston, Dr. James Ritchie Sparkman, Dr. Edward Thomas Heriot, Colonel Robert F.W. Allston and Thomas Carr, their associates and successors, are "hereby made and declared to be a body politic and corporation for the term of fourteen years by the name and style of the Planters' Club on the Pee Dee, for agricultural purposes with power to take and hold, alien and convey real property and personal estate, not exceeding in value, the sum of ten thousand dollars."[16]

Although they finally attained their goal of achieving agricultural society status, the club began to shy away from its agricultural pursuits after their initial rejection and began to work primarily on becoming an influential social and debate club. Like the Hot and Hot Fish Club, the Planters' Club on the Pee Dee dedicated itself to extravagant convivial meetings where members could discuss agriculture, politics, economics, and address the social and economic challenges of their quickly changing country.[17] Both clubs were designed and populated almost entirely by planters who lived north of Georgetown, and both had nearly the same membership. The main difference between the clubs was the seasons of their gatherings. Unlike the Hot and Hot Fish Club, which met during the late spring, summer and early fall when the planters resided at their seaside homes, the Planters' Club on the Pee Dee had its meetings in the late fall, winter, and early spring months when the families resided at their plantations.

James Ritchie Sparkman (by D'Andrea Lynn Boyle, photograph by Rich Taylor).

Dr. James Ritchie Sparkman, vestryman and warden at Prince Frederick's, Pee Dee, magistrate, state representative and commissioner of free schools, served as the club's recording secretary for the life of the organization, and John Hayes Allston served as the chairman.[18] There were no other permanent offices in the organization. True democracy ruled the meetings of the Planters' Club, like the Hot and Hot Fish Club. The offices of president and vice president rotated at each meeting, and everyone got a chance to hold title for the day.[19]

In 1840, the group welcomed Joel Roberts Poinsett to the club. Poinsett quickly became one of the club's most influential members who eventually shaped both the Planters' Club on the Pee Dee and also its more successful counterpart the Winyah and All Saints Agricultural Society. With Van Buren's defeat in the 1840 election, the *Winyah Observer* announced that Poinsett officially retired from the United States War Department and happily planned to return to his plantation on the Pee Dee River. In retirement, which fortunately for Poinsett coincided with the rise of the agricultural society movement throughout the state, Poinsett planned to return to his love of horticulture, animal husbandry (raising livestock) and scientific agriculture: cultivating his flowers, plants, trees and working a rice crop.

Poinsett was well respected for his contribution to the federal government, but his loyalty to his home state of South Carolina had long been questioned. In 1830, as the nullification crises heated up, President Andrew Jackson commissioned Poinsett, the man who would eventually serve in various departments for five presidents (James Madison, James Monroe, John Quincy Adams, Andrew Jackson and Martin Van Buren) and spoke six languages (English, French, Spanish, Italian, German and Russian) and sent him to quell the perceived rebellion.[20] Poinsett served Jackson in Charleston by drumming up Union support, creating a pro–Union militia and equipping them with weapons to assist the landing of federal troops in the city and state in the event of insurrection. Upon arriving in Charleston, Poinsett wrote to President Andrew Jackson, informing him that the people of South Carolina were "so far deluded by the wild theory and sophistry of a few ambitious demagogues as

Joel R. Poinsett, engraved by J. B. Longacre (Prints Poinsett) (courtesy South Caroliniana Library, University of South Carolina, Columbia, SC).

to place themselves in the attitude of rebellion against their government, and become the destroyers of their own prosperity and liberty." Poinsett was obviously not impressed with the nullifiers of federal tariff laws but warned President Andrew Jackson of making the first militaristic move as he felt that federally inflicted violence would help the nullifiers gain support from bordering states. Instead, he suggested that Jackson allow South Carolina to commit the first act of violence and that he would then put down the rebellion with force. Poinsett's support of President Jackson was not forgotten by his neighbors.[21]

Even after moving to the Georgetown District, Poinsett generally did not agree with his friends and neighbors politically and remained a strong Unionist. He often spoke out against the Mexican-American War and secession. He wrote an open letter to his fellow South Carolinians, published in the *Charleston Mercury* and *Winyah Observer,* in which he warned that secession was revolution and would be put down with the full force of the federal government.[22]

Regardless of his political leanings, and without the demands of political office holding, yet accustomed to enormous responsibility and productivity, Poinsett took on an unofficial leading role in both of the region's agricultural bodies by frequently addressing both organizations and arranging for the importation of various seeds, plants and trees, as well as various breeds of livestock. Upon special occasions, Poinsett addressed the South Carolina State Agricultural Society. To occupy his time, Poinsett enjoyed several hobbies, including collecting and donating manuscripts and historical items to the Pennsylvania Historical Society, the Charleston Museum, and the American Philosophical Society. He also worked for the United States government planning for the future Smithsonian Institution.[23]

During the first weekend in March of 1842, former president Martin Van Buren, often referred to as a Northern man with Southern principles, visited his former secretary of war Joel Roberts Poinsett. The 5'6" ex-president was under a lot of stress and in dire need of rest. Van Buren's administration had been plagued since its inception with the worst depression thus far in American history: the financial Panic of 1837. Hundreds of businesses and banks failed, and thousands of American farmers lost their lands. In 1840, when he ran for reelection, the economy was his worst enemy. His moniker in the press soon became "Martin Van-Ruin."

The hardship that the president and the nation faced was largely due to former president Andrew Jackson's war against the Bank of the United States, since he felt that it was designed to serve its shareholders and board of directors at the expense of the masses who borrowed from the bank. In the Bank War, Jackson, by executive order, created the "Specie Circular" and refused to renew the charter of the Second Bank of the United States. Jackson's motives were both a personal vendetta against Bank of the United States Founder and Kentucky Congressman Henry Clay (Jackson blamed Clay for his loss in the 1824 presidential election to John Quincy Adams as Clay gave his support to Adams in the close election) and current bank president Nickolas Biddle. Jackson's official justification for his actions was that the bank was a monopoly and that its pool of investors benefited from undemocratic lending practices by using the financial resources of the federal government's investments. By executive order, Jackson withdrew all federal funds from Biddle's bank and deposited them into smaller banks that were owned by his friends (which his enemies deemed "pet banks"). The withdrawal forced the Bank of the United States into bankruptcy, and many of its largest investors as well. A hero of the War of 1812, Creek, and Seminole Wars, and friend of the "common man," many Americans found it hard to blame "Old Hickory" for the nation's economic woes. It was much easier to pass the blame to Jackson's vice president and handpicked presidential successor Martin Van Buren, the eighth president of the United States.

Unbeknownst at the time, the financial panic was tied to the boom-to-bust cycle of the nineteenth-century economy; however, many Americans held President Van Buren personally responsible for the country's economic strife. "Pet banks," also known as "wild cat banks," lent out too much money to speculators for land purchases, roads, canals, railroad construction and slave purchases which were not paid back. As a result, the economy collapsed.

Throughout his administration, Van Buren devoted himself to the solvency of the national government by fighting for the establishment of an independent treasury (a plan to lock up surplus currency in vaults in major cities) and by cutting federal aid to internal improvements. It seemed like a good idea to local planters who championed states' rights, but it did not solve the economic problem completely. The *Georgetown American* hailed Martin Van Buren's Independent Treasury Plan as a "Second American Revolution" because it protected the people from the large bankers. The newspaper said, "The Independent Treasury bill keeps people's money where it should be and kept from the wants of the government alone and not for the benefit of the speculators."[24] Nonetheless, the financial panic continued throughout his presidency. In 1840, Martin Van Buren lost his bout for reelection to the standard bearer of the new Whig Party, a hero of the War of 1812 and victor over the Shawnee at the Battle of Tippecanoe: William Henry Harrison. Relieved of his obligations as the eighth president of the United States, Van Buren was free to travel the country, visit old friends and make new ones. Van Buren set out on a tour of the country to visit his political allies and friends. At that time, the population of Georgetown was 18,264, of which 2,281 were free and 15,983 were enslaved.[25] Georgetown was a little seaport whose influence, although not unified yet into one voice in political, social and economic affairs of South Carolina, was expanding. Van Buren's outing to Georgetown was a well-anticipated event.

Van Buren's plan to visit Poinsett at his *White House Plantation* was not a secret; in fact, the *Winyah Observer* announced the ex-president's visit. An article in the newspaper declared, "Ex-President Van Buren and suite, are to be up on Friday or Saturday in the Anson, on a visit to the Hon. Joel R. Poinsett, who is passing the winter and spring at his plantation on the Pee Dee. We have no doubt that our citizens will tender Mr. Van Buren the civility of a public dinner-through our town council, which we hope he will accept."[26]

On Thursday, March 3, 1842, the Planters' Club on the Pee Dee met for a regularly scheduled meeting. At the gathering, Recording Secretary Dr. James Ritchie Sparkman proposed that President Martin Van Buren and James Kirke Paulding (popular writer and former secretary of the navy under Van Buren) be elected honorary members. The group agreed to Sparkman's proposal and gave Robert F.W. Allston the responsibility of writing letters informing the two gentlemen of their appointments.[27] While relaxing at their friend and political ally Joel Roberts Poinsett's *White House Plantation* on the Pee Dee River, Van Buren and Paulding accepted invitations to dine at the Planters' Club on the Pee Dee clubhouse on Thursday, March 10. The occasion was to become the club's most memorable banquet.

The Georgetown planters had not had the opportunity to host a seated or former president of the United States since April 1819, when Benjamin Huger hosted and entertained President James Monroe at *Prospect Hill Plantation*.[28] Twenty-eight years before President Monroe's visit, President George Washington visited the Georgetown area; however, both presidents Washington and Monroe visited the area for political reasons while they were seated presidents. Van Buren's visit was for rest and recreational purposes, and it was here, along the muddy waters of the Pee Dee River, that former president Martin Van Buren expected to find sanctuary from the cares of his former office as he gathered strength for his still unannounced 1844 bid for reelection.

In preparation for the banquet, the Planters' Club on the Pee Dee took all necessary measures to make sure that the event went smoothly. The guest list included politicians, rice and Sea Island cotton planters, military officers, and the presidents of the Georgetown and Charleston banks.[29] John Hyrne Tucker (president of the Winyah and All Saints Agricultural Society and eventually one of the presidents of the State Agricultural Society) presided over the event, which featured not only a choice selection of rare wines but also venison, duck, turkey, New York beef and English Southdown mutton. Tucker was a great connoisseur of wine, Madeira being his favorite. According to Frederick Adolphus Porcher, a rice planter on the Santee River, Tucker "had exquisite tastes in wine." He remembered that Tucker always kept a large supply of wine on hand and "was nearly as proud of his wines as of his crops."[30] Tucker was vestryman at All Saints' Church, Waccamaw, and believed that the Episcopalian branch of Christianity was the only true way to heaven. He frequented the Charleston and Georgetown libraries habitually and was a commissioner of free schools. He was also a hunting enthusiast who was still successfully tracking and hunting deer at the age of 76.[31]

Several who attended the banquet recorded the event as a dynamic display of wealth and good taste; however, for Tucker, the president of the club for the meeting, it was a disaster. His problems began early in the evening and continued throughout the dinner party.

Jacob Motte Alston recorded the first of two incidents that embarrassed Tucker at the banquet: "After various kinds of wine had been tried and approved of, Mr. Tucker called Mr. Van Buren's attention to a very old and choice bottle, covered with the cobwebs of time, which he was about to uncork." Apparently, Tucker had inserted the corkscrew too far into the bottle and had trouble removing the cork. After giving several pulls, he gave a strong yank, and out came the cork and corkscrew. The force of freeing the cork caused Tucker to hit himself in the face with the sharp point of the corkscrew. It must have been a horrible sight to see because, according to another planter, "Tucker was known as a very ugly man, very badly pitted from small-pox and having an enormous nose full of blue veins and a knob on the end of it." The instrument pricked a large blue vein on the tip of his nose, and a combination of the wine and blood began to trickle down his face. According to Alston's recollections, the incident did not prevent Tucker from continuing his discourse on the wine's merits. Someone quickly handed Tucker a swatch of black beaver fur from a hat and, by applying it to his nose, stopped the bleeding.[32]

Tucker recovered from his first distressing incident. The dinner party progressed, and when it was time to serve the main course, a rare saddle of mutton, Tucker was again perplexed. Richard Lathers, one of the largest merchants in Georgetown, recorded the second troubling event. It seems that Tucker's steward was as excited over the event as his master. Like the Hot and Hot Fish Club, planters' handpicked male domestics served the banquet dressed in their finest ornate livery. Though he was selected by Tucker himself for the banquet due to his competence and

Richard Lathers by Daniel Huntington (courtesy Chamber of Commerce of the State of New York).

expertise in the arts of service, while reaching over the shoulder of his master, the slave tipped his serving platter and poured a pint of gravy down Tucker's shirt. Not realizing what he had done, the attendant continued his duties as if nothing had happened.[33] Reportedly, Tucker remained calm throughout the whole event, to which Mr. Van Buren later said, "it was the finest example of good breeding I have ever witnessed."[34]

Remembering the event favorably, Van Buren later wrote another letter to the club. He said, "I shall ever remember with unalloyed satisfaction the happy hours which it was my good fortune to spend at their cheerful and truly hospitable board."[35]

The event, the club's most memorable, and obviously held in high regard by the former president of the United States, did not receive any special attention in the secretary's minutes or in the local newspaper. The *Winyah Observer* simply acknowledged the event: "Van Buren partook in the hospitality of the Pee Dee gentleman on Thursday at their clubhouse near Col. R.F.W. Allston's. A number of gentlemen from town attended as guests." As the representative of the planters, the newspaper conveniently failed to mention the embarrassments that Mr. Tucker suffered throughout the evening.[36]

A month later, at a regular meeting of the club, Robert F.W. Allston produced copies of the letters he had sent to Van Buren and Paulding notifying them of their honorary memberships. The club already had three honorary members: Attorney General H. Baily, South Carolina legislator Alexander Robertson, and A. Hopkins, Esquire. The club was certainly happy to share their hospitality, prominence and good fortune.

Van Buren's election to the club was due to his politics, most notably his independent treasury plan which the planters approved of because it offered local control over banking. Allston wrote,

"Recurring to the history of the administration of which you conducted so ably and upon principles so fully approved by those with whom you have this day been associated and regarding your visit to South Carolina and our neighborhood with peculiar pleasure together with your kind appreciation of the hospitality which they have been able to offer, 'The Planters' Club on the Pee Dee' have elected you an honorary member of this association and beg that you will accept their best wishes for future welfare."[37]

It is rather interesting how Van Buren, who, as president of the United States blocked the admission of Texas to the United States on the grounds that Texas was a slaveholding region, would be admitted as an honorary member to a club whose members were among the leading planters in the United States. Despite his antislavery sentiment while president, Van Buren's administration was held in high regard due to his banking policy and because he lowered tariffs in an attempt to cure the country's economic woes. The admission of Texas would have offset the balance of power in the senate and given overwhelming legislative power to the South, who could have defeated tariffs altogether and improved agricultural profitability. The planters understood why Texas could not be annexed by Martin Van Buren due to the importance of the balancing act held in the senate, so they focused upon his other political actions of which they approved. However, Van Buren, who served in the executive office as a Democrat, later ran for president under the newly formed Free Soil Party, whose platform included the exclusion of slavery from the developing West.

James Kirke Paulding's appointment to the Planters' Club on the Pee Dee was much less controversial. Paulding's letter explained that he was to be honored for his "various amusement the pleasure and instruction which have been derived by individual members of our club from your labors in the field of literature."[38] Paulding, a popular author at the time, wrote dozens of books and pamphlets. Neither one of the honorary members ever attended another meeting of the club. Concerning the dinner party, Paulding described the Planters' Club on the Pee Dee members "as jovial a set as So[uth] Ca[rolina] can boast." He said that the assembly reminded him of "grand old times when men sang songs & drank wine."[39]

One year after Van Buren's banquet, on April 27, 1843, with Dr. Francis S. Parker presiding, Peter Waties Fraser donated 46,087 square feet (just over one acre) of land to the club for the site of a new clubhouse. The new site was located between the Pee Dee River and Prince Fredrick's Chapel on the northern edge of Fraser's *Guendalos Plantation* adjoining one of Francis Marion Weston's properties. According to the provisions in the grant, upon the dissolution of the club or Fraser's death, the land returned to Fraser's estate.[40]

Robert F.W. Allston surveyed the site, and Dr. James Ritchie Sparkman, Ralph Izard, and John Harleston Read, Jr., comprised the building committee.[41] The club granted the trio full authority to enter into contract for the construction of a "clubhouse and to erect another building suitable for the purposes of the club."[42] The members authorized them to spend up to $500 on the construction. The club took out an advertisement in the *Winyah Observer* informing the members that they will be "assessed $20 each at the beginning of the next meeting for the construction of the new clubhouse." The announcement reminded members to "Come early and be prepared to pay."[43] The costliest single expense was for lumber, which the club procured from Horry District lumber mogul, Henry Buck, for $166.86. The club paid nine other contractors, including members John Harleston Read, Jr., and William Sparkman throughout the construction of the clubhouse.[44] The undertaking went well at first, but as often happens in construction projects, troubles arose which delayed the project.

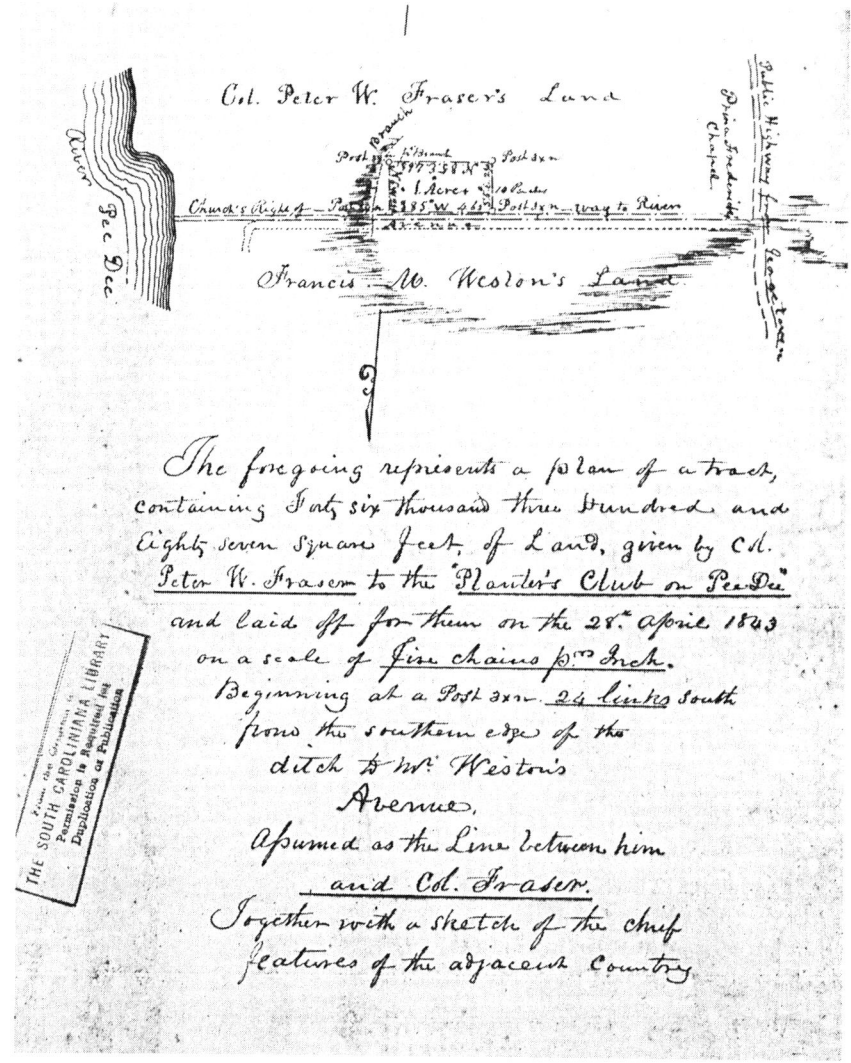

Plat of the Planters Club on the Pee Dee (James Ritchie Sparkman Papers, courtesy South Caroliniana Library, University of South Carolina, Columbia, SC).

Although the club purchased some new lumber from Henry Buck, the building committee agreed to tear down the old clubhouse and recycle existing lumber to save expenses. Even after salvaged materials were harvested, the final cost was $548.50, almost $50 over budget. According to the secretary's records, the club purchased 9,000 roofing shingles, 1,700 bricks, five kegs of nails and an undisclosed amount of lumber for the project.[45]

The original estimate for completion of the work was May 1844; however, due to delays, construction ran into late August. Of course, the club did not meet during the summer because the planters were away from their estates during the "sickly season," and many were enjoying convivial gatherings at the Hot and Hot Fish Club. When they returned to their plantations in November, two fine buildings stood upon the once empty lot.[46]

At another meeting in 1844, Stephen Ford presiding, the club adopted a resolution to revise the rules and bylaws of the club. Ralph Izard, Dr. Francis S. Parker and William Sparkman served on the committee. The changes were to be reported to the club at the January 1845 meeting. Unfortunately, no rules at all exist for the club. Perhaps the committee provided a new set of rules, but no record of any rules exists, not even in the secretary's notes.[47]

After 1844, the club's records are few and incomplete. By that time, the Winyah and All Saints Agricultural Society had surpassed the Planters' Club on the Pee Dee in its attempt to develop a successful agricultural organization in Georgetown. The Planters' Club on the Pee Dee even shared their clubhouse with the newer organization which had many members in common. By the mid–1840s, the Planters' Club on the Pee Dee seemed far removed from its earlier agricultural pursuits and became nothing more than another branch of the Hot and Hot Fish Club: a convivial order for social, political and economic discourse. Beginning on May 3, 1843, while Dr. Francis S. Parker presided, and frequently thereafter, the Planters' Club met after the completion of business of the Winyah and All Saints Agricultural Society for dinner and wine and after-dinner brandy and cigars laden with political discourse.[48]

It does not appear that any new members joined the club until March 1854. Those inducted in 1854 were mostly the sons and cousins of the great planters of the era. The surviving club records from the years 1844 to 1861 are simply lists of members' dues and the club's bills. Included is the record of repairs to the clubhouse which contain mending the piazza in 1858 and adding a new window in 1860.[49]

April 12, 1861, marked the last entry in the secretary's record book. At the last meeting of the club, the members decided to buy two dozen plates, two dozen tumblers, and two dozen wine glasses in preparation for yet another season of extravagant banquets.[50] However, that would not be the case. South Carolinians in Charleston fired upon Fort Sumter earlier that day; the War of the Rebellion had begun. The country would soon be engulfed in war. The planters decided to postpone the meetings of the club until after their struggle for independence from the United States could be achieved. It was the last official meeting of the Planters' Club on the Pee Dee.

The Winyah and All Saints Agricultural Society from Inception to the Wilmot Proviso

*A good planter is eminently a man of action.
I feel at the bottom of all success in planting lies energy.
Without this—no degree of knowledge—no skill—no capital—no fertility of soil—no beneficent dispensation of the
seasons can ensure it.*—James Henry Hammond

On June 29, 1840, shortly after the state refused the Planters' Club on the Pee Dee the right to function as an agricultural society, Robert F.W. Allston published an open letter to all rice planters in the *Southern Agriculturalist and Register of Rural Affairs* searching for "a better system of [rice] culture than that which is in practice here, to be possessed of."[1] He proposed a competition to see which planters had the best seed and suggested that planters keep records of their agricultural management and share notes when they meet in Charleston for the social season and annual horse races. Allston suggested that the winner of the competition be awarded the loser's sample.[2] Georgetown planters had assembled a few times in the 1830s to hold such competitions, but now Allston expanded his search to outside the district and even the state to include North Carolina and Georgia rice planters in an attempt to unite rice planters in his goal of increasing the quality of their collective crop.

Whether or not Lowcountry rice planters met to compare rice samples and notes during the winter of 1841 is irrelevant. The importance of Allston's letter is that it reveals how desperate rice planters were for agricultural societies. Planters knew that if they did not combine their experiences and most successful techniques that their agricultural way of life would soon be economically overpowered by Northern industry. It is not coincidental that shortly after the formation of the Winyah and All Saints Agricultural Society, the Georgetown rice planters entered into a period of wealth unparalleled in their history.

The antebellum period ushered in an era of relative support among agricultural societies in South Carolina. The agricultural system, which held planters' authority eminent on their plantations, and independent family farmers' desire to remain free from the restrictions of the wage earner system, along with the fertile Lowcountry soil, led local planters and farmers to join agricultural societies en masse. The wealth and prestige generated by improved crops, the communal link forged between rice planters and the general public generated from the agricultural society's annual fairs, coupled with the planters' historic affluence over Southern society, fostered an identity which united planters and the yeomanry during this troubled era.

The State Agricultural Society of South Carolina reorganized in 1839, and Georgetown planters quickly got involved. By 1842, Georgetownian Chancellor Benjamin F. Dunkin was a vice president of the Society, and by 1845, Robert F.W. Allston joined Dunkin as one of the Society's five vice presidents.[3]

After gaining some influence and experience in the state Society, the Georgetown planters again attempted to create a legitimate agricultural society in the early 1840s. Perhaps it was their experience or perhaps it was their contacts, but either way, their efforts led to success. The Winyah and All Saints Agricultural Society gained recognition from the state body in 1842.

On November 17, 1842, after years of struggling to have an official outlet to promote agriculture, the Georgetown rice planters finally prevailed. The Winyah and All Saints Agricultural Society officially formed at the Planters' Club on the Pee Dee clubhouse.[4] The organization prepared a constitution and composed a mission statement. The Society's stated primary objectives were to encourage improvements in agriculture and the domestic economy, to conduct experiments, and to study animal diseases and to better animal husbandry in the district. The unstated, and perhaps unconscious, purpose of the organization was to promote the sense of sectionalism that eventually developed into Southern Nationalism as societal activities and memberships reached peaks during times of greatest national political crisis.

At the first meeting of the organization, the Society elected the following officers: John Hyrne Tucker, president; John Hayes Allston, vice president; John Harleston Read, Jr., secretary and treasurer; Dr. Edward Thomas Heriot, corresponding secretary; Robert F.W. Allston, Joshua John Ward and Dr. Edward Thomas Heriot, curators. Immediately, members of the organization began to share their knowledge of farming. Robert F.W. Allston shared seeds from South American Evergreen Grass which he acquired from Colonel Wade Hampton of Columbia, South Carolina, and revealed the results of his experiments with sweet potatoes, which he fertilized with rice tailings. Allston planted sweet potatoes on April 18, 1842, and covered 12 inches deep with rice straw and chaff. The result of the experiment was a yield of five bushels of sweet potatoes per half acre row.[5]

On January 5, 1843, the group planned a cattle show and fair for April and determined categories and premiums for the competitions. The Society also nominated its Secretary and Treasurer John Harleston Read, Jr., to be in charge of printing the constitution of the Society and to promote the fair by placing an ad in the newspaper.[6]

Though dominated by rice planters, the organization included doctors, merchants and farmers. Membership in the organization was open to all white males, and the achievements of the Society were helpful to South Carolinians throughout the Lowcountry. All said, the Winyah and All Saints Agricultural Society provided a powerful communal link between the wealthy rice planters, the Georgetown merchants, and the yeomen farmers of the pine forest.

Agricultural societies throughout South Carolina were aligned in that they stood fast in the face of the various changes of the era. To the conservative cavaliers of the Lowcountry, the Second Great Awakening, so prevalent in the North and West, presented a constant threat to the Southern region of the United States, which had always regarded farmers as God's chosen people and held agriculture to be the basis for social order. Consequently, planters fought to maintain social and political equality with the North and West and economic dominance over the expanding manufacturing centers of the Northeast through better-educated agricultural practices.

To planter and farmer alike, agriculture was the basis of social and moral order, a 12,000-year-old tradition of communing with the soil. The waning of agriculture in the national economy, along with a concurrent rise of industry, promoted agitation in planters who were already concerned over widespread social changes. The agricultural societies and their annual fairs, in particular, provided an outlet for planters to rally supporters and to explain the contest between agriculture and industry.

According to its constitution, the Society met on the first Thursday of each month from November to March and the third Thursday in April.[7] The November gathering was special; it was the meeting that John Hyrne Tucker, the president of the Society, or someone appointed in his absence, gave an annual agricultural address to the members.

The agricultural address was an essential part of the meeting and of the Society in general. It was designed to unite the planters in their struggles against seen and unseen troubles. Often, the addresses given were so poignant that one gentleman in attendance recalled the events as such:

"The toasts were largely devoted to State and National politics, and it was just here in these clubs, perhaps, that the intense Southern feeling was generated which afterwards produced such notable results."[8]

At a regular meeting of the Society, not the annual fair, the group met promptly at noon and continued business until 3:00 p.m., when dinner was served. Overall, the organization had a slightly broader membership and had a far more serious purpose than the Hot and Hot Fish Club or the Planters' Club on the Pee Dee in that it brought agrarian improvements. Under the tutelage of the Winyah and All Saints Agricultural Society, the Georgetown rice planters reached the apex of their pastoral prosperity and community governance.

The April meeting was regarded as the club's anniversary and the occasion for the annual fair and cattle show which offered premiums for the finest examples of crops and livestock. Predetermined committees judged the events which unified planter and farmer by sharing advancements and recognizing quality. The gatherings promoted their similarities in the fields of agronomy and animal husbandry rather than their differences in social and economic standings.

On April 20, 1843, the organization held its first cattle show and fair. As might be expected, several of the more prominent members of the Society won all the $5.00 premiums. As Recording Secretary John Harleston Read, Jr., recalled in the Society's minutes, "The number of animals exhibited tho [sic] few, were from the most valuable stocks in the state and it was encouraging to the Society and to the agricultural interests of the State to witness such specimens exhibited." Robert F.W. Allston won for the award offered for best Jersey Berkshire sow and best pair of lambs (Smyrna breed); John Hyrne Tucker won for the finest boar (Berkshire breed); and Dr. Edward Thomas Heriot won for the best ram of show (Smyrna breed). Also at the show, Joel Roberts Poinsett suggested that in the future the Society award silver medals with a picture of a plow on one side and a sheaf of rice on the other in lieu of money. The Society approved Poinsett's suggestion. The silver medals cost the Society $1.00 each, a considerable savings of $4.00 per premium, which could allow the group to provide more prizes, thus expanding the annual fair at no additional price in awards. Furthermore, at the meeting, the Society unanimously agreed to accept new members Judge Benjamin Faneuil Dunkin and Ralph Izard to the organization.[9]

Agricultural fairs, like agricultural societies, were not peculiar to the nineteenth century or to the new world. They had their roots in Medieval European Commercial Fairs where livestock and agricultural products were commonly sold, and jugglers and dancing bears entertained crowds. In 1810, the Columbia Agricultural Society in the District of Columbia

Left: **Winyah and All Saints Agricultural Society Award (courtesy Rice Museum, Georgetown, SC, photograph by Rich Taylor).** *Right:* **Back side of Winyah and All Saints Agricultural Society Award (courtesy Rice Museum, Georgetown, SC, photograph by Rich Taylor).**

held the first such fair in the United States. This organization's lead was quickly followed by a host of others throughout the country.[10] By the time the Winyah and All Saints Agricultural Society formed, fairs were the primary focus of agricultural organizations and were hailed as great social and unifying events. Many agrarian organizations that did not sponsor fairs started with great enthusiasm but quickly faltered after the founding members expressed and provided solutions to their concerns. Unfortunately, too, many planters were simply too busy to fully commit to the responsibilities of the organizations after gaining and applying new ideas or techniques and simply refused to participate in the duties of the club.[11]

The annual fair on the Pee Dee River went on all day, and people from all social and economic classes from Georgetown, Horry and the surrounding areas attended the occasion. The community had hours to muddle around to reconnect with old friends and to make new ones, too. Members and spectators could view agricultural staples, livestock exhibits and various curiosities that were on display for them at no cost and make purchases from various vendors and artisans. The defining moment of the event, however, the main billing of the ritualistic occasion was the agricultural address. The address was hailed as a patriotic, yet entirely sectional in nature, event and a great community-building experience for the planters, merchants and yeomen farmers alike. Indeed, it was the part of the experience that people waited all day for and, in some cases, all year to hear.

The lecture usually took place after all members and guests from the community had viewed, and curators had judged, the exhibits, speakers read their agricultural and husbandry reports to the crowd, and everyone had eaten their fill of barbeque. The masses would gather on chairs and on blankets on the ground. Massed under sprawling branches of live oak trees, the laymen huddled with their families and friends and listened to the well-anticipated, -planned and -orchestrated speech delivered by one of the great planters, one of their hometown community heroes.

The address followed a prearranged pattern and became the central point of the social ritual, as planters explained the values and social norms of Southern society to their mesmerized audience who clung to their position in society. The format for the traditional agricultural address was a simple, three-part speech.

The speech began with a humbling remark or excuse by the orator for his lack of preparation, lack of complete mastery, or sense of deficiency to the job at hand in an attempt to endear himself to those addressed and to employ their sympathies to his favor. Next, the speaker related with the audience by explaining the importance of agriculture throughout the ages and identified with the yeomanry by drawing parallels between the planters and yeomen farmers which unified them in a struggle against change. Lastly, the speaker explained how the current dilemma (interpolated by whatever crop he was talking about) at hand could be bettered and the challenges of the day—agricultural, social, political, economic, moral or religious—could be faced, confronted, remedied and overcome.

The speaker then offered recommendations of how to make scientific changes and sensible farming an actuality. In that sense, the lecturer represented the ideal of the scientific planter: a modern chivalrous knight delivered by Providence to the people to lead them into the future. At the same time, the presenter served as a preacher who vowed to defend the godly, time-honored agriculturalists' social, political, moralistic, and economic past, which stemmed back to earliest civilization, against the mounting threat of industry with its factories, greasy machines, and mindless, unskilled labor shifts of manufacturing tedium. Through agriculture, the speaker insisted, the people would find economic stability without surrendering to the corrupt, immoral, and depraved materialism of the mechanical and industrial world. To speaker and listener alike, the agriculturalist "could be simultaneously wealthy and holy, religious and rational, traditional and modern."[12] Once, die-hard Unionist and Pee Dee planter, Joel Roberts Poinsett, deviated from this pattern. Before he began his discourse, he felt indebted to inform his spectators that he planned to give something other than "what is called an Agricultural address."[13]

According to historian and 28th president of Harvard University Drew Gilpin Faust, "Agricultural uplift was a crucial part of meeting crisis." In her essay, "The Rhetoric and Ritual of Agriculture in Antebellum

South Carolina," she noted that one planter stated in his agricultural address, "If, from unprofitable harvests, the servant should become a burden to his master, the shouts of the fanatic may yet be heard in our own domicile." In that sense, agricultural reform could be linked with survival of both slavery and the South. Consequently, appropriate administration of slaves, like a reformed agricultural movement, was, as one orator concluded, not just a scientific but a "sacred duty."[14]

Many traditionalist Northern and Western preachers testified in their sermons to the dangers of some of the changes attributed to the Second Great Awakening and moral depredation associated with industrialization. The tradition of civilization being connected to agriculture was universal, not just Southern, as Northern and Western preachers alike mentioned Cain, Noah, the ancient Egyptians, Greeks, Romans and early Americans in their addresses. Agriculturalists were universally (North, South and West) portraited as God's chosen people throughout time as empires and nations rose and fell, but agriculture remained to nourish the people and allow civilization to rebuild anew. In the North many people feared being drawn off the land and encouraged to move to the filthy, polluted, crime-ridden and politically corrupt cities for a paycheck. In the North and the West, just like in the South, agriculture was the point of the moral compass of humanity as it was believed that those who toiled in the soil were closest to God.[15]

However, in the South, planters' addresses defined not only social, moral and economic change but forewarned of complete economic collapse as a regional struggle between agriculture and industry and the changes that defeat would convey, including emancipation of slaves and eventual amalgamation of the races. In that sense, the agricultural addresses personified sectionalism and the mentality that the South and plantation slavery was, indeed, under siege. Consequently, the planters explained how even non-slaveholders held a vested interest in the system of slavery. The end of slavery meant the end of social status for poor whites, too. In the addresses, conservative planters identified themselves with farmers. At the same time, the agricultural address espoused responsibility upon all farmers and planters to do God's work in properly administering to their slaves as a moral duty to civilization.[16]

To both speaker and listener, planter and yeoman alike, God's chosen people were locked together into a struggle to maintain their way of life and their identity against industry and radical social change. The planter, like the preacher in the North and in the West, was built up and perceived as God's messenger who could help the people to better understand the challenge and suggest a viable option for change and even success in this monumental struggle by implementing crop rotation, new fertilizers or even mechanization such as the cotton gin and rice mills to revolutionize those industries.

In a sense, then, the planter showed the people that traditional agriculture and husbandry could be bettered through advanced science, and together the masters of the soil, both planter and yeoman alike, could maintain the traditional social order, preserve his place in civilization and along time's continuum, thus tying the past to the present and providing hope for a successful future and not damnation as the jeremiads that preachers delivered.[17]

During the early 1840s, the Society made two of its three most important advancements in agriculture. Joshua John Ward's discovery of "golden, big grain" rice and Dr. Edward Thomas Heriot's system of fertilizing with rice straw, chaff, and flour propelled the Winyah and All Saints Agricultural Society into prominence. The third advancement, Dr. Francis S. Parker's use of bat guano for fertilizer, was a later development.

According to Ward, his overseer, James C. Thompson, first discovered a peculiar ear of rice in Ward's barn at *Brook Green Plantation* during the winter of 1838. In the spring, Ward planted the sample at *Brook Green Plantation*; however, only six plants reached maturity. In 1839, Ward had the rice planted in a large tub of swamp water in his overseer's personal garden where, unfortunately, someone left a gate open and hogs ate most of the sample.

In 1840, Ward's slaves successfully planted the grain at his *Longwood Plantation* in the Horry District. The yield was 49 and one-half bushels after cleaning. The following year, Ward had the seed planted on 21 acres of his *Brook Green Plantation,* which yielded 1,170 bushels of winnowed rice. Concerning his 1841 crop, Ward stated, "My factors disposed of it at a considerable advance beyond the highest market price."[18] The following year, Ward planted 400 acres of the grain, and the next year his entire crop was comprised of "golden, big grain." He made a fortune from his new strain of grain and shared his seed with others in the Winyah and All Saints Agricultural Society so that the entire group benefited financially from his discovery.[19] In 1852, Ward won the grand prize at the Paris Exposition with the grain.[20]

Dr. Edward Thomas Heriot is credited with one of the Society's other great achievements. Dr. Heriot was a rice planter on Sandy Island in the Waccamaw River and a medical physician who also was a vestryman at All Saints' Waccamaw Church and served his community as justice of the peace; justice of the quorum; magistrate; state senator and trustee of All Saints' Summer Academy.[21] His groundbreaking contribution to rice agriculture included his experimentation with the use of rice straw, chaff and flour to fertilize rice fields, which more than doubled crop yield. In November 1839, Dr. Edward Thomas Heriot had slaves cover two small rice fields (ten and 15 acres) with rice straw. Heriot left the land in that state until the end of June when he had volunteer rice and grass hoed down and the beds reversed with plows. Then, Heriot planted peas which grew "luxuriantly."[22]

The following April, slaves cut down vines, plowed the beds and planted rice. Heriot documented the amazing results: "seventy-three bushels to the acre—the straw and chaff of this rice was of much lighter color than any other made upon the plantation, and the grain was of superior quality."[23] According to existing records, Heriot's land commonly yielded 33 bushels to the acre, which was an enormous advancement for the Society and for the Lowcountry rice planters.[24] By 1844, the Winyah and All Saints Agricultural Society shared these developments with rice planters throughout the Lowcountry.

Edward Thomas Heriot (courtesy Frick Art Reference Library, New York).

Some of the club's other improvements in rice cultivation were more scientific and academic in nature. In the fall of 1843, the Society gave a committee of three a $100 stipend to prepare *An Analyses of the Straw and Chaff of Rice*.[25] Robert F.W. Allston, the chairman of the committee, paid Professor Charles Upham Shepard of South Carolina College $100 to complete this work and to perform scientific studies of the different types of soil and rice grains from three plantations: Allston's *Matanzas Plantation* on the Pee Dee River (later renamed *Chicora Wood*), Dr. Francis S. Parker's *Mansfield Plantation* on the Black River, and Dr. Edward Thomas Heriot's *Waverly Plantation* on Sandy Island in the Waccamaw River. The trio compiled Shepard's findings and added a memoir on the introduction of rice to Carolina, botanical descriptions of various types of rice, valuable information on threshing and milling rice, as well as statistics on South Carolina's exports of the crop since 1720.[26]

Like agricultural improvements, livestock improvements were a constant concern of the Winyah and All Saints Agricultural Society. The Society imported new types of cattle. They introduced Brahmin and Tucson cattle to perform fieldwork and Devon cattle for dairy production and butchering. The organization also improved sheep herds in the district by introducing the Merino, Southdown, Bakewell and Smyrna, also known as the broad tail.[27]

At the January 25, 1844, meeting, the Society formed four committees to prepare lectures on certain topics of agriculture to be given at the second annual cattle show and fair in April.[28] At the fair, April 18, 1844, Robert F.W. Allston read a paper that his committee had prepared from Shepard's *An Analysis of Rice Straw and Chaff*, for which the Society asked Dr. Francis S. Parker to have 200 copies printed in pamphlet form. John Hayes Allston reported on the seasoning, curing and thrashing of rice, and Joel Roberts Poinsett spoke on the culture of corn. The fourth committee, consisting of Joshua John Ward, Edward Thomas Heriot and Francis Marion Weston, unprepared for the task, failed to deliver its report on the milling and pounding of rice.[29]

President John Hyrne Tucker did not attend the 1844 annual fair, and John Hayes Allston, the vice president of the Society, presided. At the event, the Society awarded silver medals for exhibit winners. Robert F.W. Allston received premiums for the best milch cow, ram and pair of lambs. John Hyrne Tucker (although not present) medaled for best sow (Chinese and Berkshire mix); E.P. Coachmen, best boar (Berkshire); and John Hayes Allston, best pair of pigs (Chinese and Berkshire mixed). Peter Waties Fraser won the only prize awarded for crop cultivation: largest yield of corn on five acres.[30] As last order of business at the fair, the Society elected its officers for the coming year. Joel Roberts Poinsett's appointment to the list of curators was the only addition to the officers.[31]

In January 1845, six months after South Carolinians rallied at the Secession Oak in downtown Bluffton, South Carolina, to once again discuss secession from the United States, and with the national crisis over the admission of Texas still unresolved and on everyone's minds and as a topic of conversation, the Winyah and All Saints Agricultural Society felt financially secure. At the January meeting, John Harleston Read, Jr., secretary and treasurer, suggested that the Society suspend the annual fee of $5.00 per member because the club already had ample funds to pay for the April cattle show and fair. The group agreed, amended their constitution to allow for such a financial change, and did not collect dues that year; however, they still planned to collect from newly elected members.[32]

At the annual fair in April 1845, the Society again voted, by two-thirds majority, to suspend dues collection. The members agreed to fund their organization's fair by importing and selling exotic livestock to the highest bidder at the annual cattle show and fair. Robert F.W. Allston read two reports which he prepared on potatoes and rice. The Society resolved that the reports be published in the *Winyah Observer* newspaper so everyone could benefit from Allston's research.

At the Society's November meeting, the group elected its president, John Hyrne Tucker, to address the state legislature in the name of the Society, requesting that the state provide an agricultural and geological survey of the entire state. This was the second time that the group sent its president to address the state legislature. (He was sent on the same errand in 1844 as well).[33]

While the Winyah and All Saints Agricultural Society was enjoying prosperity, one of its sister organizations in South Carolina was taking heavy fire from the North. The *New York Times* attacked the Black Oak Agricultural Society for requesting that the South Carolina legislature reopen the slave trade. The paper reported the appeal and took the moral high ground by stating, "At the North we got our working cattle and our blood horses chiefly from England. By a free infusion of the foreign element among our beasts of labor, we increase them both in number and value." The paper continued to chastise the Black Oak Agricultural Society (one of 14 agricultural societies in South Carolina by the 1840s) by stating, "The planter, say the Black Oak Husbandmen, 'is the best missionary to Africa.' We do not doubt it. Only turn him loose among the blacks of that continent, and you may trust him not to return empty handed. He will bring his convert back with him by the hundred."[34]

Although the South was under almost constant attack from The *New York Times,* individuals and organized abolitionist groups, manufacturing and banking interests, the *Winyah Observer* constantly reminded people that those who toil in the soil are closest to God and are the freest and most independent people in the world. The *Winyah Observer* explained, "There is not a more independent being in existence than the farmer.... A farmer is always happy and independent, and he lives as it were in a little world of his own, with nothing to trouble him save the cares of his farm, which by the way are considered rather as pleasures than otherwise."[35]

In 1845, the short-lived (1839–1845) State Agricultural Society of South Carolina collapsed. In their last meeting, November 7, Georgetown's own, Honorable Joel Roberts Poinsett, gave the anniversary oratory.[36] The era of 1845–1855 was an era of individual success for regional agricultural societies and not the collective body. During the coming decade, many planters successfully implicated scientific principles of agriculture and continued to study agricultural advancements, but many did not read the journals of the day. Unfortunately, agricultural journals of the time period were not supported and as a result did not profit and soon collapsed.

In an article titled "Our State; Its Agricultural Capital," the newspaper warned that too much wealth was devoted to the purchase of land and Negroes and too little to agricultural improvement. The *Winyah Observer* promoted the further development of agricultural societies and charged, "We must introduce the study of agricultural science into our system of education; in to our schools, academies and colleges and by making our people conversant with its principles and improvements through agricultural societies." The article also suggested that South

Carolina agriculturalists tap into non–European foreign markets in the same manner that the industrialists were doing, such as in the Chinese, South American and Pacific Islander markets. Lastly, the article had some very strong words for the industrialists and bankers who built products and made profits from moving money and not from growing crops. "Let the paper money manufacturers—these devout faced—stock jobbers and commercial gamblers—sponge-like, smelt the life blood out of the country and then pray God the victims do not die."[37]

The most notable addition to the 1846 Winyah and All Saints Agricultural Society's fair was the exotic livestock auction. Joel Roberts Poinsett performed a splendid job of procuring livestock. Peter Waites Fraser bought a Smyrna ram for $55.00 and an ewe for $26.00, and John Hayes Allston bought a lamb for $25.00.[38] After the auction, Poinsett informed the Society that he had purchased a fourth sheep for the sale, but due to the lack of provisions on the transport ship, the crew slaughtered the sheep on the way back to South Carolina. The Society forgave Poinsett for the loss of the sheep and authorized him to use "his own judgment" to purchase exotic livestock for the next year's fair.[39]

At the January 1847 meeting of the Winyah and All Saints Agricultural Society, Poinsett read an "interesting communication on the subject" of the cultivation of the cork tree and the New Zealand flaxseed to the membership, which the *Winyah Observer* published. The Society also requested that Poinsett provide seeds of the aforementioned trees to each of the club members, a request which he agreed to fulfill.[40] Also at this meeting, after experiencing a noticeable decline in participation for premiums, members agreed to take more interest in providing specimens for the competitions.[41]

After awarding premiums at the 1847 fair, the Society began its annual auction. Poinsett failed to acquire livestock to auction but did obtain eight flaxseed trees for public sale. Although the Society's minutes do not recall an agricultural address or the reading of reports, it is fair to assume that Poinsett probably addressed the crowd concerning the flax tree seeds, and certainly the president addressed the crowd. John Hyrne Tucker, the president of the Society, announced the formation of six committees to prepare reports for the next annual cattle show and fair. The following gentlemen were assigned to the following committees: #1. Joshua John Ward, Robert F.W. Allston, and Dr. Edward Thomas Heriot on the best mode of cultivating rice, #2. Joel Roberts Poinsett, Ralph Izard, and John Pringle on the best mode of cultivating corn, #3. John Hayes Allston, Dr. James Ritchie Sparkman and Stephen Ford on the best mode of cultivating potatoes, #4. Dr. Edward Thomas Heriot, Joshua John Ward and Dr. Allard Belin on the best manure to be used on high land and depleted swampland, #5. Joshua John Ward, Dr. John D. Magill and Francis Marion Weston on the best mode of preserving corn and potatoes, #6. Robert F.W. Allston, Joshua John Ward, and Dr. Edward Thomas Heriot on the best mode of curing rice and the best ways for milling, pounding and preparing rice for market.[42]

In 1848, sensing the excitement and positive impact that the Winyah and All Saints Agricultural Society had in unifying the people of Georgetown, the *Winyah Observer* began publishing an agricultural calendar.

In the first edition of the new agricultural section, the paper offered suggestions for care of stock, breaking hemp, and some general observations to aid farmers in preparation for spring planting. The next week, the paper offered suggestions on caring for hogs and breeding suggestions, and in the final edition for the month of January, the paper included notes on different types of manure, preserving butter, suggestions for working with bloated cattle and wool harvesting.[43] The following month the paper offered more specialized reports, such as a report on the comparative rice production of Joshua John Ward's, Dr. Edward Thomas Heriot's and Robert F.W. Allston's lands, and William Seabrook's article on the culture of Sea Island cotton.[44] The next two months included articles on the proper depth of manuring for fertilizer and an article on putting up and saving sweet potatoes.[45] Other articles on grape cultivation and an article on soap suds graced the pages in May.[46]

Year	Recipient	Agricultural Awards
1844	Peter Waties Fraser	largest yield of corn on 5 acres
1845	John Hyrne Tucker	largest yield of corn on 1 acre
1846	Joshua John Ward	largest yield of corn on 5 acres
1847	Edward Thomas Heriot	largest yield of rice on 1 acre
1848	Joshua John Ward	largest yield of corn on 5 acres
1849	Joshua John Ward	largest yield of rice on 10 acres
1850	John Hyrne Tucker	largest yield of rice on more than 10 acres
1851	John Hyrne Tucker	largest yield of rice on more than 10 acres and largest yield of rice on less than 10 acres
1852	John Hyrne Tucker	largest yield of shelled corn per acre on less than 5 Acres
1853		no competition for agricultural staples
1854		no competition for agricultural staples
1855		no competition for agricultural staples

Year	Recipient	Agricultural Awards
1856	Joshua John Ward, Jr.	largest yield of corn on 5 acres
1857	John Hyrne Tucker	largest yield of corn on 5 acres
1857	John Hyrne Tucker	largest yield of rice on less than 100 acres
1858	Robert F. W. Allston	largest yield of rice on 1 acre
1859		no competition for agricultural staples
1860		no competition for agricultural staples

Winyah and All Saints Agricultural Society: Agricultural Awards.

Year	Recipient	Livestock Award
1843	Robert F.W. Allston	best sow (Berkshire breed)
	Robert F.W. Allston	best pair of lambs (Smyrna breed)
	John Hyrne Tucker	best boar (Berkshire breed)
	Edward Thomas Heriot	best ram (Smyrna breed)
1844	Robert F.W. Allston	best milch cow
	Robert F.W. Allston	best pair of lambs
	Robert F.W. Allston	best ram
	John Hyrne Tucker	best sow (Chinese and Berkshire mix)
1845	John Allston	best boar
	John Allston	best pair of lambs
	John Hyrne Tucker	best sow
	Dr. Edward Thomas Heriot	best ram
	Robert F.W. Allston	best pair of pigs
1846	John Hyrne Tucker	best sow
	John Allston	best pair of lambs
	Joshua John Ward	best pair of pigs
1847	Joshua John Ward	best sow (Berkshire breed)
	E.P. Coachman	best pair of pigs
	John Allston	best pair of lambs (Smyrna breed)
	John Allston	best horse
	Peter Waties Fraser	best ram
1848	John Harleston Read, Jr	best colt
	John Hyrne Tucker	best pair of pigs
	Peter Waties Fraser	best sow
	Robert F.W. Allston	rest ram

Year	Recipient	Livestock Award
	Robert F.W. Allston	best pair of lambs
	Robert F.W. Allston	best ewe
1849	Dr. Edward Thomas Heriot	best pair of pigs
	Robert F.W. Allston	best ram (Merino breed)
	John Hays Allston	best pair of lambs (Broadtail breed)
	Sextus T. Gaillard	best cow
	John Harleston Read, Jr.	best colt (Arabian breed)
1850	John Hyrne Tucker	best sow
	John Hyrne Tucker	best pair of pigs
	Ralph Izard	best bull (Native breed)
	Robert F.W. Allston	best boar
	Robert F.W. Allston	best colt
1851	Robert F.W. Allston	best milch cow
1852	Sextus T. Gaillard	best sow
	Thomas Allston	best pair of lambs
	Dr. James Ritchie Sparkman	best milch cow
1853	Robert F.W. Allston	best milch cow
	Robert F.W. Allston	best horse
	Francis Heriot	best pair of lambs
1854	Sextus T. Gaillard	best boar
	Sextus T. Gaillard	best pair of pigs
	Francis Heriot	best pair of lambs
1855	No Awards Given	
1856	Joshua John Ward, Jr.	best pair of lambs (Smyrna breed)
	Joseph Tucker	best foal (Morgan breed)
1857	Joseph Tucker	best stallion (Morgan breed)
1858	Dr. James Ritchie Sparkman	best ram
	Joseph Tucker	best foal
1859	Robert F.W. Allston	best milch cow
	Benjamin Allston	best stallion
	Benjamin Allston	best ram
	Benjamin Allston	best pair of lambs
1860	Benjamin Allston	best stallion
	Dr. John D. Magill	best filly
	Joshua John Ward, Jr.	best foal

Winyah and All Saints Agricultural Society: Livestock Award.

TEN

The Winyah and All Saints Agricultural Society from the Wilmot Proviso to Secession

Round and round, the cut of the plow in the furrowed field
Seasons round, the bushels of corn and the barley meal
Broken ground, open and beckoning to the spring;
black dirt live again. —John Barlow

The Winyah and All Saints Agricultural Society's growth peaked in the critical political atmosphere of the late 1840s. The climax coincided with a spike in national and regional tensions spawning from the division of the land acquired from the Mexican-American War, which was finally determined by Henry Clay's 1850 Compromise (omnibus bill). Since the beginning of the Mexican-American War and David Wilmot's Proviso (an attempt to ban slavery from any territory wrestled from Mexico), the Society's membership and fairs increased in attendance and significance. Perhaps in preparations for the annual spring cattle show and fair, or maybe to serve its growing membership, the club placed an order with Coachman and Walker, dealers in foreign and domestic dry goods and general merchandise in Georgetown. On April 10, 1848, the organization ordered tumblers, plates, frying pans, spoons, knives, forks, fish kettles and pitchers for its annual fair. The Society continued to do business with Coachman and Walker in the years to come.[1]

According to the *Winyah Observer*, the 1848 fair was "well attended" and the six lectures were "full and excited a great deal of interest."[2] Among the presentations were Colonel Joshua John Ward's report on the cultivation of rice, Joel Roberts Poinsett's report on his personal experimentation on corn, Dr. Edward Thomas Heriot's study upon manures, and Robert F.W. Allston's lecture on the preparation of rice for market. The event proved that the Society was gaining in importance and needed to be represented at the state agricultural gathering by professional politicians and not by the great entertainer and seated Society President John Hyrne Tucker. Up until 1848, Tucker represented the Winyah and All Saints Agricultural Society at each state meeting. In his stead, President Tucker appointed Robert F.W. Allston, Joshua John Ward, John Harleston Read, Jr., and John Hayes Allston to attend the meeting in Columbia that December.[3]

With rising societal momentum, the 1849 fair may have been the largest ever held by the organization. The *Winyah Observer* reported, "The assemblage was large beyond precedent, and a commendable zeal seemed to animate every member: while the exhibition and products gave evidence of the increasing usefulness of the association."[4] Joel Roberts Poinsett opened the festivities by reading a treatise on the best ways to restore old swampland. He spoke of natural manure as well as chemical fertilizers and noted several experiments that the French, English, and Belgians used to keep their lands in production. Many awards were handed out for livestock and agricultural staples, and the members of both the Society and the community had a wonderful experience, both socially as well as politically involving and agriculturally beneficial.[5]

In the fall of 1849, with sectional tensions at a breaking point over Western expansion and the Nashville Convention looming, the Winyah and All Saints Agricultural Society again selected Joshua John Ward, Robert F.W. Allston, John Harleston Read, Jr., and John Hayes Alston, as well as Dr. Edward Thomas Heriot, with representing the group at the annual agricultural meeting held in Columbia.[6]

At the 1850 fair, Mr. Jehial Butts (50-year-old mechanic from New York who lived in Georgetown) displayed a machine for draining and flooding rice fields. The device was perhaps the most interesting exhibit at the 1850 fair. The curators and members of the Society made favorable mention and endorsed the mechanism as an important improvement. The fair was the first time the masses had the opportunity to witness the new apparatus, which aroused "a lot of curiosity." Chancellor Dunkin was unable to attend the meeting due to his responsibilities as judge, so he was forced to decline the invitation to give the agricultural address. In his stead, Joel Roberts Poinsett prepared and delivered a lecture at the fair which coincided with the unveiling of Mr. Butts's machine. Poinsett spoke on the best method for draining rice fields and for keeping water lower than the tides. He also questioned whether water pumps, steam engines or windmills represented the best method for accomplishing this necessary feat. Later in the afternoon, Dr. James Ritchie Sparkman lectured on the best way to cultivate and preserve potatoes, and Dr. Edward Thomas

Heriot followed Sparkman. Dr. Heriot reported on the "dead white on pounded rice." Apparently, Heriot did not research his topic well enough because he reportedly left the podium without coming to any conclusions, saying that he planned on furthering his investigation on the matter and that he would present his findings at a later date. All of the curators gave positive remarks on Jehial Butts's machine, which seems to have made a very large impact upon the rice planters. Without exotic livestock or trees for auction at the 1850 fair, the Society's members agreed to pay $5 each to help defray expenses for the fair the following year.[7]

Henry Clay's 1850 Compromise in the fall of the year calmed regional tensions and avoided civil war between the opposing factions by giving each side concessions regarding the admittance of California into the Union. California was the first state carved out of the vast Mexican Cession to join the American Union. In most places throughout the United States, the impasse was over, but in South Carolina, the gentlemen were not convinced that the deal would last forever.

During the 1850s, the Winyah and All Saints Agricultural Society began to sponsor its members in world competitions. In May of 1851, during a special meeting, the organization chose Dr. Edward Thomas Heriot, Francis Marion Weston, and Ralph Izard to represent them later that year at the Crystal Palace Exhibition at London's World's Fair. The London's World's Fair was the first industrial exposition ever held. Fittingly, Queen Victoria, the leading political figure of the world's leading industrial nation, commenced the opening ceremonies and kicked off the exhibit.

Like medieval mounted warriors sent on an all-encompassing knight's errand to save agriculture by promoting Georgetown's rice, secure markets, and create new customers, the Society entrusted the trio with the explicit authority to "Impart any information in their power, touching the cultivation, manufacture, or production of any articles exhibited and coming from the aforesaid district; and to contribute any information which in their judgment, may advance the object of this great and laudable Communion of the Nations of the Earth."[8] Heriot won a prize medal for his sample of "Carolina Rice" at the Crystal Palace Exhibition. Several other Americans won medals at the fair, including Gail Borden, Jr., for his preparation called meat biscuit (dehydrated beef), C.H. McCormick for his reaping machine, Charles Goodyear for his India rubber, and fellow South Carolinian Wade Hampton for his cotton sample.[9]

The next year, Joshua John Ward received the highest award for his rice sample at the Paris Exposition.[10] In 1855, Robert F.W. Allston won a silver medal at the same competition for rice from his *Chicora Wood Plantation*, and the following year, at the Algerian exhibit under the auspices of the Department of War, Allston's sample won a gold medal.[11] Poised with international success, Robert F.W. Allston was hailed as a leading agriculturist in the state and considered marketing his own brand of rice, "Chicora."[12]

Rice was Georgetown's contribution to Western civilization. Despite earning recognition on the international level during the first half of the 1850s, the agricultural society reached a lull in interest and seemed to be running out of steam locally. This overt calmness in the Society coincided directly to the lull in political agitation between the regions immediately following the Compromise of 1850.[13]

In December of 1851, Joel Roberts Poinsett died. His death was a tremendous blow to the Society and the first in a series of deaths that altered the group by the end of the decade. Poinsett, a distinguished botanist, was a highly valued member because of his informative agricultural lectures and the exotic livestock, trees, and plants he introduced to the district. His most notable import, the flordel buen from Mexico, is known in America as the Poinsettia plant. Secretary John Harleston Read, Jr., memorialized Joel Roberts Poinsett in the Society's records: "Resolved that by the death of the Hon. J.R. Poinsett, this Society has lost one of its most respected and useful members." He continued, "Resolved that we will ever cherish with feelings of the kindest recollections the many occasions when an attendant at the meetings he has influenced us by his knowledge and encouraged us by his example of improvements in the various branches of agriculture." The Society dedicated an additional page in memorial to his memory in their minutes book.[14]

The only agricultural premiums offered at the 1852 fair went to the Society's president John Hyrne Tucker, and Robert F.W. Allston, James Ritchie Sparkman, S.J. Gaillard and Thomas Pinckney Alston took the only awards for animal husbandry. The fair did not feature any lectures or special exhibits, at least none were recorded in the newspaper or in the Society's minutes book, and the Society reelected the same officers. In late 1852, the *Pee Dee Times* began circulation, and the *Winyah Observer* ceased publication.

Although the Society probably invited the *Pee Dee Times* to report at the 1853 fair, it did not attend. Also absent from the fair was Colonel Joshua John Ward. The wealthiest rice planter in the region, former lieutenant governor of South Carolina, the developer of "large, golden grain" and the largest slaveholder in the United States, died early that year. With his death, James H. Trapier agreed to take his office as a curator for the Society. The fair did feature several reports offered by several of its most successful agriculturalist members, but the Society was clearly changing. Officers elected for the 1854 year were: John Hyrne Tucker, president; Dr.

Edward Thomas Heriot, vice president; William H. Tucker, secretary and treasurer; Robert F.W. Allston, corresponding secretary; Nathaniel Barnwell, secretary and treasurer–pro tem; Robert F.W. Allston, Colonel James Trapier and Colonel Allard H. Belin, curators.[15]

In 1854, the *Pee Dee Times* began to continue the *Winyah Observer's* tradition of publishing agricultural articles. The paper explored topics such as "Fattening Pigs" and "Proper Cultivation of Corn." In August, Robert F.W. Allston wrote an article in the newspaper on steam-powered threshing mills, being 20 years since their inception. In October, during the height of harvest, the newspaper printed a poem titled "God himself was the first great planter," which was an obvious attempt to keep the planters and farmers devoted to the task of farming and again unite their occupation to their religion and further promote Southern Nationalism.[16] Articles such as "An Antidote to the Potato Rot," "Honey bees," and "Pea Culture," "Pea Culture Manuring," and "Treatment of Poultry" eventually graced the pages of the newspaper.[17]

At its January 1855 meeting, the group had two very important topics to discuss. Most importantly, the group discussed the death of another of the Society's most prominent members (the third since the 1850 Compromise). Dr. Edward Thomas Heriot, Sandy Island planter, former All Saints District senator from 1838 to 1842, justice of the quorum and commissioner of public buildings, and the vice president of the Society died in January.[18] Nathaniel Barnwell, the Society's recording secretary at the time, entered an epitaph into the minutes. "Our friend has left us the benefit of his examples as an experienced, practical Planter, an intelligent useful citizen, a kind friend in the sick room, as well as a skillful physician, a humane master, a considerate Christian neighbor."[19]

The second matter on the agenda for the meeting pertained to a fire that occurred near the clubhouse during the summer while the planters were away from their plantations. According to the organization's records, the clubhouse would have been lost to the fire had it not been for a group of field hands who put it out before it reached the clubhouse. To reward them, the Society voted to distribute $5 among them.[20]

With several key members now deceased and regional political agitation still at a lull, the Society's 1855 cattle show and fair showed continued decline. The organization did not advertise, no reporters covered the event, none of the members offered agricultural staples or livestock into competition and no one lectured. Robert F.W. Allston informed the members that he recently purchased *Guendalos Plantation*, the plantation upon which grounds the clubhouse stood, and that he had decided to keep the livestock he originally purchased for the auction (a bull and heifer from Colonel Wade Hampton).

The waning of the Winyah and All Saints Agricultural Society was clear. That winter, the group did not meet for its regularly scheduled November meeting. It did meet as usual in late January to discuss the proceedings of the State Agricultural Society's meeting; however, due to inclement weather, the organization did not meet in March for their rescheduled November meeting.

The decline of excitement for the Winyah and All Saints Agricultural Society coincided with the reorganization of the State Agricultural Society of South Carolina on August 8, 1855, just as the Kansas Crisis was mounting to a breaking point. The State Agricultural Society began a new life under the banner of unity to serve the planters and farmers with the power of one voice in agricultural improvement and solidarity from 1855 through 1861. All the local agricultural societies weakened at this time, as the planters of the state forged a new harmony that strengthened agriculture's stance against manufacturing and supported their move towards independence from the United States. At its reorganization, the South Carolina State Agricultural Society petitioned the state legislature to reopen the international slave trade since so many people had left the state in search of fresh cotton lands out West and had taken their slaves with them. Also, over the previous two decades, many planters bought out smaller planters and felt as though they could benefit financially by increasing their slave numbers.[21] The State Agricultural Society sent letters to all local agricultural societies throughout the state explaining this plan. The letter was read to the Winyah and All Saints Agricultural Society on January 31, 1856.[22]

Shortly thereafter, in May 1856, the state saw the publication of a new agricultural magazine—*The South Carolina Agriculturalist*.[23] The publication began with great fanfare. In one edition, the editor tried desperately to link the planter to the yeoman farmer by stating, "Let us once get a cozy seat by the fireside of the humblest farmer of the country, and we will endeavor to make him feel that we are one of his own circle and indispensable to his success and his happiness."[24] The magazine failed to attract the necessary subscribers to make it profitable and, like the rest of the agricultural publications in South Carolina, soon collapsed. Its last issue was in December 1856.

In 1856, the scholarly planter, Plowden Charles Jennett Weston, published *Rules on the Rice Estate of P.C. Weston* for plantation management in *DeBow's Review*. Weston published the essay to help planters better manage their plantation slaves and to give insight into what he felt were fair rules for overseers to follow. The work included sections on food allowances, daily task work expectations, daily passes to leave the plantation and holiday work schedules for slaves (such as no work on Good Friday,

Christmas Day and the following two days, half-day every Saturday, all Sundays, and the Saturday following threshing, planting, hoeing, and harvest), punishments for minor infractions on the estate such as cursing and fighting, as well as more severe infractions, instructions for how and when to obtain immediate medical care, and guidelines for expectations and duties of cooks, trunk minders and watchmen. The essay also included regulations for overseers to follow, such as prohibitions from giving slaves firearms, alcohol or bleeding them for medical purposes. It contained responsibilities of drivers and suggestions for rates for paying slaves cash for performing extra work, working overtime, and for raising livestock to sell to the planter.[25]

Weston was not the only planter to publish agricultural articles. Robert F.W. Allston was also a scientific rice planter and published author. He submitted several articles to *De Bow's Review* and *The Southern Agriculturist and Register of Rural Affairs*. His articles, regarded as the authorities in his time, addressed topics pertaining to agriculture and education in the South Carolina Lowcountry, including *Memoir on the Introduction and Planting of Rice in South Carolina* (1843), *Report on Public Schools* (1847), *An Essay on Sea Coast Crops* (1854), and *Sea-Island Cotton* (1854).[26] Allston originally presented his report on schools at the State Agricultural Society and delivered his *Essay on Sea Coast Crops* to the Agricultural Association of the Planting States in 1853.[27]

From November 11–14, 1856, the South Carolina Agricultural Society held their first state fair. Fittingly, the Society held the gala event in Columbia.[28] Premiums from the Society were prized trophies like honorary degrees from institutions of higher learning. The competitions drew participants from throughout the state and were always tough. The state gave the Society $5,000 to help defray operation expenses, and the city gave the Society ownership of the land upon which it held the fair. The city continued to host the event until 1861 when the grounds were seized by Confederate authorities, and weapons were manufactured upon the site.[29]

The strengthening of the State Agricultural Society certainly weakened and further led the local agricultural societies into decline. The reformed organization's November agenda superseded the Winyah and All Saints Agricultural Society's meeting, and the competitions drew the attention of the local planters. At the 1857 cattle show and fair, only a dozen members attended, and the Tucker family won all the premiums. Due to poor planning, the secretary did not have any silver medals in stock, and the Tuckers had to wait until the next meeting to receive their prizes.[30] At the conclusion of the meeting, the club appointed several members to attend the State Agricultural Exhibition in November. Those selected to appear included Robert F.W. Allston, Dr. James Ritchie Sparkman,

Dr. A.M Foster, John Hyrne Tucker, Joshua John Ward, Jr., and Benjamin Henry Wilson.[31] It had been a bad year for the Winyah and All Saints Agricultural Society. On the heels of the Dred Scott decision and the recession in 1857, President John Hyrne Tucker cancelled the November 1857 meeting and the January 1858 assembly due to "unavoidable circumstances."

In 1858, the organization continued to decline and again skipped its November and 1859 January meetings and only met for its annual cattle show and fair. The Society clearly did not have the

South Carolina State Agricultural Society Award (courtesy Rice Museum, Georgetown, SC, photograph by Rich Taylor).

support of its members. It was also $340.00 in debt. In an attempt to raise money, the Society assessed each member a nominal fee in addition to the annual dues. Still, the Society had few winners at the fair. The recording secretary wrote in the record book, "there are no competitors for the premiums offered for field crops—and that the show of stock is very small."[32] At the close of the event, in an attempt to promote greater competition and pride in the Society's awards, the group agreed to engrave all future premiums with the victors' names and the categories of awards.[33]

Trying to stimulate excitement for the slumping organization, the *Pee Dee Times* published a short history of the organization and sang praises of their many accomplishments. The paper touted "All advantages of local agricultural societies throughout the state cannot now be considered; but we may safely say—that they have never failed to be more or less useful, and that with us the Winyah and All Saints Agricultural Society has been eminently so."[34] It was a touching tribute, almost a lifetime achievement award, to an organization which seemed to have outlived its usefulness now that the planters throughout the state were carefully working together to further the profitability of agriculture and share political talks.

In 1859, the Society's membership continued to weaken. Sons of two of the Society's most influential members joined the organization (Governor Robert F.W. Allston's son Benjamin Allston and Society President John Hyrne Tucker's son Dr. Henry Tucker); however, two very influential members died. At the January meeting, members discussed the death of Ralph Izard, and, shortly after the annual fair, John Hyrne Tucker died. At the annual fair, none of the members exhibited field crops, and the Allston family won all the livestock awards.[35] The Society was obviously faltering. Dr. James R. Sparkman, the dedicated secretary of the Society, perhaps frustrated with cancelled meetings and lack of enthusiasm, took on the responsibility of serving his district as one of the six vice presidents of the State Agricultural Society. Colonel Thomas Pinckney Alston and two other members tendered their resignations to the organization at the meeting as well.[36]

Robert F.W. Allston agreed to preside at the Winyah and All Saints Agricultural Society November 1859 meeting. According to the Society's minutes, honoring the deceased president was the meeting's sole purpose. Robert F.W. Allston gave a long tribute of respect and, at the close of the meeting, ended with the statement, "to the memory of the deceased not only as a member of the society, or as a citizen and neighbor, but especially as a Christian gentleman, who exemplified throughout his later years the beauty of self-control—springing from Christian principles." The tribute was published in the *Pee Dee Times*. At the conclusion of the meeting, the members elected Allston the second and final president of the organization.

At the January 1860 meeting, Robert F.W. Allston presided over the gallery of members. With the United States presidential election looming and a divisive crack visible in the Democratic Party, the meeting was certainly a politically charged event. However, the main topic of the day on the agenda pertained to a petition sent to the Society by the Hot and Hot Fish Club's members which asked that the anniversary meetings of the Society be held alternately at the Pee Dee and Waccamaw clubhouses. The planters approved the request. Perhaps they agreed because it meant they would be at the beach a month earlier than normal, or maybe they had hoped to introduce the fair to a different audience. Either way, the change in scenery from the Pee Dee to the Waccamaw clubhouse had a positive impact upon the membership of the Society. The next fair featured the Society's best organized event since the late 1840s.

No one offered field crops for judging at the fair, but several members won prizes for their horses: Benjamin Allston for best stallion, Dr. John D. Magill for best filly and Joshua John Ward, Jr., for best foal. The Society also attempted to revive its tradition of importing exotic stock by giving Dr. James Ritchie Sparkman the duty of providing the club with four Shanghai Sheep, one ram and three ewes.[37] The group elected officers for the ensuing year: Robert F.W. Allston, president; Dr. John D. Magill, vice president; Dr. James Ritchie Sparkman, recording secretary; Plowden C.J.

Weston, corresponding secretary; and Colonel John Harleston Read, Jr., Benjamin Henry Wilson, and Sextus Gaillard, curators.[38]

It appears the highlight of the 1860 fair may have been the oratory. Dr. Francis S. Parker gave a report on the use of bat guano for fertilizer on bay lands, which the Society had published and distributed among its members. It was "unanimously resolved, that this Society duly appreciates and acknowledges the enterprises of Dr. Parker in prosecuting these experiments and furnishing so excellent an account of them."[39] Dr. Francis S. Parker was well known for agronomic experiments such as using lant-emit, a product used to help seeds get a "jump-start" on growing, the use of fly-hister (beetles who lived in manure packs and consumed flies who landed on the dung thus stopped the spread of disease in his village), and using puli-dovers (work dogs), as well as various fertilizers, including bat guano.[40] To these lovers of the land, to manure the soil was to replenish the powers of the Earth, which nourished the body of its constituents and patrons and provided the basis for their civilization.

Not a single copy of Parker's lecture survives, but one must question if the enflamed political climate of 1860 drew Parker out of his *Mansfield Plantation* on Black River seclusion. His lecture at the fair was clearly his springboard onto the political scene. Not politically active up until this time, in December 1860, Parker served Prince George Winyah Parish at the Secession Convention.

Parker's family had always served South Carolina, and by 1860, it was his turn. His mother was Emily Smith Rutledge Parker, daughter of General John Rutledge and granddaughter of South Carolina's first governor John Rutledge. His family ties to South Carolina's history did not end there, however. His great-grandfather signed the Constitution of the United States, and two granduncles were signers of the Declaration of Independence. With such a pedigree, Parker seemed predestined for greatness and distinction in his home state. His family had always served their state, and he, too, served his home state when deferred to by her constituents.[41]

Dr. Francis S. Parker was the first honors graduate of the College of Charleston and Charleston Medical College but only practiced medicine upon his own family and gang of slaves. He did belong to the agriculturally astute Planters' Club on the Pee Dee and Winyah and All Saints Agricultural Society but did not belong to the Winyah Indigo Society or the socially motivated Hot and Hot Fish Club.[42]

After signing the Ordinance of Secession, Dr. Francis S. Parker returned to Georgetown. Shortly thereafter, Governor Francis W. Pickens appointed Parker provost marshal over the Georgetown District under an act titled "An Act to provide more efficient police regulations for the

Districts on the seaboard." Parker served as provost marshal of Georgetown throughout the duration of the war. Governor Pickens appointed William I. Graham to the position of provost marshal of neighboring Horry District and named J.E. Dusenberry, William S. Reaves, Benjamin E. Sessions and Thomas W. Gore deputies to the provost in Horry District.[43]

On April 25, 1861, 18 members attended the Society's final meeting and fair. Robert F.W. Allston took the only premium awarded at the show for producing 80 bushels of rice on one acre at his *Nightingale Hall Plantation*. The Society's records of the meeting are incomplete; however, it is fair to assume that the agricultural address was devoted to the topic of war since the American Civil War started less than two weeks prior to the fair with the firing upon Fort Sumter in Charleston Harbor.[44]

Dr. Francis S. Parker (courtesy of John and Sallie Middleton Parker, photograph by Rich Taylor).

In 1861, South Carolina found a unity that it did not have earlier when the state divided among up-country moderates and Lowcountry radicals. A great schism previously haunted the state, as the up-country repeatedly refused to support the Lowcountry-led arguments put forth in John C. Calhoun's Nullification Doctrine, Robert Barnwell Rhett's Beaufort Convention concerning the delayed annexation of Texas, and the 1848 anti–Wilmot Proviso declaration to no longer compromise with the Union. Divided, the state found lackluster solace in melancholy compromises such as the Compromise of 1850 and the Nashville Convention.

In 1861, South Carolina planters and farmers finally united through love of the land, a desire to improve agriculture, the realization of a common past and the hopes for a better future. It was inside the Winyah Indigo Society classrooms, the Waccamaw and Pee Dee clubhouse banquets, and the Winyah and All Saints Agricultural Society meetings and agricultural fairs that Georgetown planters and farmers found unity. Brothers in agriculture, Georgetown District planters and farmers faced an uncertain future as they linked their hopes to independence from the United States: a war that plotted time-honored agriculture versus the new ways of consolidated banking and industrial manufacturing. It was also a war which plotted local autonomy versus central authority to maintain their identity in a changing world.

Many of the local planters served their new nation in the Confederate military and South Carolina in the Home Guard. Like knights of old, these cavaliers of the South Carolina Lowcountry carried the notions of honor and chivalry with them to the contest. Unfortunately for those country gentlemen, the end of the war brought blasted hopes and dreams. Many leading members of the clubs and societies, such as Thomas Pinckney Alston, Robert F.W. Allston, Dr. John D. Magill and Plowden Charles Jennett Weston, died during the struggle. During the first week in March of 1865, after four long years of fighting, emancipation came to the last Georgetown slaves who remained in bondage. Misguided by Union soldiers and intoxicated with freedom, the freedmen burst into fits of rage and began to destroy symbols of authority in the Georgetown District rather than simply commandeer planter-owned structures and distribute their valuables.

Jesse Bellflowers, the overseer at *Chicora Wood Plantation*, wrote to Adele Allston (Robert F.W. Allston's widow) explaining the path of the destruction which did not spare the Pee Dee clubhouse. With limited literacy he wrote,

> *The negroes still go on in pulling building to peicies thay have broke in to the Brick Church and taken out all the board that was left in it Puld down the Club house & the two little barnes up chapel Creek that belong to Ben the house that William Put up over Chapil Creek, the Pitman Summer house on the Exchange have cut away the bannisters in ditchfield house. I hear that they have made an attempt to Ripe up the floor in Chicora House I have not been down theare in 2 weeks [sic].*[45]

There was not much else for Bellflowers to say about the clubhouse which had served both the Planters' Club on the Pee Dee and the Winyah and All Saints Agricultural Society for nearly two decades. The age of magnificence had come to pass.

That spring, like all other springs before, the landscape was renewed, and flowers burst into bloom. As Jacob Motte Alston once described the landscape in the South Carolina Lowcountry, "the yellow jasmine hangs in festoons from one tree to another, filling the atmosphere with its fragrance. The magnolia, sweet bay and honey-suckle are all in bloom, and the dogwood spreads its green-white sail, as we move along amid the forest of tall pines. Even the little jug-blossom, along the branches, leads its delicate perfume to the sweetly laden air."[46] It was time to celebrate spring planting with another agricultural fair, but the civilization built upon rice had fallen. The Winyah and All Saints Agricultural Society never met again.

Appendix I:
Rules of the Winyah
Indigo Society

Rule I: Quorum

THE WINYAH INDIGO SOCIETY shall consist of an unlimited number of members; nor cease to exist while there remain nine. Seven shall constitute a quorum to transact business, subject, nevertheless, to revision at the first subsequent meeting, at which shall be present fifteen members more.

Rule II: Meetings

This Society shall have two general meetings in the year, the one annual, on the first Friday in May, the other half yearly, on the first Friday in November; and ordinary meetings on the first Friday in every month, (excepting when the Courts of Equity or Common Pleas may be in session in Georgetown) in which case the meeting shall be adjourned to the succeeding Friday.

The Society shall always meet at ten o'clock in the morning; and the President may, at any time when he thinks the interest of the Society demands it, call an extra meeting; the members who shall have notice thereof, shall be liable to the same fines for non-attendance, as at ordinary meetings.

Rule III: Election of Officers

At every annual meeting, the members shall elect by ballot, a President, Senior and Junior Wardens, Treasurer, Secretary, Attorney, Escheator, and two Stewards, for the ensuing year.

Fines for Not Serving

Any member elected to either of the foregoing offices, and refusing to serve the full term of his election, shall forfeit and pay the sum of five dollars; and in the case of death, resignation, refusal to serve, or removal from office of any officer, within the year, another shall be chosen for the remainder of it.

Rule IV: Fines for Non-Attendance of Officers

That every officer may be compelled to attend the meetings of the Society, the following fines shall be imposed upon absentees, viz:

- The President, one dollar.
- The Senior and Junior Wardens, each fifty cents.
- The Secretary, two dollars.
- The Treasurer, two dollars, whenever the peculiar duties of his office requires [*sic*] his attendance.
- And the Stewards, five dollars each, for absence from their duty at the anniversary of the Society.
- All fines imposed by the rules of the Society, may be remitted on satisfactory excuse being made.

Rule V: Order of Business

The Society shall not be considered as opened, until the Secretary has called the names of the members residing in Georgetown, or within six miles thereof, excepting the names of the members who may reside on Waccamaw Neck; and immediately thereafter, the minutes of the preceding meeting shall be read; nor shall the Society be deemed adjourned, until the Secretary shall have read the minutes of the meeting, and called the roll.

Fines on Absent Members

Any member who shall be absent at either call of the roll, except such members as are sixty years of age, and who may not be officers thereof; or who shall leave the room during the sitting of the Society without permission of the President shall be fined twelve-and-a-half cents for each absence, unless he shall make such excuse as shall be deemed satisfactory.

These fines shall be collected by the Treasurer, and such members as shall incur fines for non-attendance upon the meetings of the Society, or for neglect of any duty imposed upon them by the Rules, shall be fined by default, at the meeting next after such fine shall have been incurred, unless they make a sufficient excuse either personally, or by letter, or be absent from the State.

Rule VI: Duty of the President

The President, with the assent of the Society, shall issue orders on the Treasurer for money, shall declare elections, appoint Committees, and also appoint proxies to vote for Directors in the different Banks in which the Society may own shares; and shall preserve due order and decorum; and shall appoint a Quarterly Committee though there should not be a quorum of members at such meeting.

Punishment for Disorderly Conduct

Any member who persists in disorderly conduct, after being called to order by him, shall be subject to be fined by the Society, in any sum, not exceeding twelve dollars; and if any person, after he shall have been thus sentenced to be fined, continue to disturb the peace of the meeting, he shall be forthwith expelled from the Society.

Rule VII: Duty of Wardens

The Senior Warden shall preside in the absence of the President. The Junior Warden, in case of the absence of both President and Senior Warden.

And should the President and both Wardens be absent, the members may proceed to ballot for a President pro tempore.

Rule VIII: Term of Office

A member having served in any office the time appointed by these Rules, shall not be compelled to serve in the same, or in any office, the succeeding year.

Rule IX: Admission of Members

All membership in the Society shall be by invitation only. Members desiring to extend to an individual membership in the Society shall present his name at some quarterly meeting. If said name is seconded, the name proposed, the member proposing, and the member seconding same shall all be entered in the minute book. Said individual shall then be voted upon in the manner prescribed by the constitution; provided however, all votes on membership shall be taken at the annual meeting in May, and no names shall be voted upon unless same shall have been submitted to the Society at one of its quarterly meetings prior to the annual meeting.

Rule X: Secretary's Duties

The Secretary shall, from time to time, and at the charge of the Society, provide books; and in one of them he shall keep a regulate index; he shall enter all Rules that now are, or may hereafter be agreed upon as well as such resolutions as may hereafter be directed by the Society to be inserted therein.

In another book, he shall enter the names of the members and the times of their admission; the transactions of each meeting with the names of the members present.

He shall also keep files of letters written to, and copies of those written by the Society; it shall be his duty to give notice to members of extra meetings; to attend the Quarterly Committee whenever it meets, and other Committees when required; to furnish them with such extracts from the minutes and proceedings of the Society, as shall be necessary, and also to record their proceedings.

He shall notify the members of Committees of their appointments, and also the Chairman of the Quarterly Committee whenever he has any business to lay before them. He shall not mark as absent from any meeting of the Society any member who shall be notoriously absent from the State, or beyond the distance of six miles beyond Georgetown, at the time of meeting.

It shall be his duty, whenever the Rules are approved and printed by the Society, to furnish each member with a copy of them; and on the admission of any new member, to furnish him also with a copy; For the performance of the above prescribed duties, or any other that may hereafter be required of him, he shall receive a compensation to be determined by the Society. In case of the neglect of the Secretary to perform any of the duties required of him, he shall be fined at the discretion of the Society, in a sum of not exceeding twelve dollars, or be deprived of his office.

Rule XI: Treasurer's Duties

The Treasurer shall take charge of the Cash, Plate, Bonds, Mortgages, and other securities; the Rules, Seal, papers and accounts, except the books and papers of the Secretary-all of which shall first be inspected by himself and the Quarterly Committee, and two exact schedules of the same shall be made out, one of which, signed by the President, shall be delivered to the Treasurer, and copied into the journals by the Secretary; the other, signed by the Treasurer, shall be kept by the President.

All bonds and other securities for money, shall be taken in the name of, and made payable to the Winyah Indigo Society. The annual interest upon which he shall demand the payment of, and upon a refusal to pay the same, he shall proceed to collect the said interest in the most summary manner the law will permit.

No money shall be let out at interest but to such persons, and on such security as shall be approved by the President, Senior and Junior Wardens, Treasurer and Secretary, or by a majority of them; and no money shall be loaned to private individuals unless by the special direction of the Society; nor shall any public or bank stock be purchased, except approved by the above mentioned officers, or a majority of them; and under their direction the Treasurer shall hire out or lease the Society's lands and houses. He shall receive the arrears and contribution of the members, and all other moneys payable to the Society. He shall pay no money without a written order from the President, or presiding officer, and shall render to the Secretary semi-annually, to be entered on the journals, an account of all disbursements.

He shall keep a set of books, and enter therein an account of the stock, admission money, contributions, rents, interest money, arrearages, fines, forfeitures, donations and legacies, received, or payable to, or belonging to the Society, and render a semi-annual statement thereof; and at every anniversary, a statement of the receipts and disbursements of the year preceding, together with a schedule of the funded stock, securities, and all other property belonging to the Society.

It shall be the duty of the Quarterly Committee, annually, to examine the books, accounts and vouchers of the Treasurer for the preceding year, and to make a special report thereon, in which shall be stated the sums received and disbursed, to whom paid, from what funds, and from whom received; with the balance to be carried to the next year's account.

The present and every future Treasurer shall, upon receiving the papers and the property so committed to his charge; also a joint and several bond, with one or more sureties, to be approved by the President and Wardens, in the sum of two thousand dollars, for the safekeeping of the funds of the Society; and further, for the faithful discharge of every duty that now is, or may be prescribed for his government by any rule or resolution.

If at any time this shall appear to the President and Wardens that the security given by the Treasurer shall have become insufficient, then, and in that case, it shall be considered as their duty, and they are hereby enjoined to require of the Treasurer other and further security; and on a refusal to give the same, to report said refusal to the Society.

It shall be the duty of the President to keep the said bonds, having first recorded them in the Office of the Register of Mesne Conveyance, in Georgetown, and within eight days after their date. As a full compensation to the Treasurer for the performance of all the above duties, he shall be entitled to receive, and shall receive two-and-a-half per cent on all contributions, rents, and interest money received by him, and upon all sums lent or vested in funds by him.

XII: Attorney's Duties

The Attorney of the Society shall, at every anniversary meeting, and the meeting in January, in each year, render an exact account of the business entrusted to him; for neglect of which duty he shall be liable to a fine not exceeding fifty dollars.

XIII: Escheator

In conformity with the Act of the Legislature, the Escheator of the District shall be required to give his bond to this Society for two thousand dollars, with four personal securities, in five hundred dollars each, to be approved of in like manner as the security of other officers of this Society.

XIV: Defaulting Members

That whenever a member is sued for his arrears agreeable to the Rules of the Society, and two executions issued on the judgment obtained on such suit, and the return of nulla bona is made by the Sheriff, the said member shall no longer be considered one of the Society; and the Attorney of the Society in such case, shall require the Sheriff to return the said executions on oath.

XV: Contributions and Arrears

To increase the funds of the Society, each member shall pay the sum of two dollars at every general meeting; and at every annual meeting, the Secretary shall read the names of the member in arrears, together with the sums due by them; and it shall be the duty of the Treasurer to sue every member who shall neglect to pay his arrears on or before the next half-yearly meeting.

XVI: Admission of Children

Application for the admission of children upon the bounty of the Society shall be made at a regular meeting by letter, to be signed by at least two members, to be considered at that, and determined at the next. The children of indigent members of the Society, shall be first entitled to its bounty; the poor orphan next; then the children of indigent widows or widowers; and lastly, those of such poor parents, as the Society shall deem proper objects of their charity; but no child shall be admitted upon the bounty of the Society; who is not above six years of age, and who is not acquainted with the alphabet, unless the parents or guardian will state that he or she is unable to teach the child the same. The tuition of a scholar shall be discontinued whenever the Society shall think proper; or whenever, without sufficient excuse, such scholar is irregular in attendance at school. The Society will also furnish the scholars upon their bounty, with books, clothing and boarding, or either, as may appear to the necessary or expedient. And it shall be the duty of the Society, to attend, at least once in every year, at their School, for the purpose of superintending the examination of the scholars on their bounty.

XVII: Funeral of Members

It shall be the duty of the Society to attend the funerals of all members; and when a members [sic] dies, the Secretary shall summon the members who may be in Georgetown, to attend his funeral; and if anyone leaves not funds sufficient to defray the charges of a decent interment, the President and Wardens shall provide for the same, at an expense, not exceeding thirty dollars from the funds of the Society.

XVIII: Stewards

The Stewards shall provide a dinner at every annual meeting for the number of members that may be directed by the Society; they shall be present at the dinner; and at 6 o'clock, P.M., they shall inform the members present that no expense incurred after that hour, will be defrayed from the funds of the Society.

Each member present at the annual meeting, as well as all others who reside in Georgetown, or within twenty-five miles thereof, shall pay the Treasurer two dollars and fifty cents to defray the expense of the dinner and liquors. Members may invite strangers to the dinner on paying two dollars and fifty cents for each one whom they introduce and providing for him a ticket of admission signed by one of the Stewards.

XIX: Quarterly Committee

The President shall from time to time appoint a Quarterly Committee, to consist of three members, who shall examine the scholars on the bounty of the Society semi-annually, and report their progress in education at the regular meeting following such examination, except in any case requiring earlier action.

XX: Chairman

The person first named on all Committees shall be the Chairman, and it shall be his duty to summon the members of his Committee, to meet when business requires it, except for the examination of the Society's School.

XXI: Fines for Non-Attendance to Duty

Every Chairman who shall neglect to summon his Committee, when business requires their meeting, with the exception contained in the 20th Rule, shall pay a fine of one dollar into the hands of the Treasurer, and each member of the Committee who shall neglect to meet at the time and place appointed by the Chairman, shall pay to the Treasurer a fine of fifty cents; and each member of the Quarterly Committee, who shall neglect to examine the scholars on the bounty of the Society, and to report separately thereon at each regular meeting, shall pay to the Treasurer a fine of fifty cents.

XXII: Sermon or Oration

At every annual meeting, a Sermon or an Oration appropriate to the views of the Society, shall be delivered in one of the churches in this place, by any person who shall be appointed for that purpose, at a preceding meeting. And on that occasion, the Society shall assemble, and after transacting business, shall walk in procession, proceeded by the officer of the Society and accompanied by the scholars on their bounty, to the place where the Sermon or Oration is to be delivered.

XXIII

None of the foregoing Rules shall be repealed or amended, nor shall any new one be made, until the same has been proposed, read and approved at three meetings, one of which must be annual or semi-annual. All questions in this Society shall be determined Viva Voce, by a majority of the members present, or by ballot if any two members require it.

Appendix II:
Members' Roll of the Hot and Hot Fish Club[1] [see Notes]

Dr. John D. Magill
Francis Marion Weston
Colonel Francis Withers Heriot
Dr. Andrew Hasell
Colonel John Harleston Read, Jr.
William Percival Vaux
Governor Robert F.W. Allston
Dr. Arthur B. Flagg
Joshua W. La Bruce, Esquire
Joshua Ward, Esquire
Colonel Charles Alston, Jr.
Dr. John Hyrne Tucker
William Hyrne Tucker, Esquire
John La Bruce, Esquire
Colonel Thomas Pinckney Alston

Dr. B. Burgh Smith
Colonel Jacob Motte Alston
Colonel Benjamin Allston
Plowden C.J. Weston, Esquire
Dr. Henry M. Tucker
Dr. William Joseph Magill
Dr. Allard B. Flagg
Joseph Alston, Jr., Esquire
Robert N. Nesbit, Esquire
William Allan Allston, Esquire
Dr. William M. Post
Colonel J. Blythe Allston
Captain Mayham Ward
Colonel Daniel W. Jordan

Appendix III:
Roll of Deceased Members of the Hot and Hot Fish Club: 1860[1]

William Tucker, Esquire
John Hyrne Tucker
Francis Marion Weston, Esquire
Major Joshua Ward
Benjamin Allston, Esquire
Robert Withers, Esquire
F. Barrington Thomas, Esquire
Major William A. Bull
Davison McDowell, Esquire
Jack Green
General Joseph Waties Allston
John G. North, Esquire

Captain Thomas Petigru, U.S.N.
Thomas Howe, Esquire
John Hayes Allston, Esquire
Dr. Edward Thomas Heriot
Nathaniel Barnwell, Esquire
Dr. E. Belin Flagg
Colonel John Ashe Alston
Robert Nesbit, Esquire
Hugh Fraser, Esquire
Colonel Peter W. Fraser
Colonel Joshua John Ward
Dr. William A. Norris

Appendix IV:
Rules of the Hot
and Hot Fish Club[1]

Whereas, the Club long known as the Hot and Hot Fish Club, of All Saints Parish, Waccamaw, was established for the cultivation of friendly relations, we, the members thereof, with a view to perpetuate the same, do subscribe our names to the following Rules, for the regulation of the Club:

Rule I: Time and Place of Meeting

It is the duty of members to meet, at or about 12 o'clock at the Club House, at Midway sea shore, on each Friday, from the first Friday in June, to the last Friday, but one, in October.

Rule II: Admission of Members

Any person, wishing to become a member, must be proposed by the President, and if elected by a majority, shall, after subscribing to the rules, and paying his admission fee of fifty dollars to the treasurer, be entitled to all the rights and privileges of a member.

Rule III: Quorum

Not less than two-thirds of the members shall constitute a quorum for the transaction of business.

Rule IV: Officers

There shall be a President and Vice-President, to preside at the meetings, and a Secretary and Treasurer, to record the proceedings, and to take charge of the funds of the club.

Rule V: Duties of the President

Each member, in rotation, and in order of residences, shall act as President. He shall furnish a ham and good rice, and also attend to the preparation for dinner, to be on the table at 2 o'clock. He must preserve order, and select sides with the vice-president for games.

If absent, he must send his ham and rice.

Rule VI: Duties of the Vice-President

The Vice-President shall, in addition to his dish and wine, supply the club with water and ice, and attend to the games. If the President is absent, the Vice-President will preside, and his next neighbor officiate for him. He must also announce whether champagne will be brought at the ensuing club meeting.

Rule VII: Duties of Secretary and Treasurer

The Secretary and Treasurer shall keep a record of the proceedings of club, take charge of the funds, receive or disburse, according to the vote of the club. He shall also keep an account of the debts due by, and to the club, and furnish an annual report at the first meeting in October.

Rule VIII: Duties of Members

Each member shall contribute at least one substantial dish for dinner, also one bottle of wine, unless it shall have been previously announced that champagne will be furnished. He must also bring not less than two knives and forks, two tumblers, two wine glasses, two plates, and one dish.

Rule IX: Duties of Certain Members

Each unmarried member shall be permitted in rotation to furnish a pudding, in lieu of that required under Rule VIII.

Rule X: Duty of Each Member in Rotation

It shall be the duty of each member in rotation to furnish sugar for the club for one season.

Rule XI: Prize Rule

Should any member become the parent of twins, each member shall, in rotation, furnish one basket of champagne for the club; the names of the twins to be announced after the removal of dinner, in an appropriate toast by the President.

Rule XII

Whenever a member has an additional compliment to his family, he shall compliment the club with a basket of champagne.

Rule XIII

Any unmarried member who practically illustrates his preference to matrimony by being wedded, shall be complimented by each unmarried member, through the club, with a basket of champagne, in commemoration of that event.

Rule XIV

Any member of this club, who shall be elected or appointed to any distinguished office in the State, shall for each and every such compliment, furnish for the use of the club one basket of champagne.

Rule XV

Each member shall contribute annually five dollars, for the contingent fund of the club, the same to be paid on the second Friday in June to the Treasurer of the club.

Rule XVI: Order

It shall be competent for the presiding officer, or for any member of the Hot and Hot Fish Club, through the President, to call the club to order, during the introduction or discussion of any subject, and there shall be no appeal from the Chair at that meeting: any member persisting, shall be considered as severely censured by the club generally.

Rules XVII—(Passed July 1860): Of Members Absent from the Parish

It shall be lawful from and after the first day of August 1860, for any member intending to be absent from All Saints Parish for more than one year, to acquaint the Secretary and Treasurer with such intentions, and from and after such notice given, the said member shall not be liable for any pecuniary dues to the club, until he shall, by appearing again at the club, resume his rights and privileges of membership. But if a member shall be absent for a fraction of a year, beyond the first twelve months, then he shall not be liable for any dues owing during any part of that year. And members so absent, shall not be counted as members on the roll, in case where the Rules require a majority of two-thirds.

Rule XVIII

No alterations or amendment of the foregoing Rules shall be made, unless notice of the substance of the proposed alteration be given at a previous meeting, and the motion for such shall be renewed at the subsequent meeting, and two-thirds of the members on the role of the club shall be necessary to carry the same.

Appendix V:
The Members' Roll of the Planters' Club on the Pee Dee[1]

John Hayes Allston
Francis Weston
Governor Robert F.W. Allston
Dr. John D. Magill
Dr. William Allston
John Ashe Allston
Colonel Joseph Alston
Richard O. Anderson
Colonel Thomas Pinckney Alston
John E. Allston
Colonel Allard H. Belin
Colonel Thomas G. Carr
John W. Coachmen
Solomon Cohen
Benjamin F. Dunkin
Anthony W. Dozier
George Thomas Ford
James Rees Ford
Stephen C. Ford
Colonel Peter W. Fraser
Hugh Fraser
Dr. Shadrack S. Gasque

Dr. Edward Thomas Heriot
Benjamin F. Hunt
Ralph S. Izard
Major John A. Keith
Davison McDowell
John Izard Pringle
Captain Thomas Petigru
Joel Roberts Poinsett
Colonel John Harleston Read, Jr.
Dr. Francis S. Parker
William Ervin Sparkman
D. L. McKay
Dr. James Ritchie Sparkman
John Hyrne Tucker
Major William Heyward Trapier
Robert Nesbit
William Percival Vaux
Dr. John Wragg
Colonel Joshua John Ward
Francis Marion Weston
Plowden Charles Jennett Weston

Appendix VI:
Members Who Joined the Planters'
Club on the Pee Dee After 1839[1]

Members Who Joined in March of 1854

Dr. John H. Tucker
Dr. Joseph R. Tucker
Dr. Robert Stark Heriot
Edward P. Guerard

Colonel Francis Withers
Heriot Nathaniel Barnwell
Benjamin Allston Coachmen
Joseph Wragg Ford

Members Who Joined in January of 1857

Frederick Wentworth Ford
Joshua Ford
Dr. Henry Tucker
Dr. Daniel Tucker

Richard Green White
Dr. John D. Magill
Robert Nesbit
W. H. Ford

Members Who Joined After January of 1857

William Allan Allston
Joseph Blyth Allston
Paul Fitzsimons
John Ford Fitzsimons
Joseph R. Tucker
Benjamin Allston
William H. Tucker

Mayham Ward
Bentley Weston
Dr. John Parker
Henry Augustus Middleton
Frank Middleton
Charles Alston
Francis Parker

Appendix VII:
The Constitution of
the Winyah and All Saints
Agricultural Society[1]

The members of the Planter's Club on Pee Dee having resolved to constitute themselves an Agricultural Society as well as a convivial Club and apply for a Charter of Incorporation for agricultural purposes, the following Constitution is proposed for the government for the Corporators—

1. The Society will meet on the first Thursday in November, and on the first Thursday in December, January, February, and March, and the Thursday in December, January, February, and March, and the Thursday next before the sitting of the Court of Common Pleas in Georgetown—this last shall be the anniversary meeting.

2. The following Officers shall be elected by ballot at each anniversary meeting viz—a President, 1 Vice President, a Recording Secretary and Treasurer, a Corresponding Secretary and 3 Curators, each of whom unless excused by vote of the members present, for cause, shall serve until the anniversary ensuing and until another be chosen in his stead.

3. The President shall preside and preserve order and decorum at all meetings of the Society at Club dinner he may depute a member to act as president. If absent the V. President will act as President, if both President and Vice President be absent, a chairman pro tem shall be chosen.

4. The Recording Secretary and Treasurer shall record in a book to be provided for that purpose all the proceedings of the Society; and shall file and regularly preserve all papers, letters, and articles of intelligence after they have been reported to the Society. He shall keep his accounts methodically stated in a book to be provided for that purpose also, and when required shall produce them for inspection. At every anniversary meeting he shall produce a fair and regular statement or account current showing his receipts and disbursements for the past 12 months, which after being audited by a committee of account shall be filed and preserved by the President. He shall at the same time report in writing the names of such members as may be in arrears for a year or more,

203

which report shall be read, provided he shall have given previous notice to such defaulters of their respective dues. He shall not disburse any funds without an order from the President or his countersign, and he shall deliver the accounts, with all the Books and other property of the Society, to his successor in office, or to the order of the Society.

5. It shall be the duty of the Corresponding Secretary to correspond with our Societies or with any person or persons, touching improvements in the science or practice or agriculture, and to report both the letter and a copy of his letters in question or reply, at the monthly meeting ensuing such correspondence.

6. The Board of Curators, of which the President and Vice President shall be the Judges of the merit of all inventions, experiments, and exhibitions which shall be brought to the view of the Society and shall award the premiums.

7. Each member shall pay to the Treasurer, on the day of his admission, the sum of $15 and on the first day of every anniversary meeting after $5, but the Recording Secretary and Treasurer for the time being shall be exempt from any annual contribution.

8. Any members may propose an individual for admission to the Society, upon which a ballot shall be taken, and the affirmation votes of 2/3ds. of the members present shall be necessary to admission, but all proposition of this sort shall be made and acted upon before dinner. The individual may then be introduced, and shall be forthwith pay his admission fee and sign this constitution, as to all which it shall be the duty of the member proposing to instruct him.

9. If the arrearages and dues of any member shall be reported to have been standing for more than one year, he shall be required by the Treasurer forthwith to pay the amount, or to give his negotiable note for the same. And the Treasurer shall be allowed ten per centum on the amount of all such notes collected for the benefit of this Institution.

10. Any member may withdraw from the Society by signifying his intention in writing to the Recording Secretary and Treasurer and paying up all arrears which may at the time be due by him.

11. The funds of the Society shall be appropriated by a majority of the members present at the anniversary meeting, to the encouragement of improvements in the system and practice of agriculture, in domestic economy, in the breed of Horses, Hogs, Sheep, and Cattle, in such manner as may be deemed most beneficial.

12. Donations may be received by the Recording Secretary and Treasurer, to be added to the funds or other property of the Society and the same shall be reported at the ensuing meeting.

13. The friends of agriculture generally and the members of this Society particularly are invited to forward its views by communicating in accurate detail the incidents and results of their experiments; and also the successful methods of treating any one of the various diseases to which in our climate, horses and stock of all kinds are liable. The Cor. Secretary shall, to each article of intelligence, affix the name of the person offering it.

14. There shall be a cattle show and fair at such place as the Society shall appoint on the day of the anniversary meeting at which time the prizes that may have been offer'd shall be awarded by the curators.

15. The meeting of the Society for the business shall commence at 12 o'clock P.M. and not continue later than 3 p.m. on any one day. Seven members shall constitute a quorum.[2]

16. At the meeting in November the President[3] shall furnish an address on the subject of agriculture, to be deliver'd before the Society.

17. No new Rule shall be added, nor shall there be any alteration of the foregoing Constitution unless it be sanctioned by 2/3ds. of the members present at two successive meetings.

Appendix VIII:
The Members of the Winyah
and All Saints Agricultural Society[1]

Governor Robert Francis Withers
    Allston
John Hayes Alston
John E. Allston
William Allan Allston
Joseph Blyth Allston
Benjamin Allston
Thomas Pinckney Alston
Charles Alston
John Ashe Alston
Joseph Pringle Alston
Richard Anderson
Allard H. Belin
Nathaniel Barnwell
E. P. Coachmen
Benjamin Allston Coachmen
Benjamin F. Dunkin
James Rees Ford
Joseph Wragg Ford
The Rev. A.M. Forster
Paul Fitzsimons
Peter Waties Fraser
Hugh Fraser
Sextus Tertius Gaillard
Edward P. Guerard
Dr. Edward Thomas Heriot
B. M. Gruir
Francis Withers Heriot
Dr. Robert Stark Heriot
Cleland Kinloch Huger
Dr. Andrew Hasell

Edward Gadsden Hume
Ralph Stead Izard
Daniel W. Jordan
Archibald Ligett
John LaBruce
Henry Augustus Middleton
Henry Augustus Middleton, Jr.
Donald L. McKay
Dr. John D. Magill
Dr. William Joseph Magill
Robert Hamilton Nesbit
Joel Roberts Poinsett
Dr. W.R.J. Prior
Thomas Petigru
John Julius Pringle
Dr. Francis S. Parker
Dr. John Parker
Dr. William Post
John B. Pyatt
John Harleston Read, Jr.
William Ervin Sparkman
Joshua Ward
Dr. James Ritchie Sparkman
Thomas L. Shaw
Dr. Benjamin Burgh Smith
John Hyrne Tucker
William Heyward Trapier
James Heyward Trapier
Mayham Ward
Dr. John Hyrne Tucker
Dr. Henry Massingberd Tucker

William Hyrne Tucker
Dr. Richard Green
William White
Eleazer Waterman
Francis Weston

Plowden Charles Jennet Weston
Joshua John Ward
Benjamin Henry Wilson
William Percival Vaux

About the Author

Christopher C. Boyle is the International Baccalaureate social studies teacher at Socastee High School in Myrtle Beach, South Carolina, and a part-time teaching associate at Coastal Carolina University (CCU) in Conway, South Carolina. He grew up in New York's Hudson Valley and in 1990 began taking classes at Coastal Carolina. Upon graduating from CCU with a bachelor's degree in history in 1993, he further studied history at Winthrop University, Rock Hill, South Carolina, where he graduated in 1996 with his Master of Arts in American History degree. His thesis was titled "The Social Organizations and Leisurely Activities of the Georgetown Rice Planters: 1840–1861." After publishing various articles and minor works, he published *Mansfield Plantation: A Legacy on the Black River,* in 2014 with the History Press and *The Road to Secession in Antebellum Georgetown and Horry District* with the Arcadia Press in 2017. He lives in Loris, South Carolina, with his wife D'Andrea Lynn and has three children: Veda, Brandon Joseph and Hannah Grace. He serves as a member on the boards of directors for both Mansfield Plantation and the Horry County Historical Society. He is a member of the Horry County Museum in Conway and the Rice Museum in Georgetown, South Carolina.

Chapter Notes

Introduction

1. A.S. Salley, Jr., *The Introduction of the Rice Culture Into South Carolina* (Columbia, SC: Crowson-Stone Printing Company, 1919), 3. Daniel C. Littlefield, *Rice and Slaves* (Chicago: University of Illinois Press, 1981), 105, 107, 109. Emilia Wallace Vernon, *African-Americans at Mars Bluff, South Carolina* (Baton Rouge: Louisiana University Press, 1993), 119–123.

2. Salley, *The Introduction of the Rice Culture*, 4–5.

3. George C. Rogers, Jr., *The History of Georgetown County, South Carolina* (Columbia: University of South Carolina, 1970), 29.

4. Littlefield, *Rice and Slaves*, 8.

5. Salley, *The Introduction of the Rice Culture*, 16.

6. Kenneth Morgan, "The Organization of the Colonial American Rice Trade" (William and Mary Quarterly, July 1995, 3rd series, vol. LII), 446.

7. *Ibid.*, 435–438.

8. Robert Mills, *Statistics of South Carolina* (Charleston, SC: Hurlbut and Lloyd, 1826), 559.

9. A.W. Vernon, *African Americans at Mars Bluff* (University of South Carolina Press), 25.

10. Arney R. Childs, ed., *Rice Planter and Sportsman: The Recollections of J. Motte Alston 1821–1909* (Columbia: University of South Carolina Press, 1953), 42, 45.

11. Rogers, *History of Georgetown*, 165.

12. "1810 Population Census of Georgetown District," South Carolina.

13. David Doar, A.S. Salley and Theodore D. Ravenel, *Rice and Rice Planting in the South Carolina Low Lands* (Charleston, SC: Charleston Museum, 1936), 7–11.

14. Rogers, *History of Georgetown County*, 165.

15. Charles Joyner, *Down by the Riverside* (Chicago: University of Illinois, 1984), 49.

16. "Agricultural Survey of Horry District, South Carolina. 1850 Census Report." United States Bureau of Census.

17. Henry C. Dethloff, *A History of the American Rice Industry: 1685–1985* (College Station: Texas A&M University Press, 1988), 62–63.

18. Pete Daniel, *Breaking the Land: The Transformation of Cotton, Tobacco and Rice Cultures Since 1880* (Chicago: University of Illinois Press, 1985) 40–41.

19. *Ibid.*, 83.

20. Dennis Lawson, *No Heir To Take Its Place: The Story of Rice in Georgetown County, South Carolina* (Georgetown: The Rice Museum, 1972), 22–23.

Chapter One

1. "What Constitutes a Gentleman," *Pee Dee Times*, May 14, 1856.

2. "Profanity—don't do it," *Winyah Observer*, March 3, 1847, and "Depend upon yourself and God will lead you," *Winyah Observer*, December 14, 1850.

3. "Book of Mormon," *Winyah Observer*, July 14th, 1841.

4. "An illustration of Mormonism—the Truth is Stranger than Fiction," *Pee Dee Times*, February 2, 1857.

5. Daniel W. Hollis, III, *The ABC-Clio World History Companion to Utopian Movements* (Santa Barbara: ABC-CLIO Press), 1998. 158–59, 248–49 and 276–77.

6. "Anti-Sabbath Convention," *Winyah Observer*, March 3, 1848.

7. F. N. Boney, *Southerners All* (Mercer University Press, 1984), 25–26.

8. Alvan F. Sanborn, ed., *The Reminiscences of Richard Lathers; Sixty years of a busy life in South Carolina, Massachusetts and New York* (Grafton Press, 1907), 6.

9. "A Good Wife," *Winyah Observer*, April 7, 1841

10. "Woman: Her mission and Destiny," *Winyah Observer*, November 11, 1844, "Diffusion of Christianity," *Winyah Observer*, November 18, 1844, and "The Worth of a Woman." *Winyah Observer*, November 20, 1844, and May 23, 1852.

11. "Domestic Training," and "Women," *Winyah Observer*, November 1, 1848.

12. "A wife's devotion; or the chivalry of love" *Pee Dee Times*, April 18, 1855, "A Recipe for getting a husband" *Pee Dee Times*, July 11, 1855, "Devotion of a true woman," *Pee Dee Times*, September 19, 1855, and "Marrying advice to ladies," *Pee Dee Times*, October 7, 1857.

13. "How to treat a wife," *Winyah Observer*, July 9, 1851.

14. *Winyah Observer*, May 8, 1841.

15. "The Drinking, Vending and Making Ardent Spirits," *Georgetown American*, November 30, 1839, "The Temperance Oath," *Winyah Observer*, February 26, 1842, and "Washingtonian's Temperance Oath," *Winyah Observer*, July 23, 1842.

16. "Fanaticism," *Pee Dee Times*, June 7, 1854.

17. "A Story of the Cowpens," *Winyah Observer*, April 12, 1851, and "The First Secession of South Carolina," *Winyah Observer*, June 11, 1851.

18. "The Slavery Question," *Winyah Observer*, January 19, 1850.

19. "Slavery and the Constitution," *Winyah Observer*, May 1, 1850.

20. "New York Conventions," *Pee Dee Times*, August 10, 1853, "Is an Abolitionist a Gentleman," *Pee Dee Times*, April 6, 1853, "Charity and Philanthropy," *Pee Dee Times*, April 20, 1853, "Fanaticism," *Pee Dee Times*, June 7, 1854, and "More Abolitionist Outrages," *Pee Dee Times*, September 20, 1854.

21. "Harriet Beecher Stowe's Charity" *Pee Dee Times*, May 11, 1853.

22. "Condition of the Colored Population of the North," *Pee Dee Times*, July 20, 1853.

23. "Slavery-the Proper Condition of the Negro," *Pee Dee Times*, August 2, 1854.

24. Childs, 49.

25. James Henry Hammond, "'Mud-Sill' Speech" in *Slavery Defended: the views of the Old South*, ed., Eric L. McKitrick (Englewood Cliffs, Prentice-Hall, 1963), 123.

26. "Who were the Slave Traders," *Pee Dee Times*, November 22, 1854, and "Who were the Slave Traders," *Pee Dee Times*, November 29, 1854.

27. "Abolition of Negro slavery—its Results in the British Colonies," *Pee Dee Times*, September 3, 1856.

28. "A Day at Lowell," *Winyah Observer*, November 11, 1846.

29. "Life in Northern Cities," *Pee Dee Times*, July 22, 1857, and "White Slavery in Massachusetts" and "Kansas Bleeds No More," *Pee Dee Times*, September 30, 1857.

30. Katharine M. Jones, *The Plantation South* (New York: Bobbs-Merrill Company, 1957), 178–79.

31. "1860 United States Bureau of Census," South Carolina Industry Schedule.

32. Allston, *Eulogy on John C. Calhoun Pronounced at the Request of the Citizens of Georgetown District* (Charleston, SC: Miller and Brown, April 23, 1850), 12.

33. *Winyah Observer*, May 4, 1844.

34. Boney, *Southerners All* (Mercer University Press), 13.

35. *Ibid.*, 41–42.

36. *Ibid.*, 61.

37. *Ibid.*, 59.

38. *Ibid.*, 62.

39. J.D.B. DeBow, "The Interest In Slavery Of the Southern Non-Slaveholder," in *Slavery Defended: the views of The Old South*, ed., Eric L. McKitrick (Englewood Cliffs: Prentice-Hall, 1963), 169–77.

40. *Ibid.*, 171.

41. Sanborn, 5–6.

42. "Population Survey, 1810 Census." United States Bureau of Census, Population Survey, 1850 Census. United States Bureau of Census, Population Survey, 1860 Census. United States Bureau of Census.

Chapter Two

1. *Memorial of The Citizens of Georgetown, South Carolina, Adverse to the Increase of Duties On Coarse Woolens, And*

Other Imports, January 9, 1828 (Washington: Duff Green), 1828, 3.

2. *Ibid.*, 3.

3. *Ibid.*, 4 and 6.

4. *Ibid.*, 5.

5. Childs, 25.

6. "States' Rights Convention in Charleston," *Winyah Intelligencer*, February 8, 1832. Allard H. Belin, John A. Keith, Dr. Aaron Lopez and J. Walter Phillips attended the meeting with Alston.

7. Rogers, 239.

8. Chauncey Samuel Boucher, *The Nullification Controversy in South Carolina* (Greenwood Press, New York, 1968), 231.

9. *Ibid.*, 239–40.

10. Anthony Q. Devereux, *The Life and Times of Robert F.W. Allston* (Columbia: R.L. Bryan Company, 1976), 73.

11. *Winyah Intelligencer*, January 2, 1833.

12. Rogers, 239.

13. "The Welfare of our Town," *Winyah Observer*, April 10, 1841.

14. *Winyah Observer*, May 8, 1841, "Saturday, July 6, 1844," July 6, 1844.

15. Rogers, 208.

16. "Military Parade at Black Mingo," *Winyah Observer*, December 6, 1843, and "Celebration of the 22," *Winyah Observer*, February 24, 1844.

17. "Proceedings of the Democratic State Rights Party," *Winyah Observer*, June 9, 1841.

18. "Celebration of the 4th on the Pee Dee" *Winyah Observer*, July 13, 1844.

19. Jason H. Silverman, "In *A Nation of Sovereign States: Secession & War in the Confederacy*, by Archie P. McDonald (Murfreesboro: Southern Heritage Press, 1994), 2.

20. Scrolled across the masthead, *Winyah Observer*, December 8, 1847.

21. "Head Quarters 8th Regiment Cavalry, Order No. 8," *Winyah Observer*, May 3, 1848.

22. "Democratic Party Meeting," *Winyah Observer*, April 12, 1848, and "Whig Party Meeting," *Winyah Observer*, May 17, 1848.

23. "North and South: Van Buren, Cass and Taylor: Which can the South Support?" *Winyah Observer*, August 9, 1848.

24. Silverman, 3.

25. "District Meeting," *Winyah Observer*, April 11, 1849.

26. *Ibid.*

27. "Who has betrayed the South?" *Winyah Observer*, July 25, 1849.

28. "Southern State Convention," *Washington Union*, October 17, 1849.

29. "Railroad Convention in Memphis," *Winyah Observer*, May 12, 1852.

30. J. H. Easterby, The South Carolina Rice Plantation as revealed in the Papers of Robert F.W. Allston (Columbia: University of South Carolina Press, 1945), 102.

31. *Ibid.*, 99.

32. "The Southern Convention at Nashville," *Winyah Observer*, June 19, 1850, "The Slavery Question and the Missouri Compromise," *Winyah Observer*, August 7, 1850, and "The Battle of King's Mountain; or Hero's Revenge," *Winyah Observer*, October 9, 1850.

33. "Georgetown and All Saints Southern Rights Association," *Winyah Observer*, October 16, 1850, and "Georgetown and All Saints Southern Rights Association," *Winyah Observer*, October 23, 1850.

34. *Winyah Observer*, November 13, 1850, and November 18, 1850.

35. "Divisions of the South," *Winyah Observer*, November 18, 1850.

36. Emily Bellinger Reynolds and Joan Reynolds Faunt, *Biographical Directory of the Senate of South Carolina 1776–1964* (Columbia: SC Archives Department, 1964), 44–58.

37. *Ibid.* Rogers, 327, 242 and 250.

38. Chalmers Gaston Davidson, *The Last Foray: South Carolina Planters of 1860: A Sociological Study* (Columbia: University of South Carolina Press, 1971), 258–59.

39. "Gallery of Industry and Enterprise," *Winyah Observer*, May 12, 1852.

40. *Winyah Observer*, October 16, 1850.

41. *Winyah Observer*, October 23, 1850.

42. Elizabeth Waties Allston Pringle, *Chronicles of Chicora Wood* (Atlanta: Cherokee Publishing Company, 1976), 20. *Winyah Observer*, October 2, 1850. *Winyah Observer*, May 12, 1852. *Pee Dee Times*, March 12, 1856.

43. Reynolds and Faunt, 171–72.

44. Davidson, 52, 140, 143 and 171–72.

45. "Southern Rights Association of All Saints Parish," *Winyah Observer*, December 11, 1850.

46. "The Policy of the South," *Winyah Observer*, February 12, 1851.

47. *Winyah Observer,* September 9, 1851.

48. "The Right of Secession," *Winyah Observer,* October 8, 1851.

49. "Great Secession Demonstration: Mass-Meeting at Morris Ferry 700 Persons Present," *Winyah Observer,* October 15, 1851.

50. *Ibid.*

51. Reynold and Faunt, 172. Silverman, 4. *Winyah Observer,* May 5, 1852.

52. *Winyah Observer,* December 1, 1852, and December 15, 1852.

53. "What makes South Carolina so Great?" *Pee Dee Times,* March 9, 1853. Waterman's last edition was published on April 19, 1854.

54. "The Rising Trouble in Kansas," *Pee Dee Times,* May 30, 1855.

55. "Kansas," *Pee Dee Times,* December 12, 1855.

56. "How Changed," *Pee Dee Times,* August 29, 1855.

57. "Political Excitement," *Pee Dee Times,* August 29, 1855.

58. "Trade with the North," *Pee Dee Times,* September 5, 1855.

59. "Military Capacity of the South," *Pee Dee Times,* August 22, 1855.

60. *Pee Dee Times,* July 9, 1856.

61. "Brooks Dinner," *Pee Dee Times,* October 15, 1856.

62. Silverman, 7.

63. "The Sign of the Times," *Pee Dee Times,* August 6, 1856, and "Form A Southern Confederacy," *Pee Dee Times,* November 5, 1856.

64. "Mr. Buchanan in Favor of Adding a Foreign Slave State to the South," *Pee Dee Times,* August 20, 1856.

65. Alston, 110 and Davidson, 118, 130–31.

66. www.carolana.com/SC/1800s/antebellum/sc_antebellum_38th_general_assembly_members.htm.

67. Plowden Charles Jennett Weston, *Documents Connected with the History of South Carolina* (London: Cheswick Press, 1856), 3–4. In the editor's note, Weston claimed that he compiled the documents from English collections to help stimulate research by the South Carolina Historical Society.

68. Ulrich B. Phillips, *Plantation and Frontier Documents 1649–1863,* vol. I, 115–22.

69. Plowden Charles Jennett Weston, An Address by Plowden C. J. Weston before the Citizens of All Saints Parish at Watchesaw, July 4th, 1857 (Georgetown, SC: 1857), 7.

70. Davidson, 260–61.

71. "The Death And Funeral Of Mr. Brooks of South Carolina," *Pee Dee Times,* February 4, 1857.

72. "The Decision of the Supreme Court Case, and its Tremendous Consequences" *Pee Dee Times,* March 18, 1857.

73. "Headquarters," *Pee Dee Times,* March 4, 1857.

74. "The Governors Review," *Pee Dee Times,* March 25, 1857.

75. "Duty of Southern Men," *Pee Dee Times,* June 10, 1857.

76. "The Sign of the Times," *Pee Dee Times,* May 6, 1857.

77. Weston, Address at Watchesaw, 3.

78. *Ibid.,* 4.

79. *Ibid.,* 6–7.

80. *Ibid.,* 7–8.

81. *Ibid.,* 7.

82. *Ibid.,* 9.

83. *Ibid.,* 12–13.

84. *Ibid.,* 9.

85. *Ibid.,* 15–16.

86. Allston, Robert F.W, Message No. 1, of His Excellency R.F.W. Allston, Governor of South Carolina to the State and House of Representatives at the session of 1857 (R.W. Gibbes State Printer: Columbia, SC, 1857), 3.

87. *Ibid.,* 11–12.

88. *Ibid.,* 14.

89. *Ibid.,* 14.

90. James Henry Hammond, *Selections from letters and speeches of the Honorable James H. Hammond* (New York, 1866), 317.

91. James Henry Hammond, "'Mud-Sill' Speech" in *Slavery Defended: the views of the Old South,* ed., Eric L. McKitrick (Englewood Cliffs, Prentice-Hall, 1963), 121–22.

92. "Southern Commercial Convention in Montgomery," *Pee Dee Times,* April 21, 1858.

93. "4th of July," *Pee Dee Times,* May 12, 1858.

94. "The 4th of July," *Pee Dee Times* July 7, 1858.

95. Silverman, 6.

96. Childs, 130.

97. *Charleston Mercury,* November 8, 1860.

98. Charles H. Lesser, "Relic of the Lost Cause: The Story of South Carolina's Ordinance of Secession (Columbia, SC: South Carolina Department of Archives and History, 1990), 21–26.

99. "Delegates to the South Carolina Secession Convention of 1860, with a summary of data from manuscript returns of schedules 1 and 2 of United States Census for 1860," *South Carolina Historical Magazine*, vol. 55, 1954, 192–97.

100. Easterby, 169–70.

101. Rogers, 382.

Chapter Three

1. S. H. Dickerson, "Essay on Malaria," The Proceedings of the Agricultural Convention of the State Agricultural Society of South Carolina from 1839 to 1845 (Columbia, S.C., 1846), 169. Mr. Dickerson originally read the essay to the State Agricultural Society on November 28, 1843.

2. Arney B. Childs, *Rice Planter and Sportsman: The Recollections of J. Motte Alston, 1821–1909* (Columbia: University of South Carolina Press, 1953), 6.

3. Elizabeth Waties Allston Pringle, *Chronicles of Chicora Wood* (Atlanta: Cherokee Publishing Company, 1976), 67.

4. Elizabeth Waties Allston Pringle, *A Woman Rice Planter* (Columbia: University of South Carolina Press, 1994), 58.

5. Lawrence Fay Brewster, *Summer Migrations and Resorts of South Carolina Low Country Planters* (Durham, NC, 1947), 26.

6. Pringle, Chronicles of Chicora Wood, 158–59.

7. *Ibid.*, 159.

8. Charles Joyner, *Down by the Riverside: A South Carolina Slave Community* (Chicago: University of Illinois Press, 1984), 72.

9. Charlotte Kaminski Prevost, *Pawley's Island...A Living Legend: An historical sketch of the Blessed Isle and its environs* (Columbia, SC: State Printing Co., 1972), 1.

10. James Harold Easterby, ed., "South Carolina Through New England Eyes: Almira Coffin's Visit to the Low Country in 1851," *South Carolina Historical Magazine*, vol. 46, 1945, 133.

11. Sanborn, 6.

12. Easterby, ed., *Rice Plantation As Revealed*, 102.

13. Pringle, *Chicora Wood*, 137.

14. Reverend Alexander Glennie Parish Diary 1832–1859, South Carolina Historical Society, 34–247.

15. *Ibid.* The original officers were: President William Algernon Alston, Vice President Joshua John Ward, Secretary and Treasurer Reverend Alexander Glennie, and Thomas Alston, Edward Thomas Heriot and Francis Marion Weston served as directors.

16. Prevost, 33.

17. *Winyah Observer*, January 7, 1843.

18. Henry DeSaurre Bull, All Saints Church, Waccamaw (Columbia, SC, 1968), 33.

Reverend Alexander Glennie Parish Diary 1832–1859, SCHS 34–247. Reverend Glennie often gave several sermons on each Sunday to planter and slave alike. In All Saints Parish there were 13 slave chapels: they were located at Woodbourne, Laurel Hill, Brook Green, Oaks, Litchfield, Waverly, Midway, True Blue, Hagley, Fairfield, Sandy Knoll, Cedar Grove and Mount Arena plantations.

19. George Brown Tindall, *South Carolina Negroes, 1877–1900* (Columbia: University of South Carolina Press, 1952), 5–6, 59, 60–63.

20. Albert Sidney Thomas, *A Historical Account of the Protestant Episcopal Church in South Carolina: 1820–1957* (Columbia, SC: R.L. Bryan Company, 1957), 381.

21. *Ibid.*, 706.

22. Acts of the general Assembly of the State of South Carolina (Columbia, SC, 1853).

23. Childs, *Rice Planter and Sportsman*, 105. All Saints Church, Waccamaw, South Carolina, Historical Society, 45–77.

24. Samuel G. Stoney, ed., "Memoirs of Frederick Adolphus Porcher," *South Carolina Historical Magazine*, vol. 46, 1945, 28.

25. Sanborn, 5.

26. Pringle, *Chronicles of Chicora Wood*, 150–52.

27. Easterby, *Rice Plantation As Revealed*, 135–36.

28. Joyner, 134.

29. Davidson, 12, 80, 172–73.

30. *Ibid.*, 133–37.

31. *Ibid.*, 127: Pringle, *Chronicles of Chicora Wood*, 152–56.

32. Charleston Taxpayers List for 1859. Lance's sons-in-law each owned a home in Charleston. Dr. Francis S. Parker's Charleston house was valued at $6,500 in 1859 and was staffed year-round by four domestic servants. By comparison, Parker's brother-in-law, John Harleston Read, Jr., owned two Charleston houses with a combined value of $50,000 and staffed by 30 servants.

33. Rogers, 323.

34. Brewster, 1947.

35. Fraser, Jr., Walter J., *Charleston Charleston!* (Columbia: University of South Carolina Press, 1989), 284.

36. Pringle, 214, 219.

37. *Ibid.*, 145–46.

38. *Ibid.*, 143–44.

39. Fraser, Jr., 96.

40. Pringle, 219.

41. Geoffrey Warren, *Fashion Accessories since 1500* (New York: Drama Book Publishers, 1987) 103- 05.

42. *Ibid.*, 106–09.

43. John Beaufain Irving, *The South Carolina Jockey Club* (Charleston, SC: Walker & Evans and Co., 1857), 157–58. The 15 racetracks in the state that comprised the circuit were in Charleston, St. Matthews, Pendleton, Greenville, Barnwell, Newberry, Strawberry, Georgetown, Fulton, Camden, Columbia, Orangeburg, Cherokee Ponds, Limestone Springs and Yorkville.

44. *Ibid.*, 191.

45. Childs, 19.

46. Rogers, 19–21 and 12.

47. Irving, 192–94.

48. *Ibid.*, 196. Read Family Legal Papers, 1841–1879. South Carolina Historical Society. 0308.01(R)01, John H. Read, Jr., paid his fees biannually at $80 for two years.

49. Fraser, 181.

50. Pringle, *Chicora Wood*, 5–46.

Chapter Four

1. Winyah Indigo Society of Georgetown, South Carolina, 1755–1998, 3.

2. *Norfleet Hardy Farm, mill and classroom; a history of tax supported adult education in South Carolina in 1960* (Columbia: University of South Carolina, 1967), 19.

3. Robert Mills, *Statistics of South Carolina* (Reprint Company: Spartanburg, 1972), 568.

4. Robert F.W. Allston, Address before the members and pupils of the Winyah Indigo Society delivered in Georgetown on May 5th, 1854 (Charleston, SC: Walker, Evans and Steam Power Presses, 1859), 8.

5. Meriwether Coyler, *The History of higher education in South Carolina, with a sketch of the free school system* (Government Printing Office: Washington, 1889), 19–21.

6. Rogers, 92.

7. *Charleston Gazette*, May 22, October 16, 1775, January 5, 1760. Morgan, William D., "A Short History of the Winyah Indigo Society" (n.p., n.d.), p. 3; "Winyah Indigo Society," *Pee Dee Times*, April 25, 1855.

8. Rogers, 95.

9. *Ibid.*, 96.

10. Hardy, 19–20.

11. *Ibid.*, 25.

12. Cook, Harvey Toliver, *Rambles in the Pee Dee Basin* (Columbia, SC: State Company, 1926), 111.

13. *South Carolina Historical Magazine*, vol. 72, South Carolina Historical Society, 1971, 27.

14. Robbie L. Alford, Winyah Indigo Society historical leaflet, Georgetown, SC, 1976.

15. Minutes Book of the Winyah Indigo Society.

16. "The Georgetown Library Society," *South Carolina Historical Magazine*, XXV South Carolina Historical Society (1924), 95–96. (1799–1832) Winyah Indigo Society Collection, Georgetown County library.

17. Georgetown Library Society, *South Carolina Historical Magazine*, vol. XXV, South Carolina Historical Society, 1924. 94–95. Allston, Address before the members and pupils, 9–10.

18. "The Georgetown Library Society," *South Carolina Historical Magazine*, 25, 100.

19. Barnet Abraham Elzas, *The Jews of South Carolina from the earliest times to the present day* (Philadelphia: J.B. Lippincott Company, 1905), 243.

20. Willcox, 108.

21. Allston, Address before the members and Pupils, 14–16. Alford, leaflet.

22. Dennis Lawson, "A Guide to

historic Georgetown County" (SC: Rice Museum, 1974), 42.

23. Allston, Address before the members and pupils, 1859. 9.

24. Willcox, 139.

25. John Vaught, by C. B. Berry, The Independent Republic Quarterly, 1985, vol. 19, No. 4, p. 9.

26. Allston, Report on The Free School System, 5.

27. "School," *Winyah Intelligencer*, December 4, 1819.

28. "A Teacher for the Free School," *Winyah Intelligencer*, April 3, 1819.

29. "Winyah Indigo Society," *Winyah Intelligencer*, May 5, 1819.

30. Mills, 1972, 584.

31. *Ibid.*

32. "Sheriff Sales," *Winyah Intelligencer*, April 1, 1834.

33. *Georgetown American*, November 23, 1839.

34. "A Teacher Wanted," *Georgetown American*, November 30, 1839.

35. Allston, Report on the Free School System, 7. Statistics at Large, V, 639–41.

36. *Ibid.*, 37.

37. *Ibid.*, 39.

38. Population Survey, 1840 Census. United States Bureau of Census.

39. Allston, Report on The Free School System, 14.

40. *Ibid.*, 41–42.

41. "Report," *Georgetown American*, December 16, 1840.

42. *Ibid.*

43. "Report of the Winyah Indigo Society," *Winyah Observer*, April 21, 1841.

44. "Winyah Indigo Society," *Winyah Observer*, May 3, 1843.

45. "Winyah Indigo Society," *Georgetown American*, May 1, 1840.

46. "Winyah Indigo Society," *Winyah Observer*, May 8, 1841.

47. "Winyah Indigo Society," *Winyah Observer*, May 7, 1842.

48. "Winyah Indigo Society," *Winyah Observer*, May 6, 1843.

49. "Winyah Indigo Society," *Winyah Observer*, May 4, 1844.

50. "Winyah Indigo Society," *Winyah Observer*, May 3, 1845.

51. "Winyah Indigo Society School," *Winyah Observer*, January 11, 1843, and "Winyah Indigo Society School," *Winyah Observer*, September 21, 1844.

52. "Winyah Indigo Society School," *Winyah Observer*, September 21, 1844, "Winyah Indigo Society," *Winyah Observer*, November 21, and "Select School" and "All Saints Summer Academy," *Winyah Observer*, December 18, 1844.

53. "Mrs. M.C. Durant's School," *Winyah Observer*, September 22, 1847.

54. "Winyah Indigo Society," *Winyah Observer*, April 29, 1846.

55. "Winyah Indigo Society," *Winyah Observer*, May 6, 1846.

56. "Winyah Indigo Society School," *Winyah Observer*, May 6, 1846.

57. "Winyah Indigo Society," *Winyah Observer*, May 6, 1846.

58. "Destructive Fire reported on Front Street," *Winyah Observer*, September 23, 1846.

59. Sanborn, 17.

60. Easterby, 16.

61. Allston, Report on The Free School System, 4.

62. *Ibid.*

63. *Ibid.*, 11–12.

64. *Ibid.*, 13.

65. *Ibid.*, 13.

66. "Winyah Indigo Society School," *Winyah Observer*, November 4, 1846.

Chapter Five

1. "Winyah Indigo Society," *Winyah Observer*, April 26, 1848.

2. Reverend William G. Connor, An Address Delivered Before The Winyah Indigo Society of Georgetown, May 5th, 1848, by the Reverend William G. Connor of the South Carolina Conference (Charleston, SC: Walker and Burke Printers, 1848), 3.

3. *Ibid.*, 3–4.

4. *Ibid.*, 4.

5. *Ibid.*, 5.

6. *Ibid.*, 6.

7. *Ibid.*, 7–9.

8. *Ibid.*, 10–11.

9. *Ibid.*, 13.

10. "Winyah Indigo Society," *Winyah Observer*, May 10, 1848.

11. "On School Teaching No. 1," *Winyah Observer, May* 10, 1848, "On School Teaching No. 2," *Winyah Observer*, May 17, 1848, and "On School Teaching No. 3," *Winyah Observer*, April 25, 1848.

12. "Winyah Indigo Society," *Winyah Observer,* May 9, 1849.

13. "Treatment of Scholars," *Winyah Observer,* October 3, 1849.

14. Boney, 60.

15. Social Status Schedule of South Carolina, 1850 United States Bureau of Census.

16. *Ibid.*

17. "Winyah Indigo Society," *Winyah Observer,* May 8, 1850.

18. "Winyah Indigo Society," *Winyah Observer,* May 7, 1851.

19. "The Winyah Indigo Society," *Winyah Observer,* May 12, 1847.

20. "Winyah Indigo Society," *Winyah Observer,* December 10, 1851.

21. Minutes Book of the Winyah Indigo Society.

22. "The Winyah Indigo Society," *Pee Dee Times,* May 11, 1853.

23. "Free Schools," *Pee Dee Times,* August 10, 1853.

24. "Our Free School System," *Pee Dee Times,* August 10, 1853.

25. *Ibid.*

26. Cook, 111.

27. "Our Free School system" *Pee Dee Times,* August 10, 1853.

28. "Common Schools," *Pee Dee Times,* December 14, 1853.

29. "Winyah Indigo Society," *Pee Dee Times,* March 9, 1853, and "Winyah Indigo Society," *Pee Dee Times,* March 23, 1853.

30. "School," *Pee Dee Times,* October 5, 1853, and "School," *Pee Dee Times,* October 12, 1853.

31. "Winyah Indigo Society," *Pee Dee Times,* May 3, 1854.

32. "Winyah Indigo Society," *Pee Dee Times,* April 19, 1854.

33. "Winyah Indigo Society," *Pee Dee Times,* October 25, 1854, and "Winyah Indigo Society," *Pee Dee Times,* November 1, 1854.

34. Hardy, 21.

35. "Winyah Indigo Society," *Pee Dee Times,* November 15, 1854, and "Winyah Indigo Society, *Pee Dee Times,* November 22, 1854.

36. Winyah Indigo Society Minutes Book.

37. *Ibid.*

38. *Ibid.*

39. *Ibid.*

40. Easterby, 15. Allston, Address before the members and pupils of the Winyah Indigo Society, 7–8.

41. Pringle, *Chronicles of Chicora Wood,* 35. Hot and Hot Fish Club, Rules and History of the Hot And Hot Fish Club of All Saints Parish (Charleston, SC: Evans & Cogswell, 1860). James Ritchie Sparkman papers, South Caroliniana Library, 2602. Minutes Book of the Winyah and All Saints Agricultural Society, South Carolina Historical Society, 34 -161.

42. Alford, leaflet.

43. Allston, Address before the members and pupils, 4.

44. *Ibid.,* 5.

45. *Ibid.,* 6.

46. *Ibid.,* 7.

47. *Ibid.,* 17–18.

48. Winyah Indigo Society Minutes Book.

49. *Ibid.*

50. "Winyah Indigo Society," *Pee Dee Times,* April 25, 1855.

51. "A Warning to the South," *Pee Dee Times,* May 2, 1855.

52. Rogers, 215.

53. "Marion Female College," *Pee Dee Times,* May 23, 1855.

54. "Winyah Indigo Society," *Pee Dee Times,* April 30, 1856.

55. "Winyah Indigo Society," *Pee Dee Times,* April 7, 1856.

56. "Winyah Indigo Society," *Pee Dee Times,* October 13, 1856.

Chapter Six

1. Lawson, 42.

2. Hardy, 21.

3. "Anniversary of the Winyah Indigo Society," *Pee Dee Times,* May 6, 1857.

4. "Winyah Indigo Society," *Pee Dee Times,* December 10, 1856.

5. Minutes Book of the Winyah Indigo Society.

6. "Winyah Indigo Society School," *Pee Dee Times,* September 9, 1857.

7. "Winyah Indigo Society School," *Pee Dee Times,* September 30, 1857, "Winyah Indigo Society School," *Pee Dee Times,* April 1, 1857, "Winyah Indigo Society School," *Pee Dee Times,* June 3, 1857, "Winyah Indigo Society School," *Pee Dee Times,* March 25, 1857, and "Winyah Indigo Society School," *Pee Dee Times,* March 4, 1857.

8. Minutes Book of the Winyah Indigo Society.

9. *Ibid.*

10. Allston, Message No. 1, 5.

11. *Ibid.*, 7.

12. William Scarborough, *The Overseer: Plantation Management in the Old South* (Baton Rouge: Louisiana State University, 1966), 57.

13. "Winyah Indigo Society," *Pee Dee Times,* July 12, 1858.

14. *Georgetown American*, February 28, 1840.

15. "Report of the commissioners of the poor, for the year 1854," *Pee Dee Times,* November 14, 1855.

16. "Yellow fever in Georgetown," and "Quarantine" *Pee Dee Times,* August 20, 1856.

17. "Constitution of the Howard Society of Georgetown, South Carolina," *Pee Dee Times,* October 3, 1855.

18. Minutes Book of the Winyah Indigo Society.

19. *Ibid.*

20. *Pee Dee Times*, May 1, 1859.

21. Minutes book of the Winyah Indigo Society.

22. *Ibid.*

23. *Ibid.*

24. Plowden C.J. Weston, An Address delivered in the Indigo Society Hall, Georgetown, South Carolina, on May 4, 1860, the 105th anniversary of The Winyah Indigo Society (Charleston, SC: A.J. Burke, 1860), 7.

25. *Ibid.*, 8.

26. *Ibid.*, 9–10.

27. *Ibid.*, 12–13.

28. *Ibid.*, 13.

29. *Ibid.*, 15.

30. *Ibid.*, 17–20.

31. *Ibid.*, 22–23.

32. *Ibid.*, 25–26.

33. *Ibid.*, 29.

34. *Ibid.*, 28.

35. *Ibid.*, 29–30.

36. Minutes Book of the Winyah Indigo Society.

37. *Ibid.*

Chapter Seven

1. Hot And Hot Fish Club, Rules and History of the Hot And Hot Fish Club of All Saints Parish, South Carolina (Charleston, SC: Evans & Cogswell, 1860). Only two copies of this 1860 pamphlet are known to exist. One copy is located at the South Carolinian Library, Columbia, SC, and the other at Duke University Library, Durham, NC.

2. *Ibid.*, 5.

3. *Ibid.*, 6.

4. *Ibid.*

5. *Ibid.*

6. *Ibid.*, 6.

7. *Ibid.*, 7.

8. *Ibid.*

9. *Ibid.*, 8.

10. "Elections," *Winyah Intelligencer,* September 5, 1832.

11. Sanborn, 6.

12. Childs, 60.

13. *Ibid.*, 25–26.

14. Hot And Hot Fish Club, Rules, 17, and Journal of the Hot and Hot Fish Club, Robert F.W. Allston Papers, South Carolina Historical Society, 24–14–24.

15. Sanborn, 6.

16. *Ibid.* 83–84.

17. Childs, 84.

18. *Ibid.*, 60.

19. *Ibid.*, 60.

20. Hot And Hot Fish Club, Rules, 17, and Journal of the Hot and Hot Fish Club, Robert F.W. Allston Papers, South Carolina Historical Society, 24–14–24.

21. Easterby, 398.

22. John Michael Vlach, *Back of the Big House: The Architecture of Plantation Slavery* (Chapel Hill: University of North Carolina Press, 1993), 80–81.

23. Hot and Hot Fish Club, Rules, 10–11.

24. *Ibid.*, 11–12

25. Easterby, 36.

26. Journal of the Hot and Hot Fish Club, Robert F.W. Allston Papers, South Carolina Historical Society, 24–14–24.

27. Hot and Hot Fish Club, Rules, 13.

28. Reynolds and. Faunt, 116, 127. Peter W. Fraser represented Prince George Parish, and Robert F.W. Allston sat continuously on the state senate, serving as president after 1850 for three terms, until he was elected governor in 1856. In All Saints Parish Thomas Alston sat until 1838, when he was succeeded by Dr. Edward Thomas Heriot for two terms. Beginning in 1842, All Saints Parish

sent Joshua John Ward to the senate. He remained the senator for the parish until he was elected lieutenant governor of the state in 1850. Dr. Andrew Hasell filled the void in the senate when Joshua John Ward served as lieutenant governor, and Charles Alston filled the seat when Hasell vacated it in 1858. He retained the seat through the 1860 term.

29. Sanborn, 5–6.

30. Rogers, 270.

31. James Ritchie Sparkman Papers, Southern Historical Collection, #2732 folder 4a and 4b. Sparkman's papers contain two books of medical records and receipts that prove he tended to several planters and their families as well as their slave communities.

32. Dr. Andrew Hasell's account book, South Carolina Historical Society, 34–247, 110.

33. Reynolds and Faunt, 234.

34. Journal of the Hot and Hot Fish Club, Robert F.W. Allston Papers, South Carolina Historical Society, 12–4-12.

35. Ibid.

36. Hot And Hot Fish Club, Rules, 9.

37. Journal of the Hot and Hot Fish Club, Robert F.W. Allston Papers, South Carolina Historical Society, 12–4-12.

38. Ibid. The decision to distribute keys to these members took place on June 15, 1850.

39. "Winyah Indigo Society Tribute of Respect," Pee Dee Times, December 4, 1854. Journal of the Hot and Hot Fish Club.

40. Journal of the Hot and Hot Fish Club, Robert F.W. Allston Papers, South Carolina Historical Society 12–4-12.

41. Ibid.

42. Ibid.

43. Easterby, 142.

44. Childs, 64.

45. Ibid., 60.

46. Easterby, 123.

47. Childs, 12.

48. James Ritchie Sparkman to Benjamin Allston, Allston Family Papers, South Carolinian Library, 29.

49. Easterby, 117.

50. Ibid., 92.

51. Chalmers Gaston Davidson, The Last Foray: South Carolina Planters of 1860: A Sociological Study (Columbia: University of South Carolina Press, 1971), 216.

52. Dr. Andrew Hasell to Daniel W. Jordan, July 16, 1860, Daniel W. Jordan Papers, Duke University Library.

53. Ibid.

54. Daniel W. Jordan to Dr. Andrew Hasell, July 19, 1860, Daniel W. Jordan Papers, Duke University Library.

55. Ibid.

56. "Kansas Meeting in All Saints," Pee Dee Times, March 5, 1856.

57. "To Kansas Emigrants and to all Friends of the South," Pee Dee Times, February 6, 1856.

58. "Kansas Meeting," Pee Dee Times, March 12, 1856, "Kansas," Pee Dee Times, March 21, 1856, and "Kansas," Pee Dee Times, March 26, 1856.

59. "Kansas Meeting," Pee Dee Times, March 12, 1856.

60. Pringle, Chronicles of Chicora Wood, 20. Pee Dee Times, March 12, 1856.

61. Hot and Hot Fish Club, Rules, 11.

62. https://www.wikiwand.com/en/ Hot_and_Hot_Fish_Club

63. Hot and Hot Fish Club, Rules, 11.

64. David J. McCord, ed., Statues At Large of South Carolina, vol. XII (Columbia, SC: Republican Printing Company, 1874), 691.

65. Hot and Hot Fish Club, Rules, 14. Rule 17.

66. Ibid., 2.

Chapter Eight

1. Alexander Gregg, History of the old Cheraws (New York: Richardson and Company, 1867), 119.

2. Winyah Indigo Society, A short history of the Winyah Indigo Society of Georgetown, South Carolina: 1755–1950 (1950), 3–6, 33–37.

3. Lewis Cecil Gray, History of Agriculture in the Southern United States to 1860, vol. II (Gloucester: Peter Smith Publishing, 1958), 782–84.

4. Drew Gilpin Faust, "The Rhetoric and Ritual of Agriculture in Antebellum South Carolina," Journal of Southern History (vol. XLV, No. 4, November 1979), 545.

5. Charles S. Sydnor, The Development of Southern Sectionalism: 1819–1848 (Louisiana State University Press, 1948), 87–88.

6. Albert Lowther Demaree, American

Agricultural Press, 1819–1860 (New York: Columbia University Press, 1941), 18.

7. W.A. Clark, W.G. Hinson and D.P. Duncan, *History of the Agricultural Society of South Carolina* (Columbia, SC: R. L. Ryan Company, 1916), 5–6. The agricultural societies in South Carolina as of 1843 were: St. John's, Colleton Agricultural Society, Winnsboro-Fairfield Agricultural Society, Monticello Planter's Society, Barnwell Agricultural Society, St. Luke's Agricultural Society, St. Andrew's Agricultural Society, Stono and Ashley's Agricultural Society, India land Agricultural Society, Wateree Agricultural Society, Chester Agricultural Society, Pee Dee Agricultural Society, Fishing Creek Agricultural Society, Cambridge Agricultural Society, and, of course, the Winyah and All Saints Agricultural Society.

8. Faust, 547.

9. Mills, 558; Rogers, 325. In 1850, Georgetown produced 81 bales of cotton; the Horry District was the only district in the state that produced less cotton than Georgetown.

10. James Ritchie Sparkman Papers, South Caroliniana Library, 2606. The original 14 members were: John Hayes Allston, Dr. James Ritchie Sparkman, Dr. Edward Thomas Heriot, Robert F.W. Allston, John Hyrne Tucker, J.R. Ford, Stephen Ford, Joshua John Ward, Thomas Carr, William Sparkman, G.L. Ford, William Trapier, Francis Marion Weston and Allard Belin.

11. *Ibid.* The committee elected to write the constitution originally included Dr. Edward Thomas Heriot. Heriot declined an appointment to the committee, and Sparkman took his place.

12. South Carolina General Assembly, Petitions. South Carolina Archives, ND #3780 and #3781.

13. "Agricultural," *Georgetown American,* November 23, 1839.

14. *The Southern Agriculturalist and Register of Rural Affairs,* vol. IX (Charleston, SC: A.G. Miller Publishing, 1831), 221.

15. David J. McCord, ed., *Statues at large of South Carolina,* vol. XI. (Columbia, SC: Republican Printing Company, 1873), 72.

16. *Statutes at Large,* vol. XI (1839–49) (Columbia, SC: Republican Printing Company, State Printers, 1873), 71.

17. *Ibid.*

18. Gaston, 252.

19. "The Secretary's Records of the Planters' Club on the Pee Dee," James Ritchie Sparkman Papers, 2732 vol. II, Southern Historical Collection.

20. Helen Kohn Kennig, *Great South Carolinians from the Colonial Days to the Confederate War* (Mount Pleasant, SC: Supplemental Press, 1940), 303–04.

21. *Ibid.,* 312–13.

22. "Hon. Joel R. Poinsett," *Winyah Observer,* May 12, 1841.

23. Kenning, 313–14.

24. "Second Declaration of Independence: Laws of the United States Passed at the First Session of the Twenty-Sixth Congress," *Georgetown American,* August 5, 1840.

25. "1840 Population Census Report," *Winyah Observer,* July 7, 1842.

26. *Winyah Observer,* March 2, 1842.

27. "The Secretary's Records of the Planters' Club on the Pee Dee," James Ritchie Sparkman Papers, 2732 vol. II, Southern Historical Collection.

28. *Charleston City Gazette and Commercial Daily Advertiser,* April 24, 1819, "President Monroe Visits South Carolina," *Winyah Intelligencer,* April 23, 1819. Monroe stopped in Georgetown during the Southern leg of his tour of the country's coastal defenses.

29. Sanborn, 7. John Tucker, Robert Allston, John Allston, Thomas Allston, John Ashe Allston, Jacob Motte Alston, John Izard Middleton, member of the legislature; Henry A. Middleton; John Alexander Keith; James Smith; Col. Donald L. McKay, president of the Bank of Georgetown; Stephen Ford; J. Ress Ford; Sextus. T. Gaillard; James Sparkman; State Senator John W. Coachmen; Benjamin H. Wilson; William Bull Pringle; Dr. Prior; Reverend Alexander Glennie; Reverend Maurice Harvey Lance; Francis R. Shackelford; Thomas Carr; John Harleston Read, Jr., member of the legislature; Alexander Robertson, a commission merchant of Charleston; James G. Henning; Major William W. Trapier; Colonel John Chapman; Anthony W. Dozier; Richard Dozier; Major Samuel Atkinson; Colonel Joshua John Ward; Dr. Edward Thomas Heriot; State Senator J. W. Wilkinson; Judge Frost; Chancellor Benjamin F. Duncan; Alfred Huger, postmaster of Charleston; Colonel

Robert Hayne, United States senator; Captain Petigru of the United States Navy; General James M. Commander; Richard Lathers; E.B. Rothmakler; and Henry W. Connor, president of the Bank of Charleston, all attended the dinner.

30. Stoney, "Memoirs," 47–48.

31. Gaston, 127 and 257.

32. Childs, 34 and *Ibid.*

33. Sanborn, 7–8.

34. *Ibid.*

35. "Secretary's Records of the Planters' Club on the Pee Dee," James Ritchie Sparkman Papers, Southern Historical Society, University of North Carolina, Chapel Hill.

36. "Ex-President Van Buren," *Winyah Observer*, March 12, 1842.

37. James Ritchie Sparkman Papers, "The Secretary's Records of the Planters' Club on the Pee Dee," 2732, vol. II, Southern Historical Collection.

38. *Ibid.*

39. J.H. Easterby, ed., "Poinsett-Campbell Correspondence," *South Carolina Historical Magazine* vol. XLIIIX (1942), 30–31.

40. James Ritchie Sparkman Papers, South Caroliniana Library, April 23, 1843, and May 13, 1843.

41. James Ritchie Sparkman Papers, "Secretary's Records of the Planters' Club on the Pee Dee," 2732 vol. II, Southern Historical Collection.

42. *Ibid.*

43. "Notice," *Winyah Observer*, March 30, 1844.

44. James Ritchie Sparkman Papers, "Secretary's Records of the Planters' Club on the Pee Dee," 2732 vol. II, Southern Historical Collection.

45. *Ibid.*

46. *Ibid.*

47. *Ibid.*

48. *Ibid.*

49. *Ibid.*

50. *Ibid.*

Chapter Nine

1. Robert F.W. Allston, "A Proposition to Rice Planters," Southern Agriculturist and Register of Rural Affairs vol. VIII (Charleston, SC: A.E. Miller Publishing, 1840), 475–76.

2. *Ibid.*

3. Clark, Hinson and Duncan, 3.

4. Minutes Book of the Winyah and All Saints Agricultural Society, South Carolina Historical Society, 34–161.

5. *Ibid.*

6. *Ibid.*

7. Constitution of the Winyah and All Saints Agricultural Society (Georgetown: Winyah Observer office, 1842), 2. J.H. Easterby, ed., "The Constitution of the Winyah and All Saints Agricultural Society," *South Carolina Historical Magazine*, vol. XXXXV, 1944, 52–54. Robert F.W. Allston papers, South Carolina Historical Society, 12-4-6/9. Minutes Book of the Winyah and All Saints Agricultural Society.

8. Sanborn, 6.

9. Minutes Book of the Winyah and All Saints Agricultural Society.

10. *Ibid.*

11. *Ibid.*

12. Faust.

13. Poinsett, "A Discourse," *Southern Agriculturist*, N.S., IV, December 1844, 452.

14. Faust.

15. *Ibid.*

16. *Ibid.*, 558–59.

17. *Ibid.*

18. "Letter from Col. Ward, on the Large Grain Rice," *Proceedings of the State Agricultural Society* (Columbia, SC: Summer and Carroll Publishers 1847), 30–31. Joshua John Ward Plantation Journal. MS 34-117, South Carolina Historical Society.

19. *Ibid.*

20. Susan Lowndes Allston, *Brookgreen Waccamaw In the Carolina Low Country* (Charleston, SC: Nelson's Southern Printing and Publishing Co., 1935), 28. Ward, like his father before him, called his plantation Brook Green; however, the modern spelling for the estate is Brookgreen.

21. Davidson, 209.

22. *Ibid.*, "To Col. R.F.W. Allston," 31–33.

23. *Ibid.*

24. Rogers, 526.

25. Minutes Book of the Winyah and All Saints Agricultural Society.

26. "An Analysis of Rice Straw, Chaff, & C." and Robert F.W. Allston, "Memoir on the Introduction And Cultivation of Rice in South Carolina," Supplement to the Proceedings of The State Agricultural

Society of South Carolina (Columbia, SC: Summer and Carroll Publishing, 1847), 25–61.

27. "Winyah and All Saints Agricultural Society," *Pee Dee Times*, May 19, 1858.

28. Minutes Book of the Winyah and All Saints Agricultural Society.

29. *Ibid.*

30. "Winyah and All Saints Agricultural Society," *Winyah Observer*, April 27, 1844. The newspaper printed the orations of the committees.

31. *Ibid.*, Minutes Book of the Winyah and All Saints Agricultural Society.

32. Minutes Book of the Winyah and All Saints Agricultural Society.

33. *Ibid.*

34. "Palmetto Agriculture—Importation of Stock," *New York Times*, May 17, 1848.

35. "Agricultural," *Winyah Observer*, October 14, 1846.

36. Clark, Hinson and Duncan, 3.

37. *Winyah Observer*, November 12, 1845.

38. Minutes Book of the Winyah and All Saints Agricultural Society. *Winyah Observer*, April 22, 1846.

39. *Ibid.* After awarding premiums, the group elected their officers for the ensuing year. The only changes in the administration of the society were that Dr. Edward Thomas Heriot took John Hayes Allston's place as vice president, and Robert F.W. Allston took Heriot's office as corresponding secretary. The officers of the society remained unchanged until 1851.

40. *Ibid.*, *Winyah Observer*, May 3, 1847.

41. Minutes Book of the Winyah and All Saints Agricultural Society.

42. *Ibid.*

43. "Agricultural Calendar for January," *Winyah Observer*, January 14, 1848, "Agricultural Calendar for January," *Winyah Observer*, January 21, 1848, and "Agricultural Calendar for January," *Winyah Observer*, January 28, 1848.

44. *Winyah Observer*, February 9, 1848, and "Culture of Sea Island Cotton," *Winyah Observer*, March 16, 1848.

45. "Agricultural Calendar for March," *Winyah Observer*, March 16, 1848, and "Agricultural Calendar for April," *Winyah Observer*, April 12, 1848.

46. "Agricultural," *Winyah Observer*, May 10, 1848, and "Agricultural," *Winyah Observer*, March 19, 1848.

Chapter Ten

1. *Ibid.*

2. "Winyah and All Saints Agricultural Society," *Winyah Observer*, April 26, 1848.

3. *Ibid.*; Minutes Book of the Winyah and All Saints Agricultural Society.

4. "Winyah and All Saints Agricultural Society," *Winyah Observer*, April 26, 1848.

5. "Lecture," *Winyah Observer*, April 25, 1849.

6. *Winyah Observer*, November 15, 1849.

7. "Winyah and All Saints Agricultural Society" *Winyah Observer*, April 24, 1850. Minutes Book of the Winyah and All Saints Agricultural Society, South Carolina Historical Society, 34–161.

8. James Ritchie Sparkman Papers, South Caroliniana Library, 2606, file #2. Paul D. Weston Papers, South Carolina Historical Society, 11- 453.

9. "Industrial Exhibition of 1851," *New York Daily Times*, October 29, 1851.

10. Susan Lowndes Allston, 28.

11. Pringle, 36.

12. Easterby, 118. There are not any records that prove that Allston created his own brand of rice, but his personal letters suggest that he had at least attempted this process.

13. Minutes Book of the Winyah and Saints Agricultural Society. "Winyah and All Saints Agricultural Society," *Winyah Observer*, April 23, 1851.

14. Pringle, 156–57.

15. Minutes Book of the Winyah and All Saints Agricultural Society.

16. "Fattening Pigs," *Pee Dee Times*, March 22, and "Proper Cultivation of Corn," *Pee Dee Times*, August 9, 1854, and "God himself was the first great planter," *Pee Dee Times*, October 4, 1854.

17. "An Antidote to the Potato Rot" *Pee Dee Times*, May 16, 1855. "Honey Bees," and "Pea Culture," *Pee Dee Times*, May 30, 1855.

18. Reynolds and Faunt, 236.

19. Minutes Book of the Winyah and All Saints Agricultural Society.

20. *Ibid.*

21. Frederick Law Olmstead, *A Journey*

in the *Seaboard Slave States in the years 1853-1854* (New York: Knickerbocker Press), 158-59.

22. Minutes Book of the Winyah and All Saints Agricultural Society.

23. Clark, Hinson and Duncan, 18-19.

24. *Ibid.*, 17.

25. Weston, Plowden C.J., Rules on the Rice Estate of P.C. Weston, South Carolina, 1856. De Bow's Review (Jan. 1857), vol. xxi, 38-44. Commons, John R, et al., *Documentary History of American Industrial Society*, vol. 1, Plantation and Frontier (Cleveland: Arthur H. Clark Company, 1909), 115-122.

26. Ulrich B. Phillips, *Plantation and Frontier Documents 1649-1863: Illustrative of Industrial History in the Colonial and Ante-bellum South*, vol. I (Cleveland: Arthur H. Clark Company, 1909), 259-65, 271-75. DeBow's Review, vol. xvi, 589-615 (June 1854).

27. Easterby, 16.

28. *Pee Dee Times*, October 8, 1856.

29. Clark, Hinson and Duncan, 23.

30. *Pee Dee Times*, October 8, 1856.

31. *Ibid.*

32. *Ibid.*

33. *Ibid.*

34. "Winyah and All Saints Agricultural Society," *Pee Dee Times*, May 19, 1858.

35. Minutes Book of the Winyah and All Saints Agricultural Society, South Carolina Historical Society, 34- 161.

36. *Ibid.*

37. Minutes Book of the Winyah and All Saints Agricultural Society. The Society met at the Pee Dee clubhouse on November 23, 1860, and auctioned off the exotic sheep for a combined total of $270.

38. *Ibid.*

39. *Ibid.*

40. Dr. Francis S. Parker Plantation Records, MS 1608, South Caroliniana Library.

41. United Daughters of the Confederacy, For Love of a Rebel, 1964.

42. Parker Plantation Records.

43. "State of South Carolina Executive Office, Dec. 23, 1861," *Horry Dispatch*, January 9, 1862.

44. *Ibid.*

45. Easterby, Rice Plantation Revealed, 329.

46. Childs,13-14.

Appendix II

1. Hot and Hot Fish Club, Rules and History of the Hot And Hot Fish Club, 15.

Appendix III

1. *Ibid.*, 16.

Appendix IV

1. Hot and Hot Fish Club, Rules and History of the Hot And Hot Fish Club. Richard Harwell, "The Hot and Hot Fish Club of All Saints Parish," *South Carolina Historical Magazine*, vol. XLVIII (1947): 40-47.

Appendix V

1. The Secretary's Records of the Planters' Club on the Pee Dee, James Ritchie Sparkman Papers, Southern Historical Collection, 2732.

Appendix VI

1. *Ibid.*

Appendix VII

1. Winyah and All Saints Agricultural Society, Constitution of the Winyah and All Saints Agricultural Society (Georgetown: Observer office, 1842). J.H. Easterby, "Constitution Of The Winyah And All Saints Agricultural Society," South Carolina Historical Society vol. XLIV (1943): 52-54. Robert F.W. Allston Papers, South Carolina Historical Society, 12-4—6/9.

2. Robert F.W. Allston Papers, South Carolina Historical Society, 12-4—6/9. The following clause is inserted in pencil: "An extra meeting may be called by the Prest. by giving 2 weeks' notice."

3. *Ibid.* The following words are inserted in pencil: "or some member appointed for the purpose,"

Appendix VIII

1. James Ritchie Sparkman Papers, South Caroliniana Library, legal size folder #4, April 25, 1861.

Bibliography

Primary Sources

Manuscript Sources

Glennie, Reverend Alexander. Parish Diary 1832–1859. South Carolina Historical Society 34–247.

"Hasell, Andrew to Daniel W. Jordan." *Daniel Jordan Papers*. Duke University Library, 1860.

Hasell, Dr. Andrew. Account book. South Carolina Historical Society, 34–247.

"Jordan, Daniel W. to Andrew Hasell." *Daniel W. Jordan Papers*. Duke University Library, July 19, 1860.

Journal of the Hot and Hot Fish Club. *Robert F. W. Allston Papers*. South Carolina Historical Society, 24–14–24.

Minutes Book of the Winyah and All Saints Agricultural Society. South Carolina Historical Society.

Minutes Book of the Winyah Indigo Society. Winyah Indigo Society.

Parker, Dr. Francis S. *Plantation Journal, MS 1608*. South Caroliniana Library.

Read Family Legal Papers: 1841–1879, MS 0308.01(R)01, South Carolina Historical Society.

The Secretary's Records of the Planters Club on the Pee Dee. *James Ritchie Sparkman Papers*, Vol. II, Southern Historical Collection.

South Carolina General Assembly Petitions. South Carolina Archives, 3780 and 3781.

Sparkman, James Ritchie. *2732 Folder 4a and 4b*. Southern Historical Collection.

Sparkman, James Ritchie Papers. *2606, file #2*. South Caroliniana Library.

Sparkman, James Ritchie Papers. South Caroliniana Library.

Sparkman, James Ritchie Papers: The Secretary's Records of the Planters Club on the Pee Dee, MS 2732, Vol. 2, Southern Historical Collection.

Sparkman, James Ritchie to Benjamin Allston. *Allston Family Papers*. South Caroliniana Library.

Ward, Joshua John. *Plantation Journal*, MS 34–117, South Carolina Historical Society.

Weston, Paul D. Papers, *11–453*. South Carolina Historical Society.

Winyah Indigo Society Collection. Georgetown, SC: Georgetown County Library.

Newspapers

Charleston City Gazette and Commercial Daily Advertiser, April 23, 1819.

Charleston City Gazette and Commercial Daily Advertiser, April 24, 1819

Charleston Courier. "Meeting at Conwayboro." April 21, 1849.

Charleston Gazette. October 16, 1755.

Charleston Gazette. January 5, 1760.

Charleston Gazette. May 22, 1775.

Charleston Mercury. November 8, 1860.

Commercial Daily Advertiser. April 24, 1819.
Georgetown American. November 23, 1839.
Georgetown American. February 28, 1840.
Georgetown American. "Agricultural." November 23, 1839.
Georgetown American. "Battalion Order." July 3, 1840.
Georgetown American. "Battalion Orders." July 10, 1840.
Georgetown American. "Battalion Orders." August 12, 1840.
Georgetown American. "Battalion Orders." September 2, 1840.
Georgetown American. "Celebration of the Anniversary of Washington's Birth." February 17, 1841.
Georgetown American. "The Drinking, Vending, and Making Ardent Spirits." November 30, 1839.
Georgetown American. "Report." December 16, 1840.
Georgetown American. "Second Declaration of Independence: Laws of the United States Passed at the First Session of the Twenty-Sixth Congress." August 5, 1840.
Georgetown American. "A Teacher Wanted." November 30, 1839.
Georgetown American. "Winyah Indigo Society." May 1, 1840.
Horry Dispatch. "State of South Carolina Executive Office, Dec. 23, 1861." January 9, 1862.
New York Daily Times. "Industrial Exhibition of 1851." October 29, 1851.
New York Times. "Palmetto Agriculture-Importation of Stock." May 17, 1848.
Pee Dee Times. March 12, 1856.
Pee Dee Times. July 9, 1856.
Pee Dee Times. October 8, 1856.
Pee Dee Times. May 1, 1859.
Pee Dee Times. "Abolition of Negro slavery—its Results in the British Colonies." September 3, 1856.
Pee Dee Times. "An Address Delivered by Plowden C. J. Weston Before the Citizens of All Saints Parish at Watchesaw, 4th of July 1857." August 5, 1857.
Pee Dee Times. "An Antidote to the Potato Rot." May 16, 1855.
Pee Dee Times. "An illustration of Mormonism—the Truth is Stranger than Fiction." February 2, 1857.
Pee Dee Times. "Anniversary of the Winyah Indigo Society." May 6, 1857.
Pee Dee Times. "Brooks Dinner." October 15, 1856.
Pee Dee Times. "Charity and Philanthropy." April 20, 1853.
Pee Dee Times. "Common Schools." December 14, 1853.
Pee Dee Times. "Condition of the Colored Population of the North." July 20, 1853.
Pee Dee Times. "Constitution of the Howard Society of Georgetown, South Carolina." October 3, 1855.
Pee Dee Times. "The Death and Funeral of Mr. Brooks of South Carolina." February 4, 1857.
Pee Dee Times. "The Decisoin of the Supreme Court Case, and its Tremendous Consequences." March 18, 1857.
Pee Dee Times. "Devotion of a true woman." September 19, 1855.
Pee Dee Times. "Duty of Southern Men." June 10, 1857.
Pee Dee Times. "Election Notice." May 16, 1855.
Pee Dee Times. "Fanaticism." June 7, 1854.
Pee Dee Times. "Fattening Pigs." March 22, 1854.
Pee Dee Times. "Form a Southern Confederacy." November 5, 1856.
Pee Dee Times. "4th of July." May 12, 1858.
Pee Dee Times. "4th of July." July 7, 1858.
Pee Dee Times. "The 4th of July at Sampit." July 6, 1853.
Pee Dee Times. "Free Schools." August 10, 1853.
Pee Dee Times. "God Himself was the First Great Planter." October 4, 1854.
Pee Dee Times "The Governors Review." March 25, 1857.
Pee Dee Times. "Harriet Beecher Stowe's Charity." May 11, 1853.
Pee Dee Times. "Headquarters." March 4, 1857.
Pee Dee Times. "Honey Bees." May 30, 1855.

Pee Dee Times. "How Changed." August 29. 1855.
Pee Dee Times. "Is an Abolitionist a Gentleman?" *Pee Dee Times*, April 6, 1853.
Pee Dee Times. "Kansas." December 12, 1855.
Pee Dee Times. "Kansas." March 21, 1856.
Pee Dee Times. "Kansas." March 26, 1856.
Pee Dee Times. "Kansas Bleeds No More." September 30, 1857.
Pee Dee Times. "Kansas Meeting," March 12, 1856,
Pee Dee Times. "Kansas Meeting in All Saints." March 5, 1856.
Pee Dee Times. "Life in Northern Cities." July 22, 1857.
Pee Dee Times. "Marion Female College." May 23, 1855.
Pee Dee Times. "Marrying advice to ladies." October 7, 1857.
Pee Dee Times. "Message No. 1 of His Excellency R.F.W. Allston, Governor of South Carolina to the Senate and House of Representatives, Session 1857." December 2, 1857.
Pee Dee Times. "Military Capacity of the South." August 22, 1855.
Pee Dee Times. "More Abolitionist Outrages." September 20, 1854.
Pee Dee Times. "Mr. Buchanan in Favor of Adding a Foreign Slave State to the South." August 20, 1856.
Pee Dee Times. "New York Conventions." August 10, 1853.
Pee Dee Times. "Our Free School System." August 10, 1853.
Pee Dee Times. "Pea Culture." May 30, 1855.
Pee Dee Times. "Political Excitement." August 29, 1855.
Pee Dee Times. "Proper Cultivation of Corn." August 9, 1854.
Pee Dee Times. "Quarantine." August 20, 1856.
Pee Dee Times. "A Recipe for Getting a Husband." July 11, 1855.
Pee Dee Times. "Report of the Commissioners of the Poor for the Year 1854." November 14, 1855.
Pee Dee Times. "The Rising Trouble in Kansas." May 30, 1855.
Pee Dee Times. "School." October 5, 1853.
Pee Dee Times. "School." October 12, 1853.
Pee Dee Times. "The Sign of the Times." August 6, 1856.
Pee Dee Times. "The Sign of the Times." May 6, 1857.
Pee Dee Times. "Slavery - the Proper Condition of the Negro." August 2, 1854.
Pee Dee Times. "Southern Commercial Convention in Montgomery." April 21, 1858.
Pee Dee Times. "To Kansas Emigrants and to all Friends of the South." February 6, 1856.
Pee Dee Times. "Trade with the North." September 5, 1855.
Pee Dee Times. "A Warning to the South." May 2, 1855.
Pee Dee Times. "What Constitutes a Gentleman?" May 14, 1856.
Pee Dee Times. "What makes South Carolina so Great?" March 9, 1853.
Pee Dee Times. "White Slavery in Massachusetts." September 30, 1857.
Pee Dee Times. "Who were the Slave Traders?" November 22, 1854.
Pee Dee Times. "Who were the Slave Traders?" November 29, 1854.
Pee Dee Times. "A Wife's Devotion: or the chivalry of love." April 18, 1855.
Pee Dee Times. "Winyah and All Saints Agricultural Society." May 19, 1858.
Pee Dee Times. "Winyah Indigo Society." March 9, 1853.
Pee Dee Times. "Winyah Indigo Society." March 23, 1853.
Pee Dee Times. "Winyah Indigo Society." May 3, 1854.
Pee Dee Times. "The Winyah Indigo Society." May 11, 1853.
Pee Dee Times. "Winyah Indigo Society." April 19, 1854.
Pee Dee Times. "Winyah Indigo Society." October 25, 1854.
Pee Dee Times. "Winyah Indigo Society." November 1, 1854.
Pee Dee Times. "Winyah Indigo Society." November 15, 1854.
Pee Dee Times. "Winyah Indigo Society." November 22, 1854.
Pee Dee Times. "Winyah Indigo Society." April 25, 1855.
Pee Dee Times. "Winyah Indigo Society." April 7, 1856.
Pee Dee Times. "Winyah Indigo Society." April 30, 1856.
Pee Dee Times. "Winyah Indigo Society." October 13, 1856.

Pee Dee Times. "Winyah Indigo Society." December 10, 1856.

Pee Dee Times. "Winyah Indigo Society." July 12, 1858.

Pee Dee Times. "Winyah Indigo Society School." March 4, 1857.

Pee Dee Times. "Winyah Indigo Society School." March 25, 1857.

Pee Dee Times. "Winyah Indigo Society School." April 1, 1857.

Pee Dee Times. "Winyah Indigo Society School." June 3, 1857.

Pee Dee Times. "Winyah Indigo Society School." September 9, 1857.

Pee Dee Times. "Winyah Indigo Society School." September 30, 1857.

Pee Dee Times. "Winyah Indigo Society Tribute of Respect." December 4, 1854.

Pee Dee Times. "Yellow Fever in Georgetown." August 20, 1856.

True Republican. "Southern Convention." February 13, 1850.

Washington Union. "Southern State Convention." October 17, 1849.

Winyah Intelligencer. January 2, 1833.

Winyah Intelligencer. "Elections." September 5, 1832.

Winyah Intelligencer. "President Monroe Visits South Carolina." April 23, 1819.

Winyah Intelligencer. "School." April 3, 1819.

Winyah Intelligencer. "School" December 4, 1819.

Winyah Intelligencer. "Sheriff Sales." April 1, 1834.

Winyah Intelligencer. "States' Rights Convention in Charleston." February 8, 1832.

Winyah Intelligencer. "A Teacher for the Free School." April 3, 1819.

Winyah Intelligencer. "Winyah Indigo Society." May 5, 1819.

Winyah Observer. May 8, 1841.

Winyah Observer. March 2, 1842.

Winyah Observer, May 4, 1844.

Winyah Observer. November 12, 1845.

Winyah Observer. April 22, 1846.

Winyah Observer. May 3, 1847.

Winyah Observer. December 8, 1847.

Winyah Observer, February 9, 1848

Winyah Observer. November 15, 1849.

Winyah Observer. October 2, 1850.

Winyah Observer. October 16, 1850.

Winyah Observer. October 23, 1850.

Winyah Observer. November 13, 1850.

Winyah Observer. November 18, 1850.

Winyah Observer. September 9, 1851.

Winyah Observer May 5, 1852.

Winyah Observer. May 12, 1852.

Winyah Observer. December 1, 1852.

Winyah Observer. December 15, 1852.

Winyah Observer. "Agricultural." May 10, 1848.

Winyah Observer. "Agricultural." March 19, 1848.

Winyah Observer. "Agricultural Calendar for January." January 14, 1848.

Winyah Observer. "Agricultural Calendar for January." January 21, 1848.

Winyah Observer. "Agricultural Calendar for January." January 28, 1848.

Winyah Observer. "Agricultural Calendar for February." February 9, 1848.

Winyah Observer, "Agricultural Calendar for March." March 16, 1848.

Winyah Observer. "Agricultural Calendar for April." April 12, 1848.

Winyah Observer. "All Saints Summer Academy." December 18, 1844.

Winyah Observer. "Annexation." May 4, 1844.

Winyah Observer. "Annexation of Canada." February 8, 1845.

Winyah Observer. "Anti-Sabbath Convention." March 3, 1848.

Winyah Observer. "The Battle of King's Mountain; or Hero's Revenge." October 9, 1850.

Winyah Observer. "Book of Mormon." July 14, 1841.

Winyah Observer. "Celebration of the 4th on the Pee Dee." July 13, 1844.

Winyah Observer. "Celebration of the 22nd." February 24, 1844.

Winyah Observer. "Culture of Sea Island Cotton." March 16, 1848.

Winyah Observer. "A Day at Lowell." November 11, 1846.

Winyah Observer. "Democratic Party Meeting." April 12, 1848.

Winyah Observer. "Depend upon yourself and God will lead you." December 14, 1850.

Winyah Observer. "Destructive Fire reported on Front Street." September 23, 1846

Winyah Observer. "Diffusion of Christianity." November 18, 1844.

Winyah Observer. "District Meeting." April 11, 1849.

Winyah Observer. "Divisions of the South." November 18, 1850.

Winyah Observer. "Domestic Training." November 1, 1848.

Winyah Observer. "Ex-President Van Buren." March 12, 1842.

Winyah Observer. "The First Secession of South Carolina." June 11, 1851.

Winyah Observer. "4th of July at Johnsonville." July 18, 1849.

Winyah Observer. "Gallery of Industry and Enterprise." May 12, 1852.

Winyah Observer. "Georgetown and All Saints Southern Rights Association." October 16, 1850.

Winyah Observer. "Georgetown and All Saints Southern Rights Association." October 23, 1850.

Winyah Observer. "A Good Wife." April 7, 1841.

Winyah Observer. "Great Secession Demonstration: Mass-Meeting at Morris Ferry 700 Persons Present." October 15, 1851.

Winyah Observer. "Head Quarters 8th Brigade, S.C.M." February 27, 1850.

Winyah Observer. "Head Quarters 8th Regiment Cavalry, Order No. 8." May 3, 1848.

Winyah Observer. "Head Quarters of Lower Battalion." February 27, 1850.

Winyah Observer. "Hon. Joel R. Poinsett." May 12, 1841.

Winyah Observer. "Horry Celebration." July 4, 1845.

Winyah Observer. "How to treat a wife." July 9, 1851.

Winyah Observer. "Lecture." April 25, 1849.

Winyah Observer. "Martin Van Buren." May 4, 1844.

Winyah Observer. "Military Parade at Black Mingo." December 6, 1843.

Winyah Observer. "Mrs. M.C. Durant's School." September 22, 1847.

Winyah Observer. "North and South: Van Buren, Cass, and Taylor: Which can the South Support?" August 9, 1848.

Winyah Observer. "Notice." March 30, 1844.

Winyah Observer. "On School Teaching No. 1." May 10, 1848.

Winyah Observer. "On School Teaching No. 2." May 17, 1848.

Winyah Observer. "On School Teaching No. 3." May 25, 1848.

Winyah Observer. "The Policy of the South." February 12, 1851.

Winyah Observer. "Proceedings of the Democratic State Rights Party." June 9, 1841.

Winyah Observer. "Profanity—don't do it." March 3, 1847.

Winyah Observer. "Railroad Convention in Memphis." May 12, 1852.

Winyah Observer. "Report of the Winyah Indigo Society." April 12, 1841.

Winyah Observer. "The Right of Secession." October 8, 1851.

Winyah Observer. "Saturday, July 6, 1844." July 6, 1844.

Winyah Observer. "Select School." December 18, 1844.

Winyah Observer. "Slavery and the Constitution." May 1, 1850.

Winyah Observer. "The Slavery Question." January 19, 1850.

Winyah Observer. "The Slavery Question and the Missouri Compromise." August 7, 1850.

Winyah Observer. "The Southern Convention at Nashville." June 19, 1850.

Winyah Observer. "Southern Rights Association of All Saints Parish." December 11, 1850.

Winyah Observer. "State of the Poll." September 9, 1845.

Winyah Observer. "A Story of the Cowpens." April 12, 1851.

Winyah Observer. "The Temperance Oath." February 26, 1842.

Winyah Observer. "Treatment of Scholars." October 3, 1849.

Winyah Observer. "Washington's Temperance Oath." July 23, 1842.

Winyah Observer. "The Welfare of Our Town." April 10, 1841.

Winyah Observer. "Whig Party Meeting." April 12, 1848.

Winyah Observer. "Who has betrayed the South?" July 25, 1849.
Winyah Observer. "Winyah and All Saints Agricultural Society." April 27, 1844.
Winyah Observer. "Winyah and All Saints Agricultural Society." April 26, 1848.
Winyah Observer. "Winyah and All Saints Agricultural Society." April 24, 1850.
Winyah Observer. "Winyah and All Saints Agricultural Society." April 23, 1851.
Winyah Observer. "Winyah Indigo Society." May 8, 1841.
Winyah Observer. "Winyah Indigo Society." May 7, 1842.
Winyah Observer. "Winyah Indigo Society." May 3, 1843.
Winyah Observer. "Winyah Indigo Society." May 6, 1843.
Winyah Observer. "Winyah Indigo Society." May 4, 1844.
Winyah Observer. "Winyah Indigo Society." May 3, 1845.
Winyah Observer. "Winyah Indigo Society." April 29, 1846.
Winyah Observer. "Winyah Indigo Society ." May 6, 1846.
Winyah Observer. "The Winyah Indigo Society." May 12, 1847.
Winyah Observer. "Winyah Indigo Society." April 26, 1848.
Winyah Observer. "Winyah Indigo Society." May 10, 1848.
Winyah Observer. "Winyah Indigo Society." May 9, 1849.
Winyah Observer. "Winyah Indigo Society." May 8, 1850.
Winyah Observer. "Winyah Indigo Society." May 7, 1851.
Winyah Observer. "Winyah Indigo Society." December 10, 1851.
Winyah Observer. "Winyah Indigo Society School." January 11, 1843.
Winyah Observer. "Winyah Indigo Society School." September 21, 1844.
Winyah Observer. "Winyah Indigo Society School." May 6, 1846.
Winyah Observer. "Winyah Indigo Society School." November 4, 1846.
Winyah Observer. "Woman: Her Mission and Destiny." November 11, 1844.
Winyah Observer. "Women." November 1, 1848.
Winyah Observer. "The Worth of a Woman." November 20, 1844.

Government Publications

Acts of the General Assembly of the State of South Carolina. Columbia, SC, 1853.
Agricultural Survey of Georgetown District, South Carolina. 1850 Census Report. United States Bureau of Census.
Agricultural Survey of Georgetown District, South Carolina. 1860 Census Report. United States Bureau of Census.
Agricultural Survey of Horry District, South Carolina. 1850 Census Report. United States Bureau of Census.
Agricultural Survey of Horry District, South Carolina. 1860 Census Report. United States Bureau of Census.
Charleston Taxpayers' List for 1859.
Industry Schedule, 1850. United States Bureau of Census.
Industry Schedule, 1860 United States Bureau of Census.
Memorial of The Citizens of Georgetown, South Carolina, Adverse to the Increase of Duties On Coarse Woolens, And Other Imports, January 9, 1828 (Washington: Duff Green, 1828).
McCord, David J., ed. *Statutes at Large of South Carolina,* vol. XII. Columbia, SC: Republican Printing Company, 1874.
_____. *Statutes at Large of South Carolina,* vol. XI. Columbia, SC: Republican Printing Company, 1873.
_____. *Statutes at Large of South Carolina: 1839–1849.* vol. II. Columbia, SC: Republican Printing Company, State Printers, 1873.
Population Survey, 1790 Census. United States Bureau of Census.
Population Survey, 1810 Census. United States Bureau of Census.
Population Survey, 1820 Census. United States Bureau of Census.
Population Survey, 1830 Census. United States Bureau of Census.

Population Survey, 1840 Census. United States Bureau of Census.
Population Survey, 1850 Census. United States Bureau of Census.
Population Survey, 1860 Census. United States Bureau of Census.
Slave Schedule, 1840 Census. United States Bureau of Census.
Slave Schedule, 1850 Census. United States Bureau of Census.
Slave Schedule, 1860 Census. United States Bureau of Census.
Social Status Schedule of South Carolina. 1850 United States Bureau of Census.
Social Status Schedule of South Carolina. 1860 United States Bureau of Census.

Primary Source Books

Allston, Robert F.W. "Address before the members and pupils of the Winyah Indigo Society delivered in Georgetown SC May 5, 1854." Charleston: Walker, Evans Steam Power Presses, 1859.

_____. *Analysis of Rice Straw, Chaff & Supplement to the Proceedings of the State Agricultural Society of South Carolina.* Columbia, SC: Summer and Carroll, 1847.

_____. Eulogy on John C. Calhoun Pronounced at the Request of the Citizens of Georgetown District. Charleston, SC: Miller and Brown, April 23, 1850.

_____. "Message No. 1 of His Excellency R.F.W. Allston, Governor of South Carolina to the State and House of Representatives at the session of 1857." Columbia, SC: R.W. Gibbes State Printer, 1857.

_____. *Report on the Free School System in South Carolina.* Charleston, SC: Miller and Browne, 1847.

Childs, Arney R. *Rice Planter and Sportsman; the Recollections of J. Motte Alston, 1821–1909.* Columbia: University of South Carolina Press, 1953.

Connor, Reverend William G. "An Address Delivered Before the Winyah Indigo Society of Georgetown." Charleston, SC: Walker and Burke Printers, May 5, 1848.

"Constitution of the Winyah and All Saints Agricultural Society." Georgetown, SC: Winyah Observer Office, 1842.

DeBow, J.D.B. "The Interest in Slavery of the Southern Non-Slaveholder." In *Slavery Defended: the views of The Old South,* by Eric L. McKitrick. Englewood Cliffs: Prentice-Hall, 1963, 169–177.

Dickerson, S.H. "Essay on Malaria." The Proceedings of the Agricultural Convention of the State Agricultural Society of South Carolina from 1839 to 1845. Columbia, SC, 1846.

Easterby, J. H., *The South Carolina Rice Plantation as Revealed in the Papers of Robert F.W. Allston.* Chicago: University of Chicago Press, 1945.

Hammond, James Henry. "'Mud-Sill' Speech." In *Slavery Defended: the Views of the Old South,* edited by Eric L. McKitrick. Englewood Cliffs: Prentice-Hall, 1963, 121–25.

Jones, Katharine M. *The Plantation South.* New York: Bobbs-Merrill Company, 1957.

McKitrick, Eric L. *Slavery Defended: The views of The Old South.* Englewood Cliffs: Prentice-Hall, 1963.

Mills, Robert. *Statistics of South Carolina.* Charleston, SC: Hurlbut and Lloyd, 1826.

Olmstead, Frederick Law. *A Journey in the Seaboard Slave States in the Years 1853–1854.* New York: Knickerbocker Press, 1904.

Phillips, Ulrich. *Plantation and Frontier Documents 1649–1863: Illustrative of Industrial History in the Colonial and Ante-bellum South,* vol. I. Cleveland: Arthur H. Clark, Co., 1909.

Pringle, Elizabeth Waties Allston. *A Woman Rice Planter.* Columbia: University of South Carolina Press, 1994.

_____. *Chronicles of Chicora Wood.* Charleston, SC: C. Scribner's Sons, 1922.

Rhett, Robert Barnwell. n.d. "The Address of the People of South Carolina, Assembled in Convention, to the People of the Slaveholding States of the United States." Charleston, SC: Evans and Cogswell.

"Rules and History of the Hot and Hot Fish Club of All Saints Parish." Charleston: Evans & Cogswell, 1860.

Sanborn, Alvan F. *Reminiscences of Richard Lathers; Sixty Years of a Busy Life in South Carolina, Massachusetts, and New York.* New York: Grafton Press, 1907.

Selections from Letters and Speeches of the Honorable James H. Hammond. New York: J.F. Trow and Company Printers, 1866.

Weston, Plowden C.J. "An Address by Plowden C.J. Weston before the Citizens of All Saints Parish at Watchesaw." Georgetown: Tarbox and Company, July 4, 1857.

_____. "An Address Delivered in the Indigo Hall, Georgetown, South Carolina on the 4th day of May 1860." *The 105th Anniversary of the Winyah Indigo Society.* Charleston, SC: A. J. Burke, 1860.

_____. *Documents Connected with the History of South Carolina.* London: Cheswick Press, 1856.

Primary Source Articles

Allston, Robert F.W. "A Proposition to Rice Planters." *Southern Agriculturalist and Register of Rural Affairs.* A.E. Miller, VIII, 1840.

_____. "Sea Island Cotton." *DeBow's Review* XVI, 1854.

"Delegates to the South Carolina Secession Convention of 1860, with a summary of date from manuscript returns of schedules 1 and 2 of the United States Census for 1860." *South Carolina Historical Magazine* 55: (1954), 192–197.

Easterby, J.H., ed. Vol. XLIIIX, "The Constitution of the Winyah and All Saints Agricultural Society." *South Carolina Historical Magazine,* 1944.

_____. "Poinsett-Campbell Correspondence." *South Carolina Historical Magazine,* 1942.

_____. "South Carolina through New England Eyes: Almira Coffin's Visit to the Low Country in 1851." *South Carolina Historical Magazine* 45 (1944).

"Letter from Col. War on the Long Grain Rice." *Proceedings of the State Agricultural Society.* Columbia, SC: Summer and Carroll Publishers, 1847.

Poinsett, Joel Roberts. "A Discourse," *Southern Agriculturist,* N.S., IV (December 1844), 452.

South Carolina Historical Magazine (South Carolina Historical Society) 72, 1971.

Southern Agriculturalist and Register of Rural Affairs, vol. IX. Charleston: A. G. Miller Publishing, 1831.

Stoney, Samuel G., ed. "Memoirs of Frederick Adolphus Porcher." *South Carolina Historical Magazine,* vol. XLVII, 1946.

Weston, Plowden C.J. "Rules on the Rice Estate of P.C. Weston, South Carolina, 1856." *DeBow's Review* XXI, 1857.

Secondary Sources

Books

Alford, Robbie L. "Winyah Indigo Society Historical Leaflet." *Leaflet.* Georgetown Rice Museum, 1976.

Allston, Susan Lowndes. *Brook Green Waccamaw in the Carolina Low Country.* Charleston: Nelson's Southern Printing and Publishing Company, 1935.

A Short History of the Winyah Indigo Society of Georgetown, South Carolina, 1755–1998.

Boney, F.N. *Southerners All.* Macon, GA: Mercer University Press, 1984.

Boucher, Chauncey Samuel. *The Nullification Controversy in South Carolina.* New York: Greenwood Press, 1968.

Brewster, Lawrence Fay. *Summer Migrations and Resorts of South Carolina Low-country Planters.* Durham: Duke University Press, 1947.

Bull, Henry DeSaurre. *All Saints Church Waccamaw.* Columbia, SC, 1968.

Clark, W.A., W.G. Hinson, and D.P. Duncan. *History of the Agricultural Society of South Carolina from 1839–1845: Inclusive of the State Agricultural Society of South Carolina from 1855–1861, Inclusive of the State Agricultural and Mechanical Society of South Carolina from 1869–1916.* Columbia, SC: R.L. Bryan Company, 1916.

Cook, Harvey Toliver. *Rambles in the Pee Dee Basin.* Columbia: State Company, 1926.

Coyler, Meriwether. *The History of higher education in South Carolina, with a sketch of the free school system.* Washington: Government Printing Office, 1889.

Daniel, Peter. *Breaking the Land: The Transformation of Cotton, Tobacco and Rice Cultures Since 1880.* Chicago: University of Illinois Press, 1985.

Davidson, Chalmers Gaston. *The Last Foray: South Carolina Planters of 1860: A Sociological Study.* Columbia: University of South Carolina Press, 1971.

Demaree, Albert Lowther. *American Agricultural Press: 1819–1860.* New York: Columbia University Press, 1941.

Dethloff, Henry C. *A History of the American Rice industry: 1685–1985.* College Station: Texas A&M University Press, 1988.

Devereux, Anthony Q. *The Life and Times of Robert F. W. Allston.* Columbia, SC: R.L. Bryan Company, 1976.

Doar, David, A. S. Salley, and Theodore D. Ravenel. *Rice and Rice Planting in the South Carolina Low Country.* Charleston, SC: Charleston Museum, 1936.

Dye, John H., John T. Walker, and W. A. Rodgers. *A Short History of the Winyah Indigo Society of Georgetown, South Carolina 1755–1950; with lists of deceased and living members.* n.p., 1950.

Elzas, Barnet Abraham. *The Jews of South Carolina from the Earliest Times to the Present Day.* Philadelphia: J.B. Lippincott Company, 1905.

Fraser, Jr., Walter J. *Charleston Charleston!* Columbia: University of South Carolina Press, 1989.

Gray, Lewis Cecil. *History of Agriculture in the Southern United States to 1860,* vol. II. Gloucester, MA: Peter Smith Publishing, 1933.

Gregg, Alexander. *History of the Old Cheraws.* New York: Richardson and Company, 1867.

Hardy, Norfleet. *Farm, Mill, And Classroom; a history of tax supported adult education in South Carolina in 1960.* Columbia: University of South Carolina Press, 1967.

Hollis, III, Daniel W. *The ABC-Clio World History Companion to Utopian Movements.* Santa Barbara: ABC-CLIO Press, 1998.

Irving, John Beaufain. *The South Carolina Jockey Club.* Charleston, SC: Walker and Evans, 1857.

Joyner, Charles W. *Down by the Riverside: A South Carolina Slave Community.* Urbana: University of Illinois Press, 1984.

Kenning, Helen Kohn. *Great South Carolinians from the Colonial Days to the Confederate War.* Mount Pleasant: Supplemental Press, 1940.

Lawson, Dennis T. *A Guide to Historic Georgetown County, South Carolina.* Georgetown, SC: Rice Museum, 1974.

_____. *No Heir to Take Its Place: The Story of Rice in Georgetown County, South Carolina.* Georgetown, SC: Rice Museum, 1972.

Lesser, Charles H. *Relic of the Lost Cause: The Story of South Carolina's Ordinance of Secession.* Columbia: The South Carolina Department of Archives and History, 1990.

Littlefield, Daniel C. *Rice and Slaves: Ethnicity and the Slave Trade in Colonial South Carolina.* Baton Rouge: Louisiana State University Press, 1981.

Meriwether, Colyer. *History of Higher Education in South Carolina; with a sketch of the free school system.* Washington: Government Printing Office, 1889.

Morgan, William D., *A Short History of the Winyah Indigo Society* (n.p., n.d.).

Prevost, Charlotte Kaminski., and Effie Leland Wilder. *Pawley's Island ... a Living Legend; an Historical Sketch of The Blessed Isle and Its Environs.* Columbia, SC: State Print, 1972.

Reynolds, Emily Bellinger, and Joan Reynolds Faunt. *Biographical Directory of the Senate of South Carolina 1776–1964.* Columbia: South Carolina Archives Department, 1964.

Rogers, George C. *The History of Georgetown County, South Carolina.* Columbia: University of South Carolina Press, 1970.

Salley, A. S. *The Introduction of Rice Culture into South Carolina.* Columbia, SC: Printed for the Commission by the State, 1919.

Scarborough, William. 1966. *The Overseer: plantation management in the old south.* Baton Rouge: Louisiana State University Press.

Silverman, Jason H. "South Carolina." In *A Nation of Sovereign States: Secession & War in the Confederacy,* by Archie P. McDonald. Murfreesboro: Southern Heritage Press, 1994.

Sydnor, Charles S. *The Development of Southern Sectionalism: 1819–1848.* Baton Rouge: Louisiana State University Press, 1948.

Thomas, Albert Sidney. *A Historical Account of the Protestant Episcopal Church in South Carolina, 1820–1957; Being a Continuation of Dalcho's Account, 1670–1820.* Columbia, 1957.

Tindall, George Brown. *South Carolina Negroes, 1877–1900.* Columbia: University of South Carolina Press, 1952.

United Daughters of the Confederacy. *For Love of a Rebel.* Georgetown, SC: The Arthur Manigault Chapter of the Daughters of the Confederacy, 1964.

Vernon, Amelia Wallace. *African Americans at Mars Bluff, South Carolina.* Baton Rouge: Louisiana State University Press, 1993.

Vlach, John Michael. *Back of the Big House: the architecture of plantation slavery.* Chapel Hill: University of North Carolina Press, 1993.

Warren, Geoffrey. *Fashion Accessories since 1500.* New York: Drama Book, 1987.

Willcox, Clark A. *Musings of a Hermit at Three Score and Ten: with historical sketches of places on the Waccamaw Neck.* Charleston, SC: Evan's and Cogwell Company, 1966.

Winyah Indigo Society. *A Short History of the Winyah Indigo Society of Georgetown, South Carolina 1755–1950.*

Articles

Berry, C.B. "John Vaught." *The Independent Republic Quarterly,* 19 (4), 1985.

Faust, Drew Gilpin. "The Rhetoric and Ritual of Agriculture in Antebellum South Carolina." *Journal of Southern History* XLV, no. 4 (1979): 541–68.

"Georgetown Library Society." *South Carolina Historical Magazine.* South Carolina Historical Society XXV, 1924.

Morgan, Kenneth. "The Organization of the Colonial American Rice Trade." *The William and Mary Quarterly* 52, no. 3 (1995): 433–52.

Web page

https://www.wikiwand.com/en/Hot_and_Hot_Fish_Club.

Index

Weston, Plowden C.J. 3, 52, 61, 62, 63, 66, 74,
75, 80, 116, 124, 125, 138, 142, 143, 144, 145,
181, 184, 187, 196, 201, 207
Whig Party 46, 48, 154
White House Plantation 32, 154, 155
Wilmot, David 47, 176
Wilmot Proviso 47, 48, 49, 98, 104, 137, 186

Wilson, Benjamin Henry 49, 52, 58, 100, 108,
116, 118, 183, 185, 207
Wilson, John Lyde 33
Withers, Francis 109, 115, 118, 202

Yeoman farmers 33, 36, 37, 167, 168, 181